MOON

MAGIC

Text © 1998 by Lori Reid
Design © 1998 Carlton Books Limited

Published by Three Rivers Press,
a division of Crown Publishers Inc.,
201 East 50th Street,
New York, New York 10022.
Member of the Crown Publishing Group.
Originally published in Great Britain by Carlton Books Ltd in 1998

Random House, Inc. New York, Toronto, Sydney, Auckland
www.randomhouse.com

Three Rivers Press and colophon are trademarks of Crown Publishers, Inc.

Printed in Spain

Library of Congress Cataloguing-in-Publication Data
Reid, Lori.
    Moon magic: how to use the moon's phases to inspire and influence your
relationships, home life and business/Lori Reid. -- 1st ed.
      p.   cm.
    ISBN 0-609-80347-6 (alk. paper)
    1. Moon--Miscellanea. 2. Moon--Mythology. 3. Astrology.
    4. Conduct of life. 5. Success. I. Title.
    BF1723.R45 1998
    133.5'32--dc21   97-52685
                                                              CIP

ISBN 0-609-80347-6

10 9 8 7 6 5 4 3 2 1

First American Edition

PICTURE CREDITS

The publishers would like to thank the following sources for their kind permission to reproduce the pictures in this book:

AKG London 17tr, 23 /Bibliotheque Nationale, Paris 52, 69, 72, 88 /British Library, London 45, 49, 61, 77, 80/Musee Conde, Chantilly, France 64 /Erich Lessing 24; Ancient Art and Architecture Collection Ltd. 25tc; Bridgeman Art Library /British Library, London, January feasting: Aquarius, Bedford Hours, French (c.1423) 84 /Giraudon/Musee Conde, Chantilly, France 'The anatomy of man & Woman' Tres Riches Heures du Duc de Berry early C15th 38 /Oriental Museum, Durham University, Kitchen God with lunar calendar 1895, Chinese (woodblock on paper) Qing Dynasty 10 1 /Victoria and Albert Museum, London, July: harvesting and sheep shearing, by the Limbourg brothers, Tres Heures du Duc de Berry (early C15th) 56; Corbis UK Ltd. /Richard Bickel 110 /Richard Cummins 111/Galen Rowell 114; Equinox, The Astrology Shop, London 41; ET Archive 20tl, 26b; Mary Evans Picture Library 107; Getty Images 29, 102, 103, 112, 115; Robert Harding Picture Library 17 bl /Jutta Klee 30; Image Bank 109/David De Lossy 113; Images Colour Library 90; Kobal Collection 37, Sharon Stone in Casino (Universal Pictures 1995) 92, Anna Neagle, Herbert Wilcox and Herbert Yates (RKO) 94/5; Pictor International 15, 31br , 31t, 32, 34, 36, 97, 98, 100, 101tr, 101br, 104, 105; Topham Picturepoint 7, 18 b, 33 /Associated Press 92br/National Gallery of Oslo The Scream 1893, by Edvard Munch 35;

Every effort has been made to acknowledge correctly and contact the source and/or copyright holder of each picture, and Carlton Books Limited apologises for any unintentional errors or omissions which will be corrected in future editions of this book.

MOON MAGIC

How to Use the Moon's Phases
to Inspire and Influence
Your Relationships, Home Life
and Business

LORI REID

THREE
RIVERS
PRESS

CONTENTS

INTRODUCTION

6

Since earliest times our ancestors have recognized that, just as the Moon has the power to move the great waters of the world's oceans, so she also exerts a profound influence on the lives of all things that live on this planet.

Now, more and more people are becoming increasingly aware of the fact that the ever-changing rhythms of the Moon affect our moods and emotions, our very deepest impulses and our actions and behaviour.

As she passes through her different phases, the Moon's rhythmic movement sets up a kind of "beat" – a dynamic and constantly changing energy that washes through us like the coming and going of the tides. How we behave and how we respond to the many stimuli around us springs from our personal interaction with that lunar beat.

Learning to tap into this tempo, to work in tune with the rhythm, means that we can capitalize on the energy of the moment. It means that, rather than fight against the trends, we can go with the flow and harmonize our efforts with the prevailing forces of Nature.

Falling out of step with these natural rhythms can all too often result in frustration, depression and a feeling of dislocation, as we waste large amounts of our time and energy struggling against the tide.

The angles that the Moon forms with the Sun, the relationships that she establishes with the other planets and her alignment with the astrological signs, all form a vital part of the rich pattern of natural energies that underlies everything we do in the course of our daily lives.

It is this natural pattern – essentially subtle and yet intense – that we all need to recognize in order to harness lunar energy, harmonize with our times and make the very most of every moment.

Through the pages of *Moon Magic*, you will learn all about the fascinating life-cycle of the Moon. Discover just how the Moon exerts her power over our daily lives – from how she lights the night sky to how she influences the great tides of the world's oceans. Learn about eclipses and Moon phases and what they can mean in our lives – and, most of all, learn to capture the magic for yourself and improve your life.

✳ ☆ ✳ ☆ ✳ ☆ ✳ ☆ ✳ ☆ ✳ ☆

High in the sky, the Moon shines like a beacon in the night, guiding the wanderer and the sea-farer on their way. As regularly as clockwork, her constantly changing face marks the passage of time for each and every thing that lives on the face of the Earth.

CHAPTER 1

LUNAR RHYTHMS

Serene and romantic, the Moon's silver disc lights up the dark midnight skies and transforms everything she touches with her pallid, eerie beams. Inconstant, because of her ever-changing shape, the Moon fascinates and inspires artists, entrances lovers and illuminates the wanderer's path.

Time was when people could reckon the passing of time by a simple glance at the Moon – the cyclical pattern of her changing shape is as regular as precision clockwork. Today, huddled in our urban conurbations, city lights obscure our view of the night sky and we consult our hi-tech digital watches rather than the planetary patterns overhead. Yet the Moon's changing face follows a precise pattern that repeats itself unfailingly every month. From New Moon, through First Quarter, to Full, to Last Quarter and back to New again, the cycle takes 29½ days to complete.

The Lunar Phases

Four main lunar phases divide each month – New, First Quarter, Full and Last Quarter. But, since the Moon is constantly either waxing or waning as it travels round the Earth, changing shape each night, its cycle can be broken down further, into eight obvious stages. The first four stages are the waxing or increasing moons; the next four are the waning or decreasing moons; the ninth stage brings the cycle back to the beginning again, as follows:

1 New Moon
2 First/Waxing Crescent
3 First Quarter
4 Waxing Gibbous Moon
5 Full Moon
6 Waning Gibbous or "Disseminating" Moon
7 Last Quarter
8 Waning Crescent or "Balsamic" Moon
9 And back to – the New Moon

Each stage lasts approximately three and a half days.

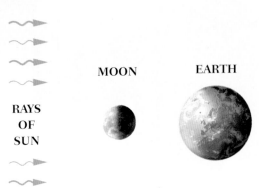

RAYS OF SUN

MOON   **EARTH**

The Moon circles the Earth and is lit by the rays of the Sun.

Waxing or Waning?

Whichever stage it is in, the waxing Moon takes the shape of a "D", and the waning Moon of a "C". Say to yourself that the "D" equals Developing, or increasing, in size, while the "C" equals Contracting, or getting smaller.

REFLECTED GLORY

The Moon actually emits no light of its own. It shines because it reflects light that it receives from the Sun. As the Moon circles the Earth, rays of sunlight strike its surface and illuminate different portions of its face. At that point in its journey, when it lies directly between us and the Sun, the Moon cannot reflect any light back to Earth since the Sun's rays strike the face of the Moon that is pointing away from us. This renders the Moon invisible from Earth – a point in its cycle known as the Moon's dark phase.

The Cycle of the Moon

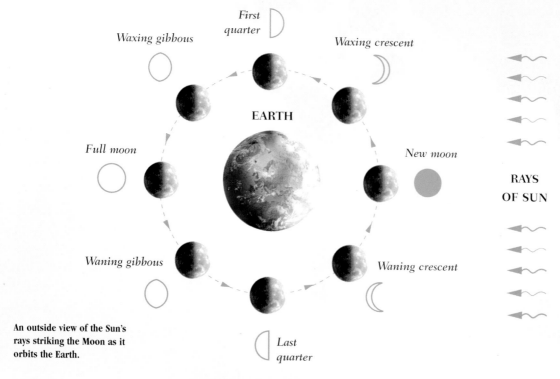

An outside view of the Sun's rays striking the Moon as it orbits the Earth.

As the Moon moves out of direct line and begins to sweep around the Earth, the Sun's rays strike at an angle. The first sign of the New Moon, a slender silver eyelash in the darkened sky, begins to appear. This is the start of the Moon's waxing phase and, from now, as more and more of its face is illuminated by the Sun, the Moon appears to increase in size each night until it reaches half-way around the Earth. At this point, the Moon is at its farthest from the Sun, in direct opposition, so that its whole face is lit up by sunlight. In this position, it is the Full Moon that is seen from the Earth.

From here, the Moon begins the second half of its journey around the Earth. As it sweeps around us in its approach to the Sun, it reverses its phases and, with less and less of its face lit up by the Sun, it appears to wane, or decrease. It wanes from Full to Last Quarter, to the Crescent and finally to invisibility again when it aligns itself between the Earth and Sun once more.

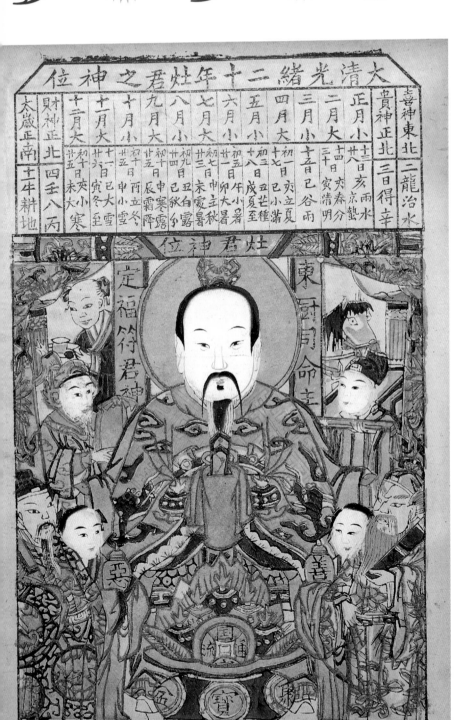

Eastern calendars, such as those traditionally used by the Chinese, are based on the movements of the Moon while those in the West are calculated according to solar time. A significant difference between these two systems can be seen with New Year's Day. In the West, this always falls on January 1. In the East, however, it varies from one year to the next.

The Full Moon

There are 12 Full Moons in the year, one occurring each month, and different cultures have given each one a name. These names not only distinguish one from another, and therefore one month from another, but also act as tags that associate a certain month with the specific activities that always take place at that time of year. Harvest Moon and Hunter's Moon, for example, are traditional European names for the Full Moons that occur in September and October respectively, coinciding with harvesting and hunting. Other cultures have names, such as Crow Moon and Big Winter Moon, to denote various times and events in their calendars.

ONCE IN A BLUE MOON...

Because the lunar cycle and the solar year are slightly out of sync with each other, once in a while we come across a month that contains two Full Moons. Since this is a fairly unusual occurrence, happening approximately every three years, we call the second Full Moon a Blue Moon. Hence the popular expression "once in a blue moon" – meaning something that happens only very infrequently.

The term "Blue Moon" is also used to refer to times when the Moon appears blue due to atmospheric pollution caused by a major volcanic eruption. This is an extremely rare phenomenon. For example, written records tell of a Blue Moon after the eruption of Krakatoa.

The Lunar Phases

For many centuries, people right across the world have recognized that the Moon influences the affairs of all living things on the Earth. Some law enforcement agencies, for example, have noticed a significant rise in violent crime around the time of the Full Moon. In a totally different area of expertise, prominent surgeons have observed certain variations in the rate of blood flow. As far as they can see, these appear to tie in with different phases of the Moon's cycle.

The waxing Moon appears to have a drawing, increasing and enhancing effect, whereas the waning Moon has a decreasing, receding and withdrawing effect. All things that come into being are stamped with the qualities of the prevailing Moon stage. So, for example, an individual who is born during the fortnight of the increasing Moon would be imbued with its corresponding waxing characteristics.

FINE DISTINCTIONS

Over the years, other observations have been made that refine these distinctions still further. So, it seems that people who are born during the other phases in the month – say, for example, the time of the Disseminating Moon – tend to share specific attributes with other people born during this time. In turn, their attributes will be subtly different from those of individuals born during any of the other stages in the Moon cycle – such as a First Quarter Moon period.

COSMIC CALENDARS

Since early times, people have used the movement of the stars and planets, and especially the movement of the Moon, with its precise sequences, as a great cosmic clock. First, the Moon marks the division of day and night. Then blocks of seven days, counted from one lunar phase to the next, create a week. From New Moon to Full Moon and Full Moon to the next New Moon forms two fortnights, so one entire cycle of the Moon constitutes a month. Indeed, the word "month" itself comes from an old Germanic term for Moon.

Throughout history, some civilizations have based their calendars purely on the movements of the Moon, while others used the Sun. The old Chinese calendar, for example, was based on the Moon, as is the Islamic month. The calendar currently in use in the West is mainly solar based, although it does incorporate elements of lunar timing. In this system, a year is calculated on the time it takes the Sun to return to exactly the same position in the sky. Months are loosely based on the phases of the Moon.

This mixture of solar and lunar influences in the Western calendar is best appreciated when looking at religious holidays. Christmas Day, for example, is fixed according to solar time and therefore always occurs on December 25. Easter Sunday, however – a vestige of an old lunar calendar – is based on complex calculations revolving around the movement of the Moon and so falls on a different date each year.

Knowing exactly which phase of the Moon you were born under gives you all kinds of extraordinarily valuable insights into your character, emotions, behaviour and motivation in life. It can make you aware of your deepest underlying drives, the fundamental purpose that you feel you have in life and the contribution that you can make to society at large during the course of your lifetime.

Armed with the knowledge that these insights give you, you can begin to understand your responses and then attune yourself to a personal cyclical pattern that you go through each and every month. This will allow you to nurture your body's needs, cope with its ever-changing demands and channel all of your energies in the most propitious direction.

LONG-TERM GOALS

Because this lunar pattern repeats itself every month, you will find that you can also pace yourself on a long-term basis. Soon you will be effectively targeting your efforts on periods of time that you know will be the most auspicious to you and your affairs.

WORKING WITH YOUR LUNAR CYCLE

You will find that your birth phase corresponds with the days of the month when you have plenty of energy and can generate new concepts with ease. During this period you should test out those ideas, process information, lay your plans, overcome obstacles, synthesize your thoughts and work towards a fruition of your efforts. Following this are the days in which you begin to take an objective view and look at your work and ideas retrospectively, making modifications if necessary to put right what might have gone wrong. At this stage you have the opportunity to spread your ideas wider and confer with like-minded people. This is the time to tie up loose ends and withdraw in order to muster your energies in anticipation of the new cycle that lies a few days ahead.

Finding Your Lunar Birth Phase

To discover how the Moon has shaped your character, find out which lunar phase was in effect at your birth by following the instructions below. Then look for the description of your Moon phase personality over the following few pages.

Discover your lunar birth phase by turning to the appropriate charts at the end of the book. These charts cover the moon phases in every month of every year between 1920 and 2020. Find the chart that refers to the year and month in which you were born. Next, find the phase closest to your date of birth. If you were born on the first day of that phase, or up to two and a half days after it, then that will be your personal lunar phase. But if you

were born up to three and a half days before the date of the given Moon phase, you will belong to the preceding lunar phase group.

Remember the order of all the phases:

1 New Moon
2 First/Waxing Crescent
3 First Quarter
4 Waxing Gibbous Moon
5 Full Moon
6 Waning Gibbous or "Disseminating" Moon
7 Last Quarter
8 Waning Crescent or "Balsamic" Moon
9 And back to – the New Moon

EXAMPLE:

The French film-star and animal rights campaigner Brigitte Bardot was born on September 28, 1934.
The listing for September 1934 looks as follows:

	Day	Hour	Min	Moon Phase
1934 Sep	09	00	20	NM
1934 Sep	16	12	26	FQ
1934 Sep	23	04	19	FM
1934 Sep	30	12	29	LQ

NM=New Moon FQ=First Quarter
FM=Full Moon LQ=Last Quarter

The nearest Moon phase date given for this birthday is the 30th, which is the day of the Last Quarter. As Brigitte's birthday is the 28th, she was born two days before the Last Quarter phase, so she falls within the previous phase of the Disseminating Moon.

A Permanent Record

Look up your lunar phase in the tables at the back of the book. Now use the space provided below to make a permanent record of this phase (along with the information needed to find it). You can use the other spaces provided to note down the lunar phases of your friends and family.

Name ....
Date of Birth:
Year.............
Month.........
Day.............
Hour...........

Your lunar birth phase is:.....................
☆

Name ....
Date of Birth:
Year.............
Month.........
Day.............
Hour...........

Your lunar birth phase is:.....................
☆

Name ....
Date of Birth:
Year.............
Month.........
Day.............
Hour...........

Your lunar birth phase is:.....................
☆

Your Lunar Phase Personality

Now that you know which lunar influences were operating at the time of your birth, and at certain times of each month, read on to find your lunar personality.

New Moon	First Crescent	First Quarter	Gibbous Moon	Full Moon	Disseminating Moon	Last Quarter	Balsamic Moon

| 1 | 2 | 3 | 4 | 5 | 6 | 7 | 8 | 9 | 10 | 11 | 12 | 13 | 14 | 15 | 16 | 17 | 18 | 19 | 20 | 21 | 22 | 23 | 24 | 25 | 26 | 27 | 28 | 29 |

1 New Moon Phase

If you were born during the New Moon phase, you have a childlike wonder and excitement about life. Open and demonstrative, you think and act spontaneously. With your bright, bubbling personality, you launch yourself into your work with tremendous enthusiasm. You are at your best when you are generating new ideas and beginning fresh projects, ever-hopeful about their outcome. Your eagerness leads you to work fast and furiously, but with the attendant danger that you can all too often exhaust yourself before reaching your goal. On the negative side, you have a habit of seeing life from a purely subjective point of view. You are likely to make your mark in life when you are comparatively young and you will need to learn how to sustain that impulse throughout the rest of your life.

2 First Crescent

As a First Crescent individual, you are assertive, adventurous and filled with joyous curiosity about life. Your creative disposition means that you have a need to expand your understanding and it also helps you to look at problems from a fresh perspective. Because of this, you may often feel torn between the conventional approach and the desire to break new ground – a conflict between established and unorthodox approaches. You may also come up against restrictions to your plans and will need to find ways of overcoming these obstacles in order to achieve your aims in life. Your twenties and early thirties are likely to be especially productive and successful.

3 First Quarter

First Quarter people are positive and strong-willed. Physically and mentally active and expressive, you are constantly on the go, taking a healthy interest in everything that you come across. You were born with an actively questioning mind and an impulse to challenge the status quo. On the negative side, this can make you appear argumentative and demanding. Used constructively, however, this also enables you to come up with new solutions to old problems. Above all else you are a builder, and, if it appears that you have a compulsion to tear down existing structures, it is merely because you have the ability to replace them with something that is not only more up-to-date, but is unquestionably an improvement on the past. You will produce some of your greatest endeavours in your thirties and early forties.

4 Gibbous Moon

Gibbous Moon individuals have a calming influence, a caring, constructive nature and a compulsion to help others. Your hope is that, through your life and work, you will contribute to the improvement of the world in some way. Whether consciously or unconsciously, this can become a "mission" with you – take care not to follow ideologies too blindly in your eagerness to accomplish your ends. Persevering in the face of obstacles will lead to maturity and will bring fulfilment and enlightenment. Look to your middle age for the recognition of your endeavours.

5 Full Moon

Being born in the middle of the cycle means that your talents lie in bringing matters to fruition. You are adept at tempering logic with instinct and practicality with creativity. Moreover, this period acts like a bridge, linking you to the past but also projecting your ideas into the future. The negative side is that you may suffer guilt and irrational fears, especially when it comes to personal relationships. Only when you learn to take control of your own feelings, rather than taking your emotional cue from your partner, will you find a way of sustaining a mutually rewarding intimate relationship. Your best efforts will find their flowering after middle age.

6 Disseminating Moon

Since "to disseminate'" means to scatter seeds, your impulse is to sow your ideas and knowledge so that others may learn from your experiences – you are a communicator and a teacher. Dedicated to your ideals, if there is a touch of the revolutionary in your nature, then it is purely and simply an urge to reform the world. In your zeal to improve people's lives, however, you may need to find a compromise and learn how to reconcile your own vision with the needs of others. Your early fifties should bring a sense of achievement and contentment to your life.

7 Last Quarter

Your understanding, sympathy, maturity and poise transcend your years and so you excel in a counselling or advisory capacity. You help others to marshal their thoughts, expand their awareness, resolve their problems and organize their lives. Some may interpret your idealism as inflexibility. Prone at times to nostalgia or melancholia, you need to put aside the past and concentrate on the future. Contentment and fulfilment will come in your later fifties.

8 Balsamic Moon

This time is essentially one of transition, a chance to contemplate what has passed, tie up loose ends, journey inwards and prepare for new beginnings ahead. You have inherited the meditative and introspective characteristics of this phase and yours is a dreamy and contemplative personality. Intuitive and far-sighted, you have innate wisdom and a mystical understanding of the workings of Mother Nature and of the human condition. For you, activity is spiritual and intellectual rather than physical. Your experiences involve endings and passings, so you are likely to live through many changes. Later life, rather than the earlier years, holds the key to your happiness and success.

CHAPTER 2

TIDES AND ECLIPSES

The Turning of the Tides

Of all the influences the Moon has upon the Earth, the one effect that is generally undisputed is the pull that the Moon exerts on our tides. Precisely how and why great oceans roll in and out was understood long ago by the ancient Chinese. The scholars of ancient Rome and Greece, however, failed to make the link between the Moon and the tides – simply because they had no need to, since the Mediterranean is virtually tideless. Julius Caesar, it is said, learned about the existence of tides only when he travelled to Britain.

Today, the rhythmic ebbing and flowing of the oceans is common knowledge, even if the precise mecha-nism is not easily understood. In addi-tion to the daily motion of high and low tides, there are also times each month when the tides are especially high (spring tide) or low (neap tide). This distinct monthly pattern strongly implicates the Moon's cyclical pattern.

THE PULL OF THE MOON

The Moon's gravitational pull upon the Earth is so strong that it draws the Earth and its waters towards it. This causes the seas to bulge at the point that is directly facing the Moon, pro-ducing a high tide at that location. At the opposite side of the Earth, the water is pulled less strongly than the land mass. This means that the oceans flow away from the surface of the Earth and form another bulge, and therefore another high tide, on the other side. As this occurs, low tide is experienced at those points of the Earth's surface that are in between – at 90° to – the bulges.

SPRING AND NEAP TIDES

Twice every month, the Sun, Moon and Earth align themselves at Full and New Moon times. With the Sun's extra draw added to the Moon's already pow-erful pull, the water bulges increase and produce the higher than normal swells that are called spring tides. Since spring tides can cause widespread flooding and danger to navigation and fishing, the ability to predict their occurrence has been of great value throughout history.

At the time of the Moon's quarters, each falling one week after the Full and the New Moons, the Moon is at 90° to the Sun and in this position its gravitational pull on the Earth coun-teracts that of the Sun. Consequently at these times, the rise of the oceans will be minimized, producing the lesser high tides – or neap tides.

Earthquakes

Since it is believed that the gravitational pull of the Earth on the Moon is a significant factor in triggering Moonquakes, it would seem likely that a similar tension created by the Moon

16

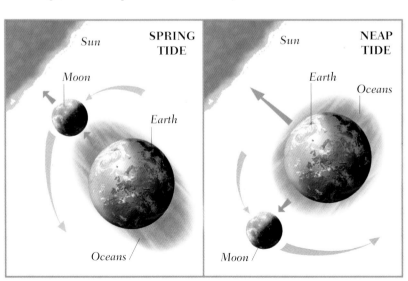

Spring tides occur when the Moon and Sun are in line. Neap tides occur when the Moon and Sun form a right angle with the Earth, which equalizes their pull on the oceans.

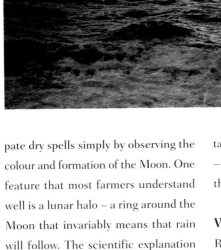

The Sun's gravitational pull at New and Full Moon times increases the tides further.

upon the Earth would have some bearing on the causes of earthquakes. And if the Moon has so much power to move the oceans, then it must also be capable of exerting stress upon the Earth's crust. Indeed, many scientists are coming to this conclusion and studies have shown a correlation between the incidence of earthquakes and volcanic eruptions and the times of Full and New Moons. Moreover, they have detected a frequency pattern of seismic activity that recurs on an 18-year cycle – a sequence that corresponds to the Moon's eclipse cycle and which has been recognized since Babylonian times.

Weather

A connection between lunar phases and the weather has long been recognized. Those living in the country have been able to predict rain or to antici-

pate dry spells simply by observing the colour and formation of the Moon. One feature that most farmers understand well is a lunar halo – a ring around the Moon that invariably means that rain will follow. The scientific explanation of this phenomenon is that ice crystals in the atmosphere – the very ice crys-

tals that will soon fall to Earth as rain – are lit up by reflected moonlight, and thus create the luminous halo.

WIND AND RAIN

Researchers have also discovered a link between hurricanes and the Full and New Moons, while data on rainfall has shown that precipitation is more likely to occur at the First Crescent than at the First Quarter, and at the Disseminating Moon phase rather than at the Third Quarter. Also, records suggest that more rainfall seems to occur during the two weeks of the waxing Moon than in the fortnight after the Full Moon. So, if you are planning a picnic, check the lunar tables first!

Many links have been made between Moon patterns and heavy rainfall.

Eclipses

Eclipses occur when the Sun, Earth and Moon come into a particular alignment with each other at special times of either the New or Full Moon. A solar eclipse occurs at the New Moon phase, while a lunar eclipse can only take place at Full Moon. There are three types of eclipses – partial, total and annular. However, it very much depends upon where on the Earth's surface the observer is situated as to whether or not he or she will be able to view the eclipse. Only those who happen to be directly within the path of the eclipse can witness it.

Eclipses do not occur at each New and Full Moon because the tilt of the Moon's orbit prevents the three celestial bodies from coming perfectly into line every single month. Between two and five solar eclipses can occur in any one year, most of which are only partial. Total eclipses of the Sun are rarer.

The Moon may be eclipsed either twice or three times per annum.

Both lunar and solar eclipses have been recorded since as far back as 3000 BC. Eclipses follow an 18-years-and-11-days pattern that is known as the Saros cycle, a name given by the Ancient Greeks. This means that each eclipse will recur in approximately the same place at this regular interval.

Eclipse Effects

Once feared as harbingers of doom that foreshadowed the sudden demise of a ruler, the destruction of crops, the maddening of livestock, pestilence and war, eclipses still fill us with awe and wonder. Moreover, many still believe that eclipses tie in with cyclical changes that are reflected on both a personal and political level.

Eclipses are said to trigger change and foretell a critical turning point or challenges ahead. Turn to the eclipse charts at the end of the book for a date-list of solar and lunar eclipses between 1920 and 2020. Check through to find any dates that are personally significant to you. Perhaps an eclipse occurred on your birthday or close to the time you met your partner.

READING THE SIGNS

Take a note, too, of the sign in which the eclipse occurred, or will occur. Those that fall in either your Sun sign (your astrological sign) or in your Moon sign (*see Chapter 6*) are also likely to have a significant effect. Eclipses that fall in your Sun sign signal new experiences, whereas those that fall in your Moon sign refer to events that will affect you emotionally – perhaps marking the start of a new romantic interest.

✳ ☆ ✳ ☆ ✳ ☆ ✳ ☆ ✳ ☆ ✳ ☆

In olden days, it was believed that eclipses were caused by dragons who swallowed up the Sun.

SOLAR AND LUNAR ECLIPSES

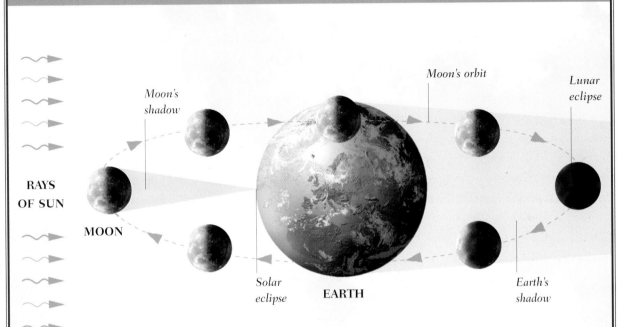

RAYS OF SUN

Moon's shadow

MOON

Moon's orbit

Lunar eclipse

Solar eclipse

EARTH

Earth's shadow

Tides and Eclipses

19

Chapter 2

Solar Eclipses

An eclipse of the Sun occurs at New Moon time when the Moon passes between the Earth and the Sun. Viewed from the Earth, the Moon appears to travel across the Sun, covering either a part (partial eclipse), or sometimes all (total eclipse), of the Sun's face.

In a total eclipse, coldness and darkness descend on Earth for up to 7½ minutes. Frightening though this can be, it is fairly rare – only three lasting over seven minutes occurred during the twentieth century. Annular eclipses are spectacular and occur when the disc of the Moon appears slightly smaller in diameter than the face of the Sun. So, when the two are perfectly aligned, a ring of brilliant sunlight is seen around the eclipsed face of the Sun.

Lunar Eclipses

The Moon can only be eclipsed when it is on the opposite side of the Earth to the Sun, since at this point it is travelling through the shadow of the Earth. This shadow is known as the umbra and, as the Moon passes through it, sections of its disc are gradually dimmed. In a partial eclipse, only part of the Moon's face will be obscured; in a total eclipse, the Moon appears to go rapidly through its phases until it reaches totality, and then it reverses the process as more and more of its face gradually returns. It is rare for the Moon to disappear completely during an eclipse and even in a total lunar eclipse the Moon usually remains visible, taking on a reddish glow that is caused by "Earthshine", or light reflected off the Earth. From start to finish a lunar eclipse can last several hours.

Galileo (1564–1642) mistook the Moon's flat basins for seas and so gave craters the name "maria".

ECLIPSE EFFECTS

In the case of the Sun, each hour of its eclipse is said to bring effects that last for one year. For the Moon, the ratio is one hour to one month.

The effects may begin to unfold before or soon after the eclipse takes place. But the full implications might not make themselves apparent until months (with the Sun) or weeks (with the Moon) after the eclipse.

Eclipses have long been thought to affect national and political affairs. If a 12-sector astrological chart is drawn up for the time of an eclipse, the house (sector) of the chart in which the eclipse occurs will indicate which aspects of the nation are likely to be affected. An eclipse in the 7th house, for example, might indicate that international relations could reach crisis point. Alternatively, an eclipse falling in the 12th house could usher in penal reforms.

The sign of the Zodiac in which the eclipse takes place will throw further light on events still to unfold. Taurus, for instance, is associated with property, Gemini with telecommunications and Aquarius with new inventions. To find out more, see the box below.

SIGNS OF THE TIMES

Signs of the Times

This gives a good idea of the areas of life affected when an eclipse occurs in a certain house or sign.

1st house	the state of the nation
2nd house	finances, trade and general fiscal resources
3rd house	communications and education
4th house	the property market, women's affairs and the family
5th house	cultural interests, the Arts, leisure, gambling, children and childbirth
6th house	employment and health matters
7th house	international affairs, agreements and alliances, diplomacy, marriage
8th house	taxation, investments, morality, matters concerning death and regeneration
9th house	the law, the Church, science, higher education, publishing, foreign travel
10th house	the head of state, the monarchy, the government
11th house	committees, associations, local authorities, trade unions and allies
12th house	institutions, hospitals, prisons, secret service, criminality, public disgrace
Aries	exploration, pioneering
Taurus	property, real estate, wealth
Gemini	communications, the media
Cancer	home, the mother, the sea
Leo	royalty, actors, the theatre
Virgo	servants, medicine, healing
Libra	music, the Arts
Scorpio	sex, investigations, psychotherapy
Sagittarius	publicity, travel, religion, education, ethics
Capricorn	business, power
Aquarius	inventions, technology
Pisces	dreams, illusions, the film industry

CHART FOR TOTAL ECLIPSE ON AUGUST 11, 1999

Here is an astrological chart drawn up for the eclipse on August 11, 1999 at 11.03 GMT. As the best vantage point for the eclipse will be in England, the chart has been compiled for London, its capital. What changes does this chart hint at for future events in this part of the world? (See "A Possible Interpretation..." below.)

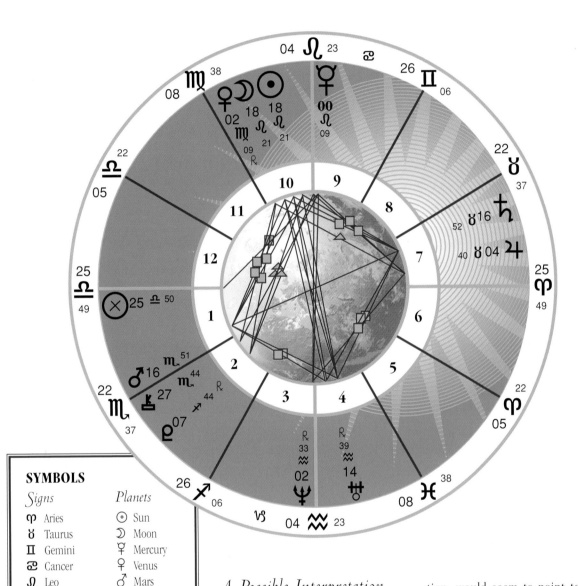

SYMBOLS

Signs		*Planets*	
♈	Aries	☉	Sun
♉	Taurus	☽	Moon
♊	Gemini	☿	Mercury
♋	Cancer	♀	Venus
♌	Leo	♂	Mars
♍	Virgo	♃	Jupiter
♎	Libra	♄	Saturn
♏	Scorpio	♅	Uranus
♐	Sagittarius	♆	Neptune
♑	Capricorn	♇	Pluto
♒	Aquarius	⚷	Chiron
♓	Pisces	⊕	Earth

A Possible Interpretation...

The eclipse falls in the 10th house, which is associated with government, rulership and heads of state. It is also taking place in the sign of Leo, which is specifically linked to the monarchy. This combination, situated in this posi-tion, would seem to point to major developments within the royal family. These patterns may coincide with general changes in the nature of the British monarchy, with the possible illness or death of a royal figure or with a new sovereign ascending the throne.

CHAPTER 3

GODDESS OF THE NIGHT

Just as Yin is to Yang, so the Moon is to the Sun. Yin and Yang, light and dark, night and day, hot and cold, feminine and masculine, Moon and Sun – the complementary forces that permeate the universe, holding all things in a precise and dynamic balance. Each in opposition, yielding by turns one to the other.

So it is that civilizations have viewed existence since the dawn of time. Our ancient ancestors looked up into the skies and saw the Sun as the life-giver, bringing heat and light into the world. The Moon, they observed, had no light of its own but absorbed and reflected that of the Sun. Holding sway in the night, its cold rays were thought to have magical properties, casting their mysterious light on the land below.

BIRTH AND REBIRTH

Moreover, while the Sun appears as a constant golden orb, the Moon is inconstant, a shape-shifter that waxes and wanes from the finest silver sliver to a full-blown yellow disc, before reversing the process back to darkness again. The repeating cycle of the Moon has been likened to the pattern of birth, death and rebirth seen in the crops, in the seasons and in Nature everywhere.

Soon people saw that the changing phases of the Moon were linked, not only to growth, destruction and re-growth in the vegetative world, but also to the female menstrual cycle that regulates human fertility, conception and birth. And so, just as the life-giving Sun became associated with masculine principles, so the Moon, his companion and receiver of life, became endowed with female qualities.

THE STUFF OF GODS

Throughout history, both the Sun and the Moon have been deified and venerated by civilizations and cultures throughout the world. Countless parallel myths grew up around the different functions of the two bodies, right across the continents.

Ra, Inti, Phoebus, Apollo, Tonatiuh, Kuat, Surya – these are just some of the incarnations of the Sun God that have been worshipped by ancient peoples. But while these mythologies centre on one predominant image of the Sun deity, driving his flaming chariot gloriously across the mid-day sky, the Moon Goddess comes in many different guises that reflect the three main stages in her cycle.

As the New Moon, she is depicted in the form of a maiden or virgin – a nubile, seductive deity of burgeoning sexuality and emergent procreative powers. As the Moon increases to fullness, so the image becomes one of the fertile Mother, pregnant with life. In the last phase, as she wanes to darkness, she is portrayed as the witch or crone, the wise woman versed in magical arts, a sorcerer and mistress of disguise with powers to heal and transform all that passes through her hands.

MYSTICAL TRINITY

These three faces of the Moon goddess represent Nature's cycles and fuse the conscious, subconscious and unconscious processes of the human mind – our material, emotional and spiritual faces. The Moon has become the archetype of creation, womanhood and the feminine psyche.

All major religions contain, in one form or another, evidence of this female trinity. Central to the ancient Greeks were Persephone, Demeter and Hecate with their Roman counterparts of Diana, Ceres and the Sibyl. In the Norse tradition, the Norns, or Weird Sisters, wove together the past, present

and future. And for the Hindus, Kali incorporates the three-fold-goddess-in-one as "the light", "the dark" and "the mother of the world".

The maiden goddesses venerated in civilizations far and wide include Persephone, Aphrodite, Al-Uzza, Athene, Diana and Minerva. Mother goddesses of creation and of the Full Moon include Astarte, Demeter, Ceres, Al-lat, Kwan-Yin, Hathor, Isis, Selene and Wahini-Hai. And of the group belonging to the "dark" goddesses may be added Kali, Skadi, Hecate,

＊ ☆ ＊ ☆ ＊ ☆ ＊ ☆ ＊ ☆ ＊ ☆

Mythologically, the Moon has come to represent all that is considered feminine.

Tlazolteotl, Circe, Hathor, Lilith, the serpent-headed Medusa and Nemesis, goddess of all retribution.

The Three Faces of the Moon

The three faces, or stages, of the Moon are symbolized by goddesses who, in turn, embody the powers of transformation through the processes of birth, growth and decay.

Among the first group, who display the qualities of innocence, creative energy, youthful hope and vigour, and who bring with them the promise of the new, are the Greek goddess Aphrodite, the Roman goddess Diana, and Freya, the Norse goddess of love and fertility.

APHRODITE

Tall, fair and lovely, Aphrodite is the symbol of beauty and the goddess of love and fertility. Born of the sea, she emerged from the waves with her feet treading the tide's white foam. Passionate, sensual and giving, she embodies seductive power, the joys of instinctive love-making and feminine love-giving. Her name is synonymous with charm and grace and she is goddess and patroness of the Arts. It is Aphrodite who has inspired artists through the centuries and who continues to inspire all those with a creative turn of mind.

Aphrodite holds sway over relationships, partners and lovers everywhere. Voluptuous and fertile, her connection with the waters of the oceans make her a deity of the Moon. Her counterpart in Roman mythology is Venus, from whom the beautiful city of Venice, "Bride of the Sea", derives its name.

DIANA

Also known as the Greek goddess Artemis, Diana was the twin sister of Apollo, who was responsible for driving the Sun's chariot across the skies. She therefore stands for the feminine principle – the Moon to his Sun.

Usually portrayed in a short white tunic and with a distinctive head-dress adorned with a Crescent Moon, Diana is the virgin huntress and the goddess of hunting. She is a young, free spirit who roams the woodlands far and wide, armed with her bow and arrow and accompanied by her trusty dogs and stags.

＊ ☆ ＊ ☆ ＊ ☆ ＊ ☆ ＊ ☆ ＊ ☆

Venus, born of the waves, beautiful and nubile goddess of the sea.

Like the Moon itself, Diana too is a skilled shape-shifter, adopting an animal guise at will to turn herself into a hare – the sacred animal of the Moon. A powerful deity, she was well versed in the healing arts and was known by many for her fierce protection of innocence, and of animals and young girls everywhere.

FREYA

Venerated by the ancient Scandinavians, Freya was the daughter of the sea god, Njord. Deity of love, she was the most beautiful of all the goddesses and, as a warrior queen, she led the Valkyries, the personal handmaidens of Odin.

Freya's name, which may also be written as Freyja, means "Lady", and she stands as the feminine archetype and sister to the lord Frey. She was patroness of the oceans and has sometimes been known, rather poetically, as "She who shines over the sea".

Freya weeps golden tear-drops that fall like beads of amber into the water. This goddess's animal emblem is the cat, which is seen as a sacred link with the Moon, and she is often depicted riding a carriage pulled by two of her feline companions.

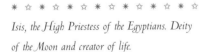

Isis, the High Priestess of the Egyptians. Deity of the Moon and creator of life.

Of the goddesses who were extolled for their ability to nurture and who were held in great esteem for their fruitfulness and their powers to bring forth life are Isis, great priestess and goddess of the Egyptians; Selene, Moon goddess of the Greeks; and Ceres,

Roman goddess of ripened corn. All deities of the Full Moon and embodiments of motherhood and abundance, these goddesses were empowered with the gifts of growth and expansion, able to bestow fecundity and bring all endeavours to their fruition.

ISIS

Mother goddess of ancient Egypt, and both wife and sister to the great lord Osiris, Isis was the deity of the Moon and ruled over home life, marriage, fertility and childbirth.

Often depicted suckling Horus, her son, and wearing the horns of a cow, a symbol of the Crescent Moon, Isis was known as the "Giver of Life". Versed in the arts of magic and healing, her personal emblems were the cow and the cat, both creatures being associated with the feminine archetype and sacred to the Moon.

SELENE

As sister of Helios, the Sun god, Selene represents the Moon and, according to mythology, was responsible for guiding the Moon across the skies. It is said that, one night, Selene looked down and caught sight of Endymion, the handsome shepherd.

She fell in love instantly. Unable to resist his beauty, she abandoned her nocturnal duties and crept down to lie gently beside her lover. Zeus, angered by the darkened sky, decided to punish Selene and ordered that Endymion should sleep forever. But even that could not break the love she had for her beautiful swain and, to this day, Selene slips away for a few nights each month to caress her sleeping lover, leaving behind her the darkened moonless skies.

It is from Selene, that selenology, the term given to the scientific study of the Moon, is derived.

CERES

As goddess of the grain and an emblem of the harvest, Ceres is often depicted holding a sheaf of corn. She is the Roman equivalent of the Greek goddess, Demeter, and her daughter is Proserpina, a parallel to Demeter's daughter Persephone. In both traditions, the daughters were abducted and taken away to the Underworld. The mothers, distraught by the loss, struck a very special bargain with the lord of the Underworld. Under the terms of this bargain, they could have their daughters returned to them at least for part of the year.

✳ ☆ ✳ ☆ ✳ ☆ ✳ ☆ ✳ ☆ ✳ ☆

Kali the Terrible, known in Indian mythology as the Black Mother. She is truly a goddess of the dark Moon, since she holds power simultaneously over both life and death.

So it is that the sorrows of motherhood, when Ceres is parted from Proserpina, result in the bleakness of winter, and the joys that a mother experiences, when Ceres is reunited once more with her daughter, are celebrated in the delights and triumphs of the summer.

Both Ceres and Demeter, goddesses of the Full Moon, embody the protective spirit of the mother and rule over vegetation and the fruitfulness of the crops, bringing forth increase and abundance.

In the natural cycle, everything is in constant flux, with each stage yielding inevitably to the next. So the Moon must inevitably decrease and disappear in order for the new cycle to begin all over again.

The next group of goddesses reflect the wisdom and experience that have been gained through the process of birth and fruition. With their accumulated knowledge, these deities have developed an acute understanding of the transformational powers of Nature, and so have become seers – the guardians of mysticism, who are versed in the many magical arts.

Lilith, Kali and Hecate, goddesses of the Dark Moon and feared for their powers of destruction, possess great wisdom and maturity and teach us the need for reflection and spiritual enlightenment. Behind their darkest moods, they offer healing, solace, peace and rest. But, above all else, these goddesses of the Dark Moon bring with them the promise of rebirth and regeneration.

LILITH

Known long ago to the Sumerio-Babylonian people of the Middle East as the "Beautiful Maiden" who gave birth to the Moon, Lilith's legendary beauty and sexual charms were later distorted by Hebraic lore. This was done in order to subvert the popular Sumerian cult of goddess worship.

And so it was that the beautiful Lilith became transformed from the free-spirited and winged "Bird Goddess" into a female demon – a dangerous, evil beauty whose powerful eroticism drove men inevitably to total madness.

In her earlier incarnation, Lilith was associated with the owl – a strong symbol of wisdom, the night and the Moon. Her name itself is a translation of the word "screech" – the cry of the owl – but even this was later corrupted into the blood-curdling screech of the she-devil.

Lilith was transformed into an evil sorceress with powers of darkness. And yet, even in this dramatic transformation of identity, we see the pattern of the ever-changing Moon from New through Full to Dark again.

KALI

In Kali, the Hindu goddess of death, we see the destroyer. Depicted with a third eye in the centre of a face that is smeared with blood and crawling with snakes, she wears a necklace of skulls and presents a truly terrifying image of destruction.

This fearsome and four-armed creature has a double-edged power – power both to deal out dreadful retribution and to offer love. Once she is bent on a frenzy of destruction, only Shiva – Kali's consort, whose seed she carries as the promise of new life – is able to control her insatiable lust for blood.

HECATE

In Hecate, the Moon goddess of the Ancient Greeks, we see the wise woman of the waning Moon, revered as the great mother figure who wore Nature itself as her mantle. As the deity of the dark hours and also known by some as "the distant one", she is often personified as a witch or a hag.

Versed in the black arts, Hecate is a shape-shifter par excellence, with the power to alter both her age and form at will – a fitting metaphor for her dominion over the changing stages of life. The owl and the bat, both well-known creatures of the night, as well as the dog and the toad – both symbols of conception – were her particular animal totems.

Drawn to tombs and crossroads, where opposing forces meet, she was worshipped in the hours of darkness with blazing torches to light up the black skies of the night.

CHAPTER 4

SEX, FERTILITY AND CHILDBIRTH

I n a pioneering study, which was conducted by American doctors (Walter and Abraham Menaker) over an eight-year period during the 1960s, and which took into account half a million births, it was discovered that more babies are born during the three days around the Full Moon than at any other time in the month.

28

Gathering statistics on the clustering of births is comparatively easy because hospital records are fairly accessible. But can this data tell us anything at all about the times of conception and, by implication, reflect any information on times of increased sexual activity? Dr Walter Menaker and his team think it can, and their research has produced some interesting findings.

The first factor they addressed was the length of pregnancy, from conception to birth. Working on a lunar month of 29½ days, they found that the average period of human gestation takes 265½ days, or 9 lunar months. The second factor they discovered was that birth takes place at the same lunar phase of the month as when conception took place. They found, in fact, that it corresponds to the very day.

REACHING A SEXUAL PEAK

This astounding piece of research shows that if more births take place during the Full Moon, then it must be that more women conceive when the Moon is full. These findings, in turn, suggest that this is the time in the month when sexual activity hits a peak.

Interestingly, the same study found that the smallest number of births occurs in the three-day period of the New Moon. So, by implication, it suggests that libido and sexual activity are generally reduced at that particular time of the month.

Sex and the Sea

People whose lives are closely linked to the sea have known since earliest times that sexual activity increases at the time of the Full Moon. For centuries it has been recognized that the mating cycles of sea urchins, shellfish and other aquatic creatures are regulated by the cycle of lunar phases. As far back as the first millennium BC, Aristotle observed that sea urchins tasted better if caught when the Moon was full. He also noted that the creatures were plumper and their ovaries heavier at that time of the month.

Over the years, similar observations have confirmed that many molluscs, crustaceans and other marine creatures spawn at Full Moon time. Their reproductive organs have been found to swell up gradually through the waxing Moon phase as their gonads fill with eggs and sperm. These then mature halfway through the cycle and are released into the water as the Moon reaches fullness. Caught during the waning phase, the creatures are thinner and less plumped up and their sexual organs are considerably reduced in size and bulk.

BOILING WATERS

One of the best demonstrations of this mass Moon-triggered spawning can be seen around the islands of Fiji. Here, on just two specific dates each year, the seas boil with swarming palolo worms as they come up to the surface to mate. So punctual are these creatures that the Fijians confidently await their coming at the appointed dates with fishing nets at the ready to catch their record hauls.

Similar evidence of lunar rhythms at work on aquatic life may be seen along the beaches of California. Here,

a slender fish called the grunion comes ashore to mate and spawn during the breeding season – but only on the nights after either the New or the Full Moon. Indeed, so many grunion come ashore on those particular nights that the beaches shimmer in a luminous mass of silver, writhing bodies as far as the eye can see.

THE POWER OF THE MOON

Crabs, lobsters, scallops, oysters and many more creatures of the seas and oceans follow breeding cycles that can be timed according to lunar movements. Migratory journeys too, such as

that of the eel, are undertaken at a precise time during the waning of the Moon. This means that they reach their spawning grounds at a time when the pull of the Moon is at its greatest. Ruled by the lunar tides, these journeys provide yet more persuasive evidence of the power of the Moon.

＊☆＊☆＊☆＊☆＊☆＊☆
In the Fijian islands, great nets are laid by local people in anticipation of the huge mass of swarming palolo worms. This worm comes to the surface of the sea to mate at just two specific times of the year – a truly dramatic example of spawning under the influence of the Moon.

A NOTE OF CAUTION...

Please note that this chapter is not intended to replace medical advice, and the author and publishers take no responsibility for individuals' choices and actions where conception and childbirth are concerned.

Fertility and Reproduction

THE FEMALE MENSTRUAL CYCLE

The human menstrual cycle, the process of ovulation, takes its name from the Latin word *mensis*, which means month. In fact, menstruation itself used to be called "the menses" – literally an event that occurred at monthly intervals. Menstruation and the very concept of a month are in turn linked to the Moon in that both the lunar cycle and a regular menstrual cycle lasts for 29½ days.

So much for regular menstrual cycles, but what about those women whose periods go haywire? How can erratic menstrual cycles be connected in any way with the Moon? This was the interesting conundrum that drew the attention, in 1967, of Edmond Dewan, a physicist working with the US Air Force.

NATURAL RHYTHM

What Dewan suggested was that the Moon seems to act like a clock – it regulates the menstrual cycle and its

light at Full Moon triggers ovulation. So, under natural circumstances, a woman's menstrual pattern would always be governed by the lunar phases. The existence of electric lighting, however, has confused many women's sensitive biological rhythms and made their cycles irregular.

✳ ☆ ✳ ☆ ✳ ☆ ✳ ☆ ✳ ☆ ✳ ☆

It has been estimated that levels of general sexual activity increase by as much as 30 per cent in the three days around the Full Moon.

* ☆ * ☆ * ☆ * ☆ * ☆ * ☆

Women have known for centuries that the Moon triggers menstruation. By understanding the lunar rhythms that govern their menstrual cycles, women can regulate their fertility and develop a system of family planning that is both natural and accurate.

Working on this theory, Dr Dewan proposed an experiment. He suggested that women with irregular periods could set up artificial "Full Moon" conditions for themselves by leaving the light on in their bedrooms for three consecutive nights, starting from the 14th day after their last period. In terms of lunar phases, the 14th day marks a mid-point between one New Moon and the next and, thus, is equivalent to the period of a Full Moon. The results were astounding. Without exception, every woman who took part in the experiment found that her menstrual cycle became as regular as clockwork – even if her electricity bills increased in the process!

CONCEPTION AND CONTRACEPTION

It was in the 1960s that the Czechoslovakian gynaecologist, Dr Eugen Jonas, set up a clinic and research centre that dealt with the problems of fertility and contraception. What was unique about Dr Jonas' approach was that, while much of the world was beginning to use the Pill as a form of birth control, he was advocating a system which, medically speaking, smacked of quackery and superstition. And yet his method seemed to be 98 per cent effective. Moreover, it was natural, inexpensive, simple to use, totally drug-free and, more importantly, it had no side-effects. This system was based on the workings of the lunar cycle.

What Dr Jonas had "discovered" was a method of family planning that had actually been recognized and used by women for centuries. Essentially, the method is based on the idea that a woman is at the peak of her fertility at that time of the month when the Moon is in the same phase as it was at the time of her own birth. So, if she was born during the gibbous Moon, for example, then it would be during the three days around that same period of each month that she would be at her most fertile and have the best chance of conceiving.

Choosing the Sex of Your Child

For the majority of women, part of the excitement of pregnancy has been the anticipation of finding out whether the baby she is expecting will be a boy or a girl. The advent of scans, however, has taken much of the uncertainty away, and now, weeks before the actual birth, a doctor can inform the mother-to-be, with a good degree of accuracy, what gender her baby will be .

But what about actively choosing the gender of your child-to-be even before conception takes place? All kinds of theories and possible future products have been suggested to help people to do this, but there may be a more natural method that we have actually known about all along. Perhaps we simply have to get in sync with the movements of the Moon.

FEMALE AND MALE PRINCIPLES

For centuries it has been recognized that astrological signs tend to be either masculine or feminine. Every month, the Moon travels through all of the signs, spending about two and a quarter days in each one. One research team discovered that the sex of the child tends to be determined by whichever gender of sign the Moon is in when conception takes place. You might like to try this theory out for yourself. Turn to the charts at the end of the book and work out which sign the Moon is in on the days you think you are likely to conceive.

The astrological signs alternate in gender as follows:

Masculine signs	Feminine signs
Aries	Taurus
Gemini	Cancer
Leo	Virgo
Libra	Scorpio
Sagittarius	Capricorn
Aquarius	Pisces

MAKE YOUR OWN FERTILITY CALENDAR

If you have been trying unsuccessfully to have a baby, and there are no medical reasons preventing you from conceiving, perhaps you have simply been unlucky with your timing and may have been missing your personal fertility peak. Learning to tune in to your own body rhythms and synchronizing your cycle with that of the Moon may well provide the answer. By following a few simple steps each month (*see below*), you can make your own fertility calendar and target those few days in your cycle when you are at your most fertile.

1 Buy a calendar that displays a whole month on one page.
2 Turn to the charts at the end of the book to find the Moon Phases for each month of each year. Find the Moon Phases for the current month and mark them on your calendar.
3 Look back to the year in which you were born and find out which Moon phase prevailed at the time of your birth. Now, using a coloured pen, colour in the equivalent Moon Phase on your current calendar. This phase will be your peak fertility period.
4 Now, using the charts at the end of the book once again, work out which astrological sign the Moon will be in on each day of the month. Using two different colours to distinguish the masculine from the feminine signs, colour in each two and a quarter day block in your calendar with the appropriate colour.
5 Exactly which astrological sign coincides with your peak fertility period? If it is a masculine sign and you conceive, chances are that you will have a boy; a feminine sign is likely to produce a girl. If your fertility period overlaps with a masculine sign, but you've set your heart on a girl, skip this month and wait until your next fertility period corresponds with a feminine sign. Vice versa if your preference is for a boy.

33

PREGNANCY PREDICTORS

Working with a sample of around 8000 women, and by calculating the day on which each had conceived, Dr Jonas was able to predict the sex of their babies with astounding accuracy.

He also discovered that women who were themselves born at the Full Moon – that is, when the Sun and Moon are 180° apart – run a higher than average risk of bearing infants with birth defects if these are also conceived at the Full Moon. However, the risk is minimized if conception occurs during any of the other lunar phases.

CHAPTER 5

CRIME AND PASSION

"Experts" have stated publicly time and time again that the Moon and her cycles have absolutely no influence on human behaviour. Despite this, many people's personal experiences tell a very different tale – and a growing number of psychiatrists and law enforcement agents also have plenty of reasons to believe otherwise.

Members of police forces across the world are only too aware of the rise in violent crimes around the time of the Full Moon. At this same time in the lunar cycle, nurses and doctors in psychiatric institutions have also observed that many of their patients become more agitated than usual. Calls to emergency or crisis centres increase, as do road traffic accidents and other acts of general mindless vandalism.

Those on the ground, so to speak – officers on the beat, fire-fighters and intake clerks working on hospital receptions – recognize these trends and acknowledge that there is some kind of monthly pattern. One senior police officer was recently quoted as saying that people seem to go out of control on a regular basis every 28 days when, to use his words – "they start acting and drinking like idiots".

A FORCE FOR GOOD OR EVIL?
Curiously, despite the fact that we think of the Moon as a serene presence in the night sky, astrologically speaking the Moon represents instability. The effects of the strong gravitational pull that the Moon exerts, not only on our tides and on our weather, but also on the state of our minds, were being noted as far back as the days of Hippocrates, the Greek physician now regarded as the father of medicine.

What all this points to is that at certain times in the Moon's cycle, we experience its influence more strongly than usual. The periods of the Full Moon, when Moon, Sun and Earth are aligned, are particularly significant, since at those times the Sun's gravitational pull is added to that of the Moon. And it is then that the pressure can have an adverse affect on us, heightening tensions and bringing emotions to the boil.

The Moon has long been implicated as a significant trigger in instances of mental instability and illness. In fact, the term "lunacy", once used to denote insanity, is derived from **luna**, *the Latin word for moon.*

34

This is when people start to act irrationally. They get edgy and jumpy, blow things out of all proportion, become accident-prone and start acting violently towards others.

CRIMES OF PASSION

As the police officer mentioned above observed, irrational behaviour, that can lead to crimes of passion and violence of a bizarre nature, occurs on a monthly basis, coinciding with the Full Moon.

Another lunar event that can exert a very powerful influence on our behaviour is known as the Moon reaching perigee (*see the box opposite for a full explanation*). This event takes place every few years and, when it

The mythical transformation at Full Moon of a human into a werewolf abounds in popular culture. The technical term for this dramatic transformation is "lycanthropy". Historically, legends about werewolves were widespread and have formed part of the folklore of many different peoples around the world.

REACHING PERIGEE

Because the Moon's orbit is elliptical, there is a point in its cycle when it is at its farthest distance from the Earth. There is also a point when it is at its nearest. The farthest point is known as apogee, while the closest point to Earth is called perigee.

This process of travelling farther out and coming closer in is simply part and parcel of the Moon's monthly cycle around the Earth, but when perigee coincides with the Full Moon, then the fireworks can really begin. It is at these times that all kinds of extreme weather conditions and freak natural phenomena are often produced. Passions are also inflamed to fever-pitch and crimes involving unusual or widespread violence, such as riots, tend to occur.

occurs at the same time as the Full Moon, the effects can be extremely dramatic. So, just what forms does this link between the Moon and our darker passions take?

Moon-influenced Crimes

While records show a normal distribution of what might be termed "straightforward" crimes throughout the month, those that occur around the time of the Full Moon tend to be especially unpleasant.

Behaviour at Full Moon time becomes psychotic, and criminal acts bear all the hallmarks of mental imbalance. The following are just some of the examples that various people have noted:

- Sportsmen and women incur more penalties during events that take place at the Full Moon than at other times of the month.
- Those who are the worse for wear after heavy drinking might wander home and sleep it off during the Moon's First Crescent, but they can all too easily become aggressive and dangerous at Full Moon.
- Motorists can literally go into dangerous overdrive at this time, becoming irate and unreasonably intolerant of other drivers on the road.
- Attacks on people and burglaries show psychopathic tendencies around this phase of the Moon.
- Records have shown that the Full Moon, especially when it is combined with the Moon at perigee, creates a dangerous climate where assassinations occur, racial tensions are inflamed, riots are sparked and all manner of dreadful atrocities and massacres are committed.

The history of showbusiness is filled with tragic stories of talented but vulnerable individuals, such as Judy Garland (above), whose troubled lives are undermined by addiction to drink and drugs. Astrologers believe that adverse aspects to the Moon at the time of an individual's birth may make a person more susceptible to potentially addictive substances. Suicides too, such as that of Kurt Cobain, lead singer of Nirvana, have been found to cluster around particular times in the lunar cycle.

CRIMES AND THE NEW MOON

Records suggest that, although crimes at and following the New Moon, either show a slight decline or are at what might be considered a more normal level, there does seem to be a slight increase in crimes in the days preceding the New Moon. However, this minor peak is minimal in comparison with the sharp peak that occurs when the Moon is full. It seems that the Moon does indeed have a strong pull on the very deepest of our passions and emotions.

CHAPTER 6

AstroMoon

SUN SIGN DATES

Aries	March 21–April 20
Taurus	April 21 –May 21
Gemini	May 22–June 21
Cancer	June 22–July 22
Leo	July 23–Aug 23
Virgo	Aug 24–Sept 22

Libra	Sept 23–Oct 23
Scorpio	Oct 24–Nov 22
Sagittarius	Nov 23–Dec 21
Capricorn	Dec 22–Jan 20
Aquarius	Jan 21–Feb 18
Pisces	Feb 19–March 20

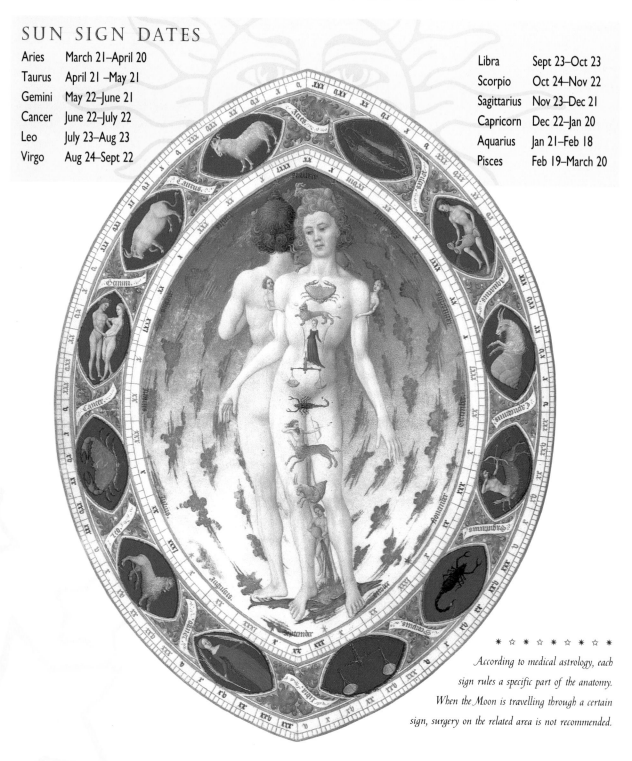

✳ ☆ ✳ ☆ ✳ ☆ ✳

*According to medical astrology, each
sign rules a specific part of the anatomy.
When the Moon is travelling through a certain
sign, surgery on the related area is not recommended.*

Most of us know which sign of the Zodiac we belong to. When we say we are Taurean or Libran, what we mean is that the Sun was in that particular sign on the day we were born. And the sign we belong to is a shorthand method of describing our personalities and the trends in our lives.

Sun and Moon

In astrological terms, we say that the Sun travels roughly one degree per day, moving through each sign in 30 or 31 days, and through all 12 in one year. The Moon, however, is much swifter of foot. While the Sun spends roughly one month in each sign, the Moon whizzes through in about two and a quarter days and passes in and out of the whole lot in just four weeks.

Because the Sun spends a comparatively lengthy time in each sign, it is fairly easy for each of us to know where it was positioned at our time of birth – apart, that is, from those born on the cusp (the end of one sign and the beginning of the next). Though we probably know our Sun signs, few of us know the sign through which the Moon was passing at our birth – yet this is just as important to our understanding of ourselves.

SUN SIGN VERSUS MOON SIGN

Your Sun sign describes how you present yourself to others and the impression that they have of you. It underlines your ego, your mannerisms and idiosyncrasies, the strength of your willpower and the impact you have on your environment – in fact, everything to do with your facade, the outer you, is contained within the parameters of your Sun sign.

Your Moon sign, on the other hand, describes the fundamental inner you – the private person you know yourself to be. It reveals your passive role in life, how you express your feelings and deal with your emotions. It reflects how you interact with people, the sort of relationships you are likely to form and how you come across to others emotionally. By understanding your Moon sign, you will gain a deeper insight into your moods and reactions, your deepest needs and personal sensitivities.

Your Moon sign describes and affects:

- your instinctive responses
- your deepest longings and needs
- your secret wishes and desires
- your innermost loves and hates
- your emotional highs and lows
- your jealousies and joys
- your imaginative potential
- your fears and obsessions
- how other people perceive you
- how you behave in private
- how you react to others on first meeting
- how you interact emotionally with the people you love
- your daily habits and preferred routines
- your home environment and domestic lifestyle
- your family history
- your security dependencies
- your relationship with your mother
- the relationship you have with other important females in your life
- your creative and artistic inclinations
- the areas in life in which you find emotional satisfaction
- the ups and downs you experience on a cyclical basis
- your subconscious memories
- your nurturing instincts
- your early conditioning
- your unconscious programming
- your family influences
- the behaviour you learned as a child and which affects you as an adult

FINDING YOUR MOON SIGN

Because the Moon stays in each sign for just under two and a quarter days, simply knowing your date of birth may be enough to find out where it was when you were born. But if you were born on one of the days when the Moon was changing from one sign to another, you may need to know your time of birth fairly accurately to be sure of the exact sign.

The Moon sign tables at the end of the book give a step-by-step guide to help you discover your personal Moon sign by calculating the Moon's position on the day you were born. You can also find out which Moon sign prevails on days of special importance, such as your wedding day. Work out signs for yourself and for the people you love and then read on to find out how the Moon affects you all.

EARTH

**Taurus
Virgo
Capricorn**

If your Moon is in an Earth sign, your emotions are stable and well balanced. In relationships, you are practical and solid as a rock. Down-to-earth and unpretentious, you take a sensible, no-nonsense attitude to affairs of the heart. Partners find you reliable but also predictable and stubborn. Rarely prone to verbalizing your feelings, your actions speak louder than words. Routine is important in your life and you need a settled, structured framework in which to live and work.

FIRE

**Aries
Leo
Sagittarius**

Warm, vibrant, out-going and physically expressive describes your emotional disposition if your Moon is placed in one of the Fire signs. You are passionate by nature, an enthusiastic and often lusty lover. Characteristically fiery, you generate a lot of heat – physically, emotionally and mentally, and in some situations there is the risk that you might over-heat! You like to be where the action is and preferably centre-stage. A feisty, challenging, loving partner maintains your interest.

AIR

**Gemini
Libra
Aquarius**

If your Moon is situated in one of the Air signs, you are a bright and breezy lover. Friendship is important to you and you need to be on the same mental wavelength as your partner. Curious about how people tick, you take an intellectual interest in sexual matters, and probably find it easier to express your feelings verbally than physically. Indeed, partners can find you cool and detached, sometimes off-hand and unpredictable. Not over-fond of too much body contact, you need your own freedom and your own space.

WATER

**Cancer
Scorpio
Pisces**

Having your Moon in one of the Water signs means that you are inherently sensitive and are ruled by your emotions. Indeed, your feelings, never very far from the surface, sweep over you in great tidal waves of emotion, often taking you by surprise and sometimes threatening to overwhelm you altogether. Mostly, you tend to be inward-looking and subjective in outlook, and so are easily hurt by the merest slight. Nurturing and deeply caring, you are emotionally clinging and have lots of love to share with an empathetic partner.

Your Element and Natal Chart

Each Zodiac sign is associated with one of the four elements – Earth, Air, Fire or Water. People of the same element group are said to be more compatible with each other than with members of other element groups.

A natal chart is a map of the positions of the planets in the sky at the moment of an individual's birth. The chart is divided into 12 sectors (houses), and each is governed by a Zodiac sign. Each sector represents a region of the skies, and the planets are plotted into the sectors according to their actual positions above.

Analysis of a person's character and possible future events in their life is made by considering the planets' position and the relationships they form with one another. These relationships are known as "aspects" and the patterns that they create suggest either harmonious or challenging energies within a person's psyche.

The position of the Moon in the chart is crucial to understanding a person's emotional nature, unconscious motivations, moods and attitudes to relationships. First, the sign that the Moon inhabits, as well as its element and house position, are considered. Next, the Moon's

relationship with the Sun is assessed in order to gauge the person's physical/emotional integration. Lastly, the aspects between the Sun, the Moon and the rest of the planets are brought into play.

YOUR PERSONAL CHART

To have a complete astrological chart drawn up, you need to consult a professional astrologer, who will ask you for three vital pieces of information: your date, time and place of birth. Astrologers use glyphs (universally recognized symbols; *see page 21 and Diana's chart*), to represent the planets and Zodiac signs.

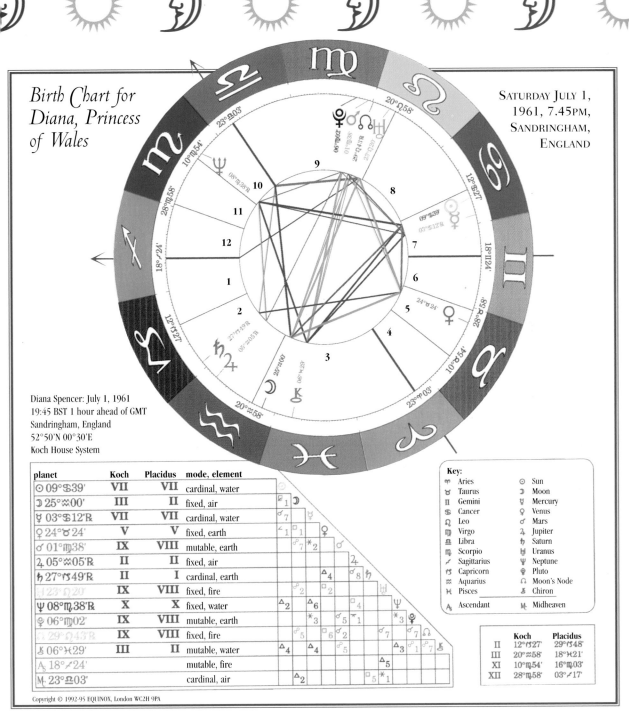

Birth Chart for Diana, Princess of Wales

SATURDAY JULY 1, 1961, 7.45PM, SANDRINGHAM, ENGLAND

Diana Spencer: July 1, 1961
19:45 BST 1 hour ahead of GMT
Sandringham, England
52°50'N 00°30'E
Koch House System

planet	Koch	Placidus	mode, element
☉ 09°♋39'	VII	VII	cardinal, water
☽ 25°♒00'	III	II	fixed, air
☿ 03°♋12'R	VII	VII	cardinal, water
♀ 24°♉24'	V	V	fixed, earth
♂ 01°♍38'	IX	VIII	mutable, earth
♃ 05°♒05'R	II	II	fixed, air
♄ 27°♑49'R	II	I	cardinal, earth
⚷ 23°♌20'	IX	VIII	fixed, fire
♆ 08°♏38'R	X	X	fixed, water
♇ 06°♍02'	IX	VIII	mutable, earth
☊ 29°♌43'R	IX	VIII	fixed, fire
⚷ 06°♓29'	III	II	mutable, water
A₅ 18°♐24'			mutable, fire
M₊ 23°♎03'			cardinal, air

Key:

♈	Aries	☉	Sun
♉	Taurus	☽	Moon
♊	Gemini	☿	Mercury
♋	Cancer	♀	Venus
♌	Leo	♂	Mars
♍	Virgo	♃	Jupiter
♎	Libra	♄	Saturn
♏	Scorpio	♅	Uranus
♐	Sagittarius	♆	Neptune
♑	Capricorn	♇	Pluto
♒	Aquarius	☊	Moon's Node
♓	Pisces	⚷	Chiron
A	Ascendant	M₊	Midheaven

	Koch	Placidus
II	12°♑27'	29°♑48'
III	20°♒58'	18°♓21'
XI	10°♏54'	16°♏03'
XII	28°♏58'	03°♐17'

✳ ☆ ✳ ☆ ✳ ☆ ✳ ☆ ✳ ☆ ✳ ☆ ✳ ☆ ✳ ☆ ✳ ☆ ✳ ☆ ✳ ☆ ✳

Diana's rising sign was Sagittarius. Since she was a Cancerian, we can see that her Sun was positioned in the sign of Cancer. Her Moon was in Aquarius at the time of her birth. Interestingly, her Sun was situated in the seventh sector of the chart, which represents partnerships and marriage – often a sign of marrying into wealth. Here we should note that, in predictive astrology, potential difficulties and times of crisis in a person's life can be picked up many years in advance. However, the actual ending of a person's life cannot, and indeed never should be, predicted.

NOW READ ON...

The following pages contain information about you and your life according to your Moon sign. First, work out your Moon sign by using the charts at the end of the book, then turn to the section that deals with your sign.

Moon in Aries

42 Key Character Points

Your instinctive response is:
enthusiastic and positive

Your best characteristics are:
courage and strength of character

Your negative qualities are:
impatience and insensitivity

You dislike:
weakness or indecision

You need:
a constant supply of new interests to keep your mind active and alive

You must:
learn to consider other people

PEOPLE WHO SHARE YOUR MOON SIGN

Jerry Hall   Leonard Bernstein

Marlon Brando   Stevie Wonder

Salvador Dali   Barbara Cartland

Whitney Houston   Al Capone

Luciano Pavarotti   Anton Chekhov

THE ESSENTIAL YOU

The Moon in this sign reveals an independent spirit with a dynamic, outgoing personality. You have a fundamental need to excel, so you are, by nature, competitive and you work hard to achieve your ambitions in life. It is leadership, making decisions and taking charge of situations that bring you the greatest satisfaction in life. Since this Moon placement confers courage, you also enjoy the thrill of challenging situations and adventure and are usually to be found right at the forefront of the action.

Lifestyle

THE ARIES MOON AT HOME

Because the Moon in Aries imbues you with masses of physical stamina, there will be much evidence of sporting activities around your house.

Travel, too, is a leisure-time passion so there are likely to be souvenirs, artefacts and memorabilia from past excursions around the world.

YOU AND YOUR FAMILY

You were probably encouraged to stand on your own two feet from a very young age and although your parents were supportive, they were highly ambitious for you too. In turn, you are likely to become a pushy parent, anxious that your own children do well in life. You may have had difficulties relating to your father, and the women in your family are likely to be strong and dominant characters, with seemingly inexhaustible energy.

AT WORK

With a mind that teems with original and far-sighted ideas, and the courage to see your projects through to their conclusions, it is inevitable that sooner or later you will make a success of your career. Moreover, you are ambitious and thrusting and will not allow obstacles to stand in your way when you are in pursuit of your goals. A born leader, you have the gift to inspire those who work under you.

Unwind by:

driving, hiking, going on survival training, travelling to foreign lands

MONEY MATTERS

As an Aries-Moon subject you are likely to possess a nose for good investments and are always ready to spot a bargain.

HEALTH NOTES

Aries-Moon people are usually robust individuals. However, because they also have a tendency to be impulsive, they are prone to accidents, especially cuts and burns.

CHILDREN BORN WITH THE MOON IN ARIES

Noisy, active and adventurous, these youngsters are bursting with life and constantly on the go. They are born with an innate competitive spirit that will usually find its true forte out on the sports field. Much happier leading rather than being led, they will always be found at the front of the queue or wherever the action is at its thickest.

The Moon in Aries can produce loveable firebrands, but look out for any signs of early aggression – these need to be channelled smartly into creative pursuits.

YOUR SUN AND MOON SIGN COMBINATION CHART

Moon in Aries

This shows just how well your outward persona (Sun sign) and inner personality (Moon sign) are integrated.

Your Sun in	Combination keynotes	Star rating
Aries	Strong, robust, insensitive	★
Taurus	Conflicting desires	★★★
Gemini	Dynamic but short attention span	★★★★
Cancer	Push and pull	★★
Leo	Powerful	★★★★★
Virgo	Spirited	★★★
Libra	Ups and downs	★★
Scorpio	Deep and intense	★★★
Sagittarius	A winning combination	★★★★★
Capricorn	Ruthlessly determined	★★★★
Aquarius	Charismatic	★★★
Pisces	Strong yet shy	★★

★ *Highly subjective* ★★ *At odds with yourself* ★★★ *Need to work towards achieving inner balance*

★★★★ *In harmony* ★★★★★ *Strongly integrated*

Relating to Others

YOUR EMOTIONAL PATTERN

In a tough, rugged, independent and egocentric sign such as Aries, there is little room for sentiment, or any patience for subtle sensitivities. Here, the softness and nurturing instincts of the Moon's influence are overlaid by a feisty, robust approach to life. As an Aries-Moon subject, therefore, you do not appreciate weakness or shilly-shallying of any kind.

In fact, you may actually find it difficult to deal with emotions – your own or those of other people. You are a spontaneous sort of person. Decisions must be made instantly and life must be lived now because, in your scheme of things, it is important to keep ahead of the game.

Your passion, too, is immediate: loving or loathing at a glance. Indeed, there is a tendency amongst most Aries-Moons to fall in love all too hastily and to pursue the object of their desire with such zeal that it can actually frighten off potential partners, who may need more time to allow their feelings to develop. Sooner or later, natives of this Moon sign learn to control their ardour and find, often to their surprise, that a little patience will yield just the response they want.

Belonging to this sign means that you like to take the lead in intimate relationships. You are a fiery lover, easily aroused and with desires that need to be satisfied urgently. And though you

Your Partner's Moon in	HOW YOU RELATE TO YOUR PARTNER *Your Moon in Aries*
Aries	Sharing this Moon sign means you both feel the same emotions in equal intensity. You are both fiery and adventurous but also as independent as each other. Neither is likely to give in to the other and the lack of compromise is bound to cause conflict.
Taurus	This partner was not born to rough it in life, for it is luxury and ease that the Taurus-Moon craves. You, on the other hand, prefer life with a sharper edge and plenty of grist to hone the senses. Needless to say, there is a fundamental discrepancy here in your outlooks.
Gemini	Both restless and curious, your Aries-Moon and your partner's Gemini-Moon will keep each of you searching for adventure. Whether you are on the same quest, however, is debatable. Perhaps you may have to agree to disagree.
Cancer	Not an easy pairing since Cancerian-Moon people are cuddly individuals while you are uncomfortable with too much billing and cooing. Additionally, this partner is a natural homebody while you prefer the rugged outdoors.
Leo	An exciting partnership, whether intimate or professional. There is masses of energy in this combination and together you should have tremendous fun. Entertainment, adventure and an active sexual life will colour your days – and nights.
Virgo	The Virgo-Moon's need for order, tidiness and discipline will undoubtedly contrast markedly with your cavalier attitude to domestic life. Sex, too, is likely to be a problem since your ardour may not be reciprocated quite so eagerly.

Your Partner's Moon in	
	## Your Moon in Aries
Libra	You will be enchanted by the grace of your Libra-Moon companion and would do well to allow some of that charm and elegance to smooth your rougher edges. You are opposites but, in relationships, opposites can so often attract!
Scorpio	The jealousy and intense emotions that are so characteristic of a Scorpio-Moon subject will impinge on your compulsive need for independence and personal freedom. Despite this, the passion and desire between you will be red-hot.
Sagittarius	Both adventurous and highly charged, both seeking challenge and distant horizons, this partnership offers excellent prospects and very few dull moments – in or out of bed.
Capricorn	The chances of this combination lasting will be greatly improved if you and your partner happen to be in business together, because you will be able to channel your considerable, but disparate, passions into the success of your company.
Aquarius	Moon-Aquarians are the first to respect another's need for independence and personal freedom, so this partnership promises tolerance and understanding from the outset.
Pisces	For this relationship to work, you would need the patience of a saint and your Pisces-Moon partner would have to develop a very thick skin – and fast! Miracles are rare so this combination may prove unrealistic.

Astro Moon

45

Chapter 6

may be quick to anger, you are unlikely to bear grudges or to seethe with lasting resentment. Aries-Moon subjects readily forgive and forget.

In life, your ideal partner needs to be as fiery and as passionate as you are yourself. A person who is adventurous, and who has plenty of stamina to keep up the pace you set, would gain both your admiration and respect.

✳ ☆ ✳ ☆ ✳ ☆ ✳ ☆ ✳ ☆ ✳ ☆

Aries rules the head so, if the Moon was in this sign at your birth, you may be prone to maladies such as headache and toothache.

Moon in Taurus

46 Key Character Points

Your instinctive response is:
cautious and pragmatic

Your best characteristics are:
charm and tenacity of purpose

Your negative qualities are:
stubbornness and self-indulgence

You dislike:
anything or anybody that makes you uncomfortable

You need:
physical, emotional and financial security

You must:
learn to let go

PEOPLE WHO SHARE YOUR MOON SIGN

Elton John
Irving Berlin
Meryl Streep
CG Jung
Mother Theresa
Ronald Reagan

Diana Ross
Joan Collins
Bill Clinton
Yasser Arafat
Busby Berkeley
Fats Domino
Bob Dylan

Prince Charles
Che Guevara
Mick Jagger
Greta Garbo
Isaac Asimov
Karl Marx

THE ESSENTIAL YOU

People who are born with the Moon in Taurus are noted for their reliability, strong sense of responsibility and level-headedness. You have your feet firmly on the ground and you know just what you want and what will make you happy in life.

Fundamentally, you are driven by a need for personal security, something that will influence almost everything you do in life. You have innate artistic talents and are endowed with immense charm.

Lifestyle

THE TAURUS MOON AT HOME

Because you are unashamedly sensual by nature, comfort and plush surroundings will be given top priority when it comes to furnishing and decorating your home.

YOU AND YOUR FAMILY

The generation gap that causes problems in so many families has never really been an issue between you and your parents because your mature attitude has always ensured that you get on well with older people. It is quite possible that one of your parents was strict, but your shrewdness and charm helped you to find a way to cope with that.

In your own turn, you make a fiercely proud and protective parent and the more responsible, polite and well mannered your children are, the happier you will be.

AT WORK

Practical, hard-working and down to earth, you are never afraid to pitch in wherever you are needed and, in your drive for security and prosperity, it is not unusual for you to take on several jobs at once.

Any occupations involving music and the Arts draw you, although the fashion and financial industries will attract you, too. You are usually quite stubborn in the way that you work and tend to resist the slightest hint of enforced change.

Unwind by:

having a relaxing aromatherapy massage or a session of reflexology

MONEY MATTERS

You are a hoarder of money and will save diligently throughout your whole life. You choose your investments

---

YOUR SUN AND MOON SIGN COMBINATION CHART

Moon in Taurus

This shows just how well your outward persona (Sun sign) and inner personality (Moon sign) are integrated.

Your Sun in	Combination keynotes	Star rating
Aries	Gutsy	★★★
Taurus	Solid but stolid	★
Gemini	Surface tension	★★
Cancer	Emotionally together	★★★★
Leo	A united front	★★★★
Virgo	Mental harmony	★★★★★
Libra	A happy mean	★★★★
Scorpio	Powerful	★★★
Sagittarius	Mismatched	★★
Capricorn	Totally together	★★★★
Aquarius	Certain discrepancies	★★
Pisces	Self-oriented	★★★

★ *Highly subjective*   ★★ *At odds with yourself*   ★★★ *Need to work towards achieving inner balance*
★★★★ *In harmony*   ★★★★★ *Strongly integrated*

---

extremely wisely and are careful to make sure that you never put all your eggs in one basket.

HEALTH NOTES

Putting on weight can be a major problem for people born in this group as the pear body shape is often associated with a Taurus-Moon placement. You may also find that you are prone to throat infections, laryngitis and various other ailments that affect this part of the body.

CHILDREN BORN WITH THE MOON IN TAURUS

Nice plump babies are often born when the Moon is in the sign of Taurus. As long as they are warm and well fed, these infants are usually perfectly contented and undemanding. Taurus-Moon children tend to be born either to parents who are well-to-do, or who have a rural or agricultural background. They have a strong sense of family and healthy appetites and grow into happy, helpful and positive young people.

Your Partner's Moon in	HOW YOU RELATE TO YOUR PARTNER
	Your Moon in Taurus
Aries	Your love of comfort and ease does not match the Aries-Moon subject's driving need to experience the challenges at the sharper end of life. Sexually, though, the atmosphere can be hot and satisfying.
Taurus	A splendid combination, with both partners sharing identical emotional needs. You will feel comfortable in each other's company and will grow happy and prosperous together.
Gemini	Certainly you both have plenty to say but you may not exactly speak the same language. Your Taurus-Moon demands stability but your partner likes to be loose and fancy-free.
Cancer	A Moon in Taurus matched with a Moon in Cancer makes a delightful combination. You are both loving, gentle and attentive to each other and to your family and friends.
Leo	Apart from the occasional battle of wills, there is every potential here to form a vibrant and enduring relationship together.
Virgo	With both Moons in strong, reliable and earthy signs, you two will have plenty in common. This has all the makings of a sexy, stable and lasting union.
Libra	Shared creative tastes offer excellent prospects for a successful combination. You and your gentle Libran-Moon partner will forge an artistic and highly sensual relationship together.
Scorpio	Your Moon is in an Earth sign, that of your partner is in Water. Earth and water mixed can produce a muddy swamp. Alternatively, they can form the basis of creation. The choice is yours.
Sagittarius	As a Taurus-Moon individual, you need a sense of permanence and stability under your feet. But your partner's Sagittarian-Moon hates to be tied down. There is little in common between you, it appears.
Capricorn	There is a wonderful meeting of hearts between these two Moon signs which bodes extremely well for a compatible and lasting relationship together. Top marks for a solid and stable union.
Aquarius	A Taurus Moon has little in common with an Aquarian Moon since each has different needs and wants different things from life. Consequently, there is no real meeting ground here.
Pisces	With these two Moon placements there are potentially good spin-offs from one to the other. You two, therefore, could be very good for each other.

Relating to Others

YOUR EMOTIONAL PATTERN

Emotionally stable and solid as a rock, you take a sensible, pragmatic approach to life. Security is perhaps your most important consideration, so you soon develop a cautious nature underpinned by an extremely strong sense of self-preservation.

So vital is your need for security that Taurus-Moon people tend to surround themselves with material possessions, which they feel give their lives structure and support. Many, too, grow over-possessive, jealously – even neurotically – guarding what (or whom) they believe to be theirs.

You are not the sort of individual who leaps blindly into a new relationship. Before you give your affections, you will carefully weigh up all the pros and cons in order to satisfy yourself that this individual is really trustworthy and will offer you the stability you require, as well as providing the physical, financial and emotional anchors that are essential to your wellbeing.

To your relationships you pledge commitment and loyalty. You work hard to make your partnership successful, comfortable and prosperous and your domestic environment a pleasant place in which to live. Innately sensual, you like to indulge yourself and your loved ones whenever possible, so ensuring that you and your family have all the creature comforts you need will be high on your list of priorities.

Sociable and outgoing, you enjoy people and get-togethers. But with such strong nurturing instincts, you are a formidable nest-builder and like to tuck your loved ones, and your possessions, under your wing to keep them safe from harm.

✳ ☆ ✳ ☆ ✳ ☆ ✳ ☆ ✳ ☆ ✳ ☆

Taurus traditionally rules the neck and the throat. For those born with the Moon in this sign, their neck may be a pronounced feature — either strong and muscular or long and graceful.

Moon in Gemini

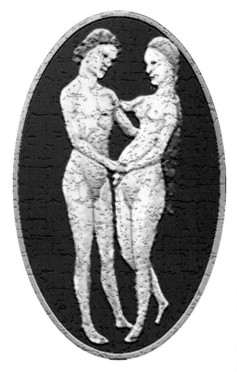

50 Key Character Points

Your instinctive response is:
flexible and sociable

Your best characteristics are:
wit and a generally youthful
outlook on life

Your negative qualities are:
a tendency towards superficiality
and craftiness

You dislike:
routine

You need:
lots of intellectual stimulation

You must:
learn to see your projects through
to the end

THE ESSENTIAL YOU

Bright as a button, as well as being
both clever and amusing, you are
blessed with a wit that is razor-sharp.

Communications are your forte and,
ever-questioning, you take a lively
interest in everything around you –
from how a gadget might work to
precisely what makes a person tick.
But you also suffer from a very short
attention span, flitting like a butter-
fly from one interest to another,
without giving yourself time to learn
a subject in depth or to finish the
projects you undertake.

PEOPLE WHO SHARE YOUR MOON SIGN

Brigitte Bardot	Doris Day	Omar Sharif
Spencer Tracy	Fred Astaire	Stan Laurel
Amelia Earhart	Mae West	Pablo Casals
T S Eliot	Groucho Marx	Edith Piaf
Joan Baez	Sigmund Freud	Dorothy Sayers
J D Rockefeller	Noel Coward	Fyodor Dostoevsky

Lifestyle

THE GEMINI MOON AT HOME

All the latest in technological wizardry will be very much in evidence in this home – anything to take the tedium out of all those routine domestic chores. And since you are so restless and have a strong need to experience new environments, you are likely to move house several times in your life.

YOU AND YOUR FAMILY

You treat everyone close to you as your friend, in a brotherly or sisterly way – including your own offspring and parents. And, because the Moon in Gemini means you are young at heart, when it's your turn to be a parent, there is unlikely to be a noticeable generation gap between you and your children – you really enjoy the outlook of young people and are happy to share their interests, their music, their games and their fun.

YOUR SUN AND MOON SIGN COMBINATION CHART

Moon in Gemini

This shows just how well your outward persona (Sun sign) and inner personality (Moon sign) are integrated.

Your Sun in	Combination keynotes	Star rating
Aries	On the go	★★★★
Taurus	Creative and clever	★★★
Gemini	Young at heart	★
Cancer	Caring but too easily bored	★★
Leo	Charismatic	★★★★
Virgo	Inventive	★★★
Libra	Persuasive	★★★★★
Scorpio	Cool customer	★★★★
Sagittarius	Restless	★★
Capricorn	Ambitious	★★★
Aquarius	Visionary	★★★★★
Pisces	Whimsical	★★

★ *Highly subjective*   ★★ *At odds with yourself*   ★★★ *Need to work towards achieving inner balance*

★★★★ *In harmony*   ★★★★★ *Strongly integrated*

AT WORK

Moon-Gemini people are quick with their brains and dextrous with their hands. You can pick up new skills as fast as lightning – all you need to do is have something demonstrated or explained once and you are able to grasp the essentials immediately.

Your versatility lends itself to a wide variety of occupations although communications, entertainment, the media and travel industries will be the most appealing to you.

Unwind by:

surfing the net

MONEY MATTERS

You need to curb your tendency to spend, spend, spend.

HEALTH NOTES

With your nervous and tense disposition you, more than any of the Moon signs, really do need to take some time out to relax. Make sure this isn't an area that you overlook.

CHILDREN BORN WITH THE MOON IN GEMINI

True to their Mercurial Moon sign, children belonging to this group develop language skills from a very early age and, once they begin to talk, never seem to stop again!

Highly socially skilled, Moon-Gemini youngsters tend to be very amusing. They are fascinated by anything that moves and they can drive their parents mad with a constant bombardment of questions.

Relating to Others

YOUR EMOTIONAL PATTERN

It has been said that those born with the Moon in this sign display the characteristics of a chameleon. Whichever crowd they happen to be with, they find a way of blending in, reflecting the mood of their companions and saying what they think other people want to hear rather than revealing their own true opinions or feelings. As a member of this sign, it is hardly surprising, then, that many people find it rather hard to get to know the real you.

Since variety is the spice of life to a Gemini-Moon, you tend to be emotionally changeable, or perhaps whimsical might be a better description. You like to feel free – light as the air that is the Geminian element. Commitments, in particular, overwhelm you and too many responsibilities leave you champing at the bit. In fact, any situation that bogs you down, for example a relationship that you feel restricts your movements, will soon become suffocating and intolerable.

If truth be told, you are a monumental flirt, whether you are in or out of a relationship, for neither constancy nor fidelity are particularly strong suits where this Moon sign is concerned.

Just as you need a good supply of interests for mental stimulation, so you also need a wide social network of friends and acquaintances that you can call up whenever you begin to feel bored. An address book brimming over with the phone numbers of friends, acquaintances – and even various past lovers – is an absolute must for anyone who has the Moon in Gemini.

You may flit from one thing to another and from one person to the next, but you do tend to have good control over your emotions. You are usually able to rationalize your feelings and work out precisely what it is that's affecting you. A Gemini-Moon individual will very rarely let their heart rule their head.

A partner who is intelligent will intrigue you. But for a truly successful relationship, he or she must also be clever enough to recognize that, just as long as you are given enough freedom, you will always want to come home.

Astro Moon

Chapter 6

✳ ☆ ✳ ☆ ✳ ☆ ✳ ☆ ✳ ☆ ✳ ☆

The sign of Gemini rules the following areas of the body: the respiratory organs, the nerves, the shoulders, the arms and the hands. Individuals who are born with the Moon in this sign may discover that they have more than an average tendency to problems affecting these parts of the body.

Your Partner's Moon in	HOW YOU RELATE TO YOUR PARTNER
	Your Moon in Gemini
Aries	Both restless and curious, your Gemini-Moon and your partner's Aries-Moon will keep you both searching for adventure. Whether you are on the same quest, however, is debatable. Perhaps you may have to agree to disagree.
Taurus	Certainly you both have plenty to say but you may not exactly speak the same language. Your partner's Taurus-Moon demands constancy – something which, alas, would bore you rigid.
Gemini	A bright and breezy union with many intellectual interests in common but little sticking power, since the Moon in Gemini exacerbates restlessness.
Cancer	Cancerian-Moon individuals like to be close to hearth and home while Gemini-Moon people are only happy when they are out and about. You and your partner, therefore, seem to be at odds.
Leo	A light and airy combination, full of fun and frivolity. If you can keep laughing with each other and not at each other, this relationship could be amusing as well as sexually exciting.
Virgo	Differences of attitude and opinion between your Moon sign and that of your partner make the divide too great to guarantee lasting romance with this union.
Libra	Definitely on the same emotional wavelength. Gemini-Moon combined with a Libran-Moon make one of the best matches in the Zodiac. This is a potentially brilliant relationship.
Scorpio	Your Gemini-Moon demands freedom whereas your partner's Scorpio-Moon is jealous and possessive. Consequently, this makes for a highly volatile situation.
Sagittarius	Despite the fact that Sagittarian-Moons are at the opposite end of the spectrum to Gemini-Moons, this combination has been known to work very nicely.
Capricorn	There is very little meeting of minds and hearts between Gemini-Moons and Capricorn-Moons. As a result, you and your partner would irritate each other and trying to stay together could prove an uphill struggle.
Aquarius	A splendidly amicable relationship, where each partner is cool and independent, yet both see eye-to-eye. An easy pairing with every chance of long-term success.
Pisces	A Pisces-Moon is perhaps the most emotionally clinging of the Moon signs. A Gemini-Moon is the most elusive. Neither has a true grasp of the other's feelings.

AstroMoon

53

Chapter 6

Moon in Cancer

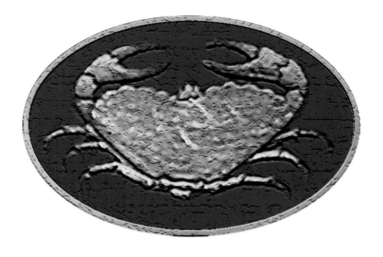

54 Key Character Points

Your instinctive response is:
emotional and sensitive

Your best characteristics are:
good intuition and a nurturing
instinct

Your negative qualities are:
a tendency towards defensiveness
and a severe sense of insecurity

You dislike:
throwing anything away

You need:
the security of a happy and settled
home life

You must:
learn to take less seriously whatever
other people say to you

PEOPLE WHO SHARE YOUR MOON SIGN

Humphrey Bogart
George Orwell
Thomas Hardy
Georgio Armani
Julio Iglesias
Christian Dior
Clarke Gable

Jimi Hendrix
Jeffrey Archer
Bob Hope
Emma Thompson
Graham Greene
Boris Yeltsin

Tom Cruise
Burt Bacharach
Igor Stravinksy
Harrison Ford
Paul Simon
Liza Minnelli

THE ESSENTIAL YOU

Just as the crab has a hard external
shell into which it climbs for protection, so you have learned to hide
your tender feelings behind a tough
facade. This is essentially because
Cancer-Moon people are so very, very
sensitive. Being born under this sign
means that you are by nature intuitive, and you characteristically feel
your way through life. If you sense
that something is right, you do it. If
you feel it is wrong, you don't. For
you, home is where the heart is and
you are at your happiest in your own
environment, surrounded by all the
people that you love.

Lifestyle

THE CANCER MOON AT HOME

An innate homemaker, but also a
terrific collector, your home will be

cosy and comfortable but crammed with all the things you cannot bear to throw away. Domesticity pleases you and, with your creative talents, you have the knack of turning the humblest hovel into a palace.

YOU AND YOUR FAMILY

All Moon-in-Cancer subjects are both strongly family-oriented and nurturing by instinct, so you will delight in looking after the people you love. As a child, you felt responsible for your brothers and sisters, even if they were older than yourself, and it is this tender, caring role that you carry through to your partner and your own offspring. Your mother is a very significant figure in your life and you are unlikely ever to lose the close attachment you formed with her as a child.

AT WORK

Cancer-Moon individuals are life's carers, so you would do well in the medical or counselling fields. Charity work, the voluntary sector and working with children would also appeal. Since you are happiest in your own environment, working from your own home might well give you immense satisfaction. Setting up your own business as an interior decorator, a landscape designer or an antiques dealer would all be suitable.

Unwind by:

creating an elaborate dish for the family to enjoy

YOUR SUN AND MOON SIGN COMBINATION CHART

Moon in Cancer

This shows just how well your outward persona (Sun sign) and inner personality (Moon sign) are integrated.

Your Sun in	Combination keynotes	Star rating
Aries	Restless spirit	★★
Taurus	Practical sense	★★★★★
Gemini	Gossip, gossip, gossip	★★
Cancer	Cuddly	★
Leo	Warm-hearted	★★★★
Virgo	Solid and sensible	★★★★
Libra	Charming and eloquent	★★★
Scorpio	Hidden depths	★★★★
Sagittarius	A searching soul	★★★
Capricorn	Responsible	★★
Aquarius	Divided	★★
Pisces	Super-sensitive	★★★★★

★ *Highly subjective*   ★★ *At odds with yourself*   ★★★ *Need to work towards achieving inner balance*

★★★★ *In harmony*   ★★★★★ *Strongly integrated*

MONEY MATTERS

You are a compulsive hoarder, so saving money will come naturally to you. Something among your eclectic possessions is bound to prove valuable one day.

HEALTH NOTES

You are physically tougher than you appear, although you are sensitively attuned to every ache and pain. But it is your habitual worrying that tends to lay you low.

CHILDREN BORN WITH THE MOON IN CANCER

Cancer-Moon babies are loving and cuddly and especially bonded to their mothers – features that they take with them into adulthood. They readily demonstrate their feelings and emotions and, when they are little, they tend to cry easily. As a consequence they may be bullied or teased at school – a possibility that all parents of these Cancer-Moon children need to keep in mind.

Relating to Others

YOUR EMOTIONAL PATTERN

Soft and sentimental, you are a consummate romantic with a tendency to slip on rose-tinted spectacles at every opportunity. Born with an innate nurturing instinct, your caring nature will reach out to help anyone in need. Protective of the people and possessions that belong to you, your family and home are the centre of your universe and you tend to fret if you are kept away from your own environment for too long.

Because the Moon is in her own sign here, her sensitivity is especially strong, so you are likely to find your emotional response to others intensified. Instinctively, you are able to tap into other people's feelings and pick up on their moods, something that can affect you deeply. Indeed, so infectious do you find the emotions of those you are with that you become happy or sad according to the prevailing atmosphere around you. And of course, it is this intuitive capacity that makes you such an understanding and sympathetic companion to your partner, your family and your friends.

Cancer-Moon and mother-figures are inseparably associated with each other. For a start, whether male or female, you have a close rapport with your own mother, taking after her in some notable way or sharing particular physical or mental characteristics. And when choosing a mate, you may be drawn to someone who will "mother" you in the same way that your own mother did when you were a child. Or else, because of your own nurturing instincts, you will naturally gravitate towards a partner who, for some reason, needs to be "mothered" and the relationship will enable you to assume the role you know so well, and which brings you so much satisfaction in your life. But perhaps the greatest fulfilment of all for you is the creation of your own family and the opportunity of watching your children grow into happy, well-rounded individuals.

＊ ☆ ＊ ☆ ＊ ☆ ＊ ☆ ＊ ☆ ＊ ☆ ＊

Being born with the Moon in Cancer may mean that you are vulnerable to problems associated with this sign. The parts of the body that are ruled by Cancer are the chest, breasts, stomach and alimentary canal. Incidentally, Cancer-born individuals are no more susceptible to cancerous diseases than members of any other Zodiac sign.

Your Partner's Moon in	HOW YOU RELATE TO YOUR PARTNER
	Your Moon in Cancer
Aries	You prefer to reminisce rather than look forward, but your Aries-Moon partner wants to live in the present and not the past. You like cuddling, but your partner cannot tolerate too much body contact. These are the sort of differences that will come between you.
Taurus	A Moon in Cancer matched with a Moon in Taurus makes a delightful combination. You are both loving, gentle and attentive to each other and to your family and friends.
Gemini	Gemini-Moon people like to be out and about while Cancerian-Moon individuals are only happy when they are close to hearth and home. You and your partner, therefore, seem to be at odds.
Cancer	A lovely combination, producing a gentle, quiet union and a somewhat old-fashioned relationship, reminiscent of lavender and lace. You are loving, tender and solicitous of one another.
Leo	Here is a relationship that could just work – but only if you are all-adoring and your Leo-Moon partner refrains from being too bossy and overbearing.
Virgo	Pairing up with a Virgo-Moon partner has all the ingredients of a mutually beneficial relationship. You could find this match stimulating and enriching for both of you.
Libra	Your Libra-Moon partner is much too cool and aloof for your liking while he or she will probably find you too physically and emotionally demanding. Altogether, then, an uphill struggle.
Scorpio	Intense feelings and deep love will underlie this union, despite occasional moods and temperamental outbursts. There will be plenty of passion and sex will be both satisfying and rewarding.
Sagittarius	With different attitudes and disparate ambitions, you and your partner are unlikely to want the same things in life. At the end of the day, neither finds the other truly understanding.
Capricorn	Despite the fact that your Moons are in opposite signs, this combination has all the makings of a highly successful partnership. All in all, a splendid match.
Aquarius	Cancer-Moons and Aquarius-Moons are poles apart emotionally – one is clinging and dependent, the other is distant and remote. Such differences are difficult to reconcile.
Pisces	Moons in Cancer and Pisces produce gentle, caring people with a loving and affectionate nature, so there will be shared feelings and understanding here. This is an ideal match.

Moon in Leo

58 Key Character Points

Your instinctive response is:
dramatic and enthusiastic

Your best characteristics are:
warmth and generosity

Your negative qualities are:
egotism and a tendency to boast

You dislike:
being ignored

You need:
to be admired

You must:
learn to see through empty flattery

PEOPLE WHO SHARE YOUR MOON SIGN

James Joyce

Peter Ustinov

H M Queen Elizabeth I

Paul McCartney

Tom Hanks

Twiggy

Winston Churchill

David Bowie

Dolly Parton

Barbra Streisand

Andrew Lloyd Webber

Clint Eastwood

Leon Trotsky

Reverend Desmond Tutu

Prince Philip

Jane Fonda

Marlene Dietrich

THE ESSENTIAL YOU

The Moon in Leo endows you with a happy, sunny nature that makes you a charismatic, popular and attractive figure among your contemporaries. You come across as honest, warm-hearted and generous to a fault. In fact, extravagance can be your downfall since you tend to have expensive tastes. You like to live life to the full and, if you can live it in luxury, then all the better! With the Moon in this placement, you feel your natural role in life is centre-stage. Being overshadowed or pushed to the sidelines would profoundly rock your inner confidence.

Lifestyle

THE LEO MOON AT HOME

There is invariably a sense of grandeur about a Leo-Moon's house. Here, luxury will be much in evidence, with

ibrant colours and rich textures that give an overall opulent effect. To be complimented on their homes gives Leo-Moon subjects tremendous satisfaction.

YOU AND YOUR FAMILY

ndividuals belonging to your Moon ign often have mothers who are olourful, demonstrative and flamoyant figures, and you respond well o this warmth.

Fathers, however, are often a different kettle of fish, possibly authorarian or difficult in some way. They ere deeply proud of, and ambitious or you, and you have the same feelngs for your own offspring. As a arent you are very generous and ave a tendency to indulge your chilren's every whim.

T WORK

etter in the limelight than in the hadows, and at the top of the hierrchy rather than at the bottom, hatever your line of work, you uickly establish yourself in a posiion of leadership and control. With our ambitious, upwardly mobile rive, you soon attract recognition nd success. Whenever possible, you ill mix business with pleasure. In articular, you have a talent for ransforming any hobby into a thrivng and lucrative business.

Unwind by:

oining a local amateur dramatics roup

MONEY MATTERS

Because of your extravagant nature, you may tend to be a big spender. If you have anything at all left over to invest, then you should put your money into luxury goods or blue chip companies.

HEALTH NOTES

The heart and the spine are this sign's weak links, so you need to watch your diet carefully and ensure that you take regular exercise.

CHILDREN BORN WITH THE MOON IN LEO

These children come into the world equipped with a regal bearing thatseems to command respect even when they are still tiny. So much so that, whatever the financial status of the family, they tend to be treated almost like royalty. Because of this, and because of their formidable, precocious talent, there is a danger that these youngsters may become arrogant or boastful, showing off in front of their friends.

YOUR SUN AND MOON SIGN COMBINATION CHART

Moon in Leo

This shows just how well your outward persona (Sun sign) and inner personality (Moon sign) are integrated.

Your Sun in	Combination keynotes	Star rating
Aries	A ball of fire	★★★★★
Taurus	Luxury-loving	★★★★
Gemini	Colourful	★★★
Cancer	Very affectionate	★★★★
Leo	Self-centred	★
Virgo	Fussy	★★
Libra	Stylish	★★★★
Scorpio	Unpredictable	★★
Sagittarius	Plenty of charisma	★★★★★
Capricorn	Upwardly mobile	★★★
Aquarius	Passionate ideals	★★
Pisces	Creative	★★

★ *Highly subjective*   ★★ *At odds with yourself*   ★★★ *Need to work towards achieving inner balance*

★★★★ *In harmony*   ★★★★★ *Strongly integrated*

Relating to Others

YOUR EMOTIONAL PATTERN

Because Leo is the sign of the king of the Zodiac, to be born with the Moon in this placement means that you have a great need for recognition, or for others to treat you as a special person of some importance. Consequently, you project a high profile and give off an air of authority which, you find, most people do respect. Above all else, you need constant reassurance, so it is essential that you get lots of praise from those around you. To be appreciated, to be patted on the back for your achievements or to be thanked for your trouble, is as important to you as the air that you breathe.

Emotionally demonstrative and openly affectionate, you come across as warm and loving. You are out-going and extroverted, and happier in the limelight than in the shade, so you seek a crowd where you can be the centre of attention. It is important that people like you and that you feel loved. But in your search for praise, you must be careful not to fall for empty flattery, nor for the ingratiating compliments of the sycophant.

In love, you are warm and generous, spontaneously affectionate and enthusiastic in your lovemaking. You can be fiery and passionate, giving your love joyfully and voluptuously. But you do expect your feelings to be reciprocated just as eagerly and abundantly as they have been given. If this doesn't happen or if, for any reason, your partner withholds his or her love from you, then you will instantly shut down all feelings and cut yourself off from that person altogether.

In relationships generally, you like to take charge and, in an ideal world

HOW YOU RELATE TO YOUR PARTNER

Your Moon in Leo

Your Partner's Moon in	
Aries	An exciting partnership, whether intimate or professional. There is masses of energy in this combination and together you should have tremendous fun. Entertainment, adventure and an active sexual life will colour your time together.
Taurus	Apart from the occasional battle of wills, there is every potential in these two Moon placements to form a vibrant and enduring relationship together.
Gemini	A light and airy combination, full of fun and frivolity. If you can keep laughing with each other and not at each other, this relationship could be amusing as well as sexually exciting.
Cancer	Here is a relationship that could feasibly work – but only if your Cancer-Moon partner is all-adoring and you refrain from being bossy and overbearing.
Leo	A fiery and highly combustible combination. Although there is a great deal of passion at the start of the relationship, you are each much too competitive and self-oriented to make this union viable.
Pisces	The Leo-Moon is emotionally driven while your Virgo-Moon partner is all reason and analysis. Such contrasting needs and approaches suggests that this relationship is not highly rated for lasting success.

you would choose a partner who allows you to shine and who is contented to bask in your reflected glory. All in all you are a happy and out-going person – and you take the greatest pleasure in making those you love happy, too.

☆ ☆ ☆ ☆ ☆ ☆ ☆ ☆ ☆ ☆ ☆ ☆

The sign of Leo rules the heart as well as the dorsal areas and the spinal column. People born with the Moon in this sign are advised to keep healthy by watching their diet and taking daily exercise. It is important that they should regulate their weight, keep their heart healthy and avoid getting a stiff back.

Your Partner's Moon in	HOW YOU RELATE TO YOUR PARTNER
	Your Moon in Leo
Libra	With a Leo-Moon and a Libra-Moon in the same house, it has to be five-star living all the way. This is certainly a fun-loving combination, but the relationship will only work with give and take on both sides.
Scorpio	Though emotionally very different types, there is a powerful and magnetic attraction that draws the two of you together. Sexually sultry, your union will sizzle and smoulder on.
Sagittarius	What a fiery, dynamic duo you two make! This has all the ingredients of a powerful love affair. With your shared interests and similar ways of experiencing the world, you are bound to go far together.
Capricorn	Not the easiest of pairings, since a Capricorn-Moon will unhesitatingly deflate your pride and your Leo-Moon generosity would affront your economically minded partner.
Aquarius	In many ways chalk and cheese, this combination has been known to work surprisingly successfully. Though you come from opposite ends of the spectrum, yet there is much to unite you.
Pisces	Although this might appear a strange combination on the surface, yet there is a great deal of romance and enchantment between you and your Pisces-Moon partner that will bind you together.

Moon in Virgo

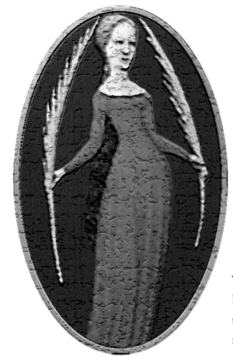

62 Key Character Points

Your instinctive response is:
cool and off-hand

Your best characteristics are:
practical know-how and attention
to detail

Your negative qualities are:
fastidiousness and a tendency to worry

You dislike:
flamboyance and ostentation

You need:
a well-ordered routine

PEOPLE WHO SHARE YOUR MOON SIGN

J F Kennedy	Kenneth Branagh	Shirley Maclaine
Gloria Vanderbilt	Madonna	Leo Tolstoy
Bill Cosby	Dustin Hoffman	Gina Lollobrigida
Princess Anne	Robert Redford	Lenny Bruce
Mel Gibson	Benjamin Britten	Thomas Carlyle
Stephen Hawking	Vanessa Redgrave	Jack Kerouac
Glenn Miller		

You must:
learn to relax in general and, in particular, don't worry about what the neighbours might think

THE ESSENTIAL YOU

If you were born when the Moon was in the sign of Virgo, you may be described as serious in outlook and modest of demeanour. Though you possess quick and instinctive reactions, there is, nevertheless, something quiet and retiring about your nature so that, rather than push yourself forwards, you prefer to take a step back. But onlookers would do well not to be deceived, for this quietness belies an intelligent and incisive mind, a wise and critical judgement and a clever, discriminating eye that can sort the wheat from the chaff from a mile away.

Lifestyle

THE VIRGO MOON AT HOME

People born with the Moon in Virgo tend to change residences several times in their lives, often uprooting themselves from their early environment and setting up home far away from where they grew up. Drawn to the country rather than to an urban setting, their homes are usually neat and tidy and many are quite happy living completely on their own.

YOU AND YOUR FAMILY

Early family life may have been strict or difficult in some way. As a result, the relationship between you and your parents may have been strained. As a parent yourself, you approach family life in a cool, dispassionate manner, expecting your home to run like clockwork and taking a fair, but firm and disciplined control over your offspring.

AT WORK

With your clever, methodical approach to work, you would find both satisfaction and success in any occupation that demands precision skills coupled with a keen eye for detail. Several areas draw your interest. The first might be in the technological, mechanical or engineering industries. The second includes the medical or scientific fields. And, because of your green fingers, the third involves gardening or horticulture. Lastly, any form of research, whether in these areas or in academic life, would also suit you well.

Unwind by:

going for a walk in the countryside

YOUR SUN AND MOON SIGN COMBINATION CHART

Moon in Virgo

This shows just how well your outward persona (Sun sign) and inner personality (Moon sign) are integrated.

Your Sun in	Combination keynotes	Star rating
Aries	Sharp and decisive	★★
Taurus	Level-headed	★★★★★
Gemini	Silver-tongued	★★★
Cancer	Caring	★★★★
Leo	Warm but reserved	★★
Virgo	Critical	★
Libra	Discerning eye	★★★
Scorpio	Determined	★★★
Sagittarius	Wise and thoughtful	★★★
Capricorn	Serious	★★★★★
Aquarius	Intelligent	★★★★
Pisces	Medically minded	★★

★ Highly subjective ★★ At odds with yourself ★★★ Need to work towards achieving inner balance

★★★★ In harmony ★★★★★ Strongly integrated

MONEY MATTERS

You are as organized and careful in your financial affairs as you are in all other areas of your life, so you will undoubtedly have made some wise investments as well as sound provisions for your future.

HEALTH NOTES

Tension headaches from pouring over intricate detail, or because you get wound up worrying about your work, seem to be the Virgo-Moon bugbear.

CHILDREN BORN WITH THE MOON IN VIRGO

Whether male or female, children born with the Moon in Virgo tend to be timid and shy, in some cases even nervous and withdrawn. Mostly self-resourceful and self-contained, they often need encouragement to express their inner talents. They possess excellent powers of concentration and can work away diligently and systematically until they are satisfied that they have achieved their objective.

Relating to Others

YOUR EMOTIONAL PATTERN

Having the Moon in Virgo means you were born with a sense of service and a deep-seated instinct for helping others. Above all else, you need to be needed. Sometimes, though, there may be a danger that you will take on too much and then find yourself over-burdened by commitments or by other people's problems.

Perhaps it is because you are innately shy, or perhaps because you are afraid of being let down and hurt, that you tend not to express your innermost feelings openly to others. This means that, emotionally, you come across as cool and reserved. For whatever reason, you are cautious about giving your love and trust to others. In addition, you have very high standards of excellence that you impose on yourself as well as on those with whom you interact. Always searching for perfection, you fuss over details, scrupulous about your own appearance and behaviour and expecting others to feel the same.

In truth, the Moon in this placement is not in the most passionate of signs. Rather, it imbues you with a logical and practical approach to relationships. You say to yourself that if you enter a partnership with your eyes open and with no illusions, then you cannot be disappointed.

The key for you, however, is finding the right partner. You need someone you can respect and who is on your wavelength; a person who will not criticize you or pick holes in the things you do. Someone who appreciates your cool efficiency and tidy mind; who will encourage you to articulate your feelings and remind you to let your hair down and relax. A partner, above all else, who knows how to make you laugh. With such a partner as this at your side, you will discover the true solace of your heart. For this soulmate will help you to flower and reach the heights of joy.

* ☆ * ☆ * ☆ * ☆ * ☆ * ☆ *

The stomach and intestines are the anatomical areas that are ruled by Virgo. If your Moon was in this sign at the time of your birth, it is possible that these are your physiological weak spots. Since Virgo also rules the nervous system, then relaxation exercises, Yoga or meditation would be beneficial to your wellbeing.

Your Partner's Moon in	HOW YOU RELATE TO YOUR PARTNER
	## Your Moon in Virgo
Aries	Your Virgo-Moon calls for order, tidiness and discipline, which is not at all well matched with your partner's cavalier attitude to domestic life. Sex, too, is likely to be a problem, since you do not always appreciate the Aries-Moon's need for urgency when it comes to satisfying passion and desire.
Taurus	With both Moons in strong, reliable and earthy signs, you two will have plenty in common. This has all the makings of a sensual, stable and lasting relationship.
Gemini	Differences of attitude and opinion between your Moon sign and that of your partner make the divide too great to guarantee lasting romance for this union.
Cancer	Pairing up with a Cancer-Moon partner has all the ingredients of a mutually beneficial relationship. You could find this match stimulating and enriching for both of you.
Leo	The Virgo-Moon is all reason and analysis, while your partner is emotionally driven. Such contrasting needs and diverse approaches suggest that this relationship is not highly rated for lasting success.
Virgo	Though you undoubtedly have plenty in common, there is the danger that, with both your Moons in this sign, your relationship could become a touch too stolid. You work hard, but neither of you knows how to relax.
Libra	Verbal communications between you will be very satisfying, with long conversations and debates well into the night. But when it comes to passion, you each look for different things.
Scorpio	Potentially, a relationship together could be a scorcher in more ways than one. In reality, however, Scorpio-Moons are physically demanding while Virgo-Moons can be prudish. So sex can be a problem here.
Sagittarius	Virgo-Moons like to feel that they have their feet on terra firma, but Sagittarius-Moons dislike being pinned down. You are both too self-sufficient in your own ways to expect this relationship to work in the long-term.
Capricorn	With both Moons in Earth signs, you both know exactly what the other wants and needs. This, therefore, is a splendid combination, with excellent chances for durability and success.
Aquarius	Your Virgo-Moon delights in the punctilious. Your partner's Aquarius-Moon relishes the unpredictable. Unless you both find a compromise, the odds would seem to be stacked against you.
Pisces	There is no doubt that friendship between you and your Pisces-Moon companion is a sure bet. But when it comes to a more intimate relationship, you may find that each soon loses patience with the other.

Moon in Libra

66 Key Character Points

Your instinctive response is:
affable and charming

Your best characteristics are:
tact and a strong sense of fair play

Your negative qualities are:
indecision and a tendency to pass the buck

You dislike:
unpleasantness of any sort

You need:
to be surrounded by beauty and
aesthetic harmony

You must:
learn to take the rough with
the smooth

PEOPLE WHO SHARE YOUR MOON SIGN

Katherine Hepburn	Simone Signoret	Rudolph Nureyev
Bertrand Russell	Ella Fitzgerald	Josephine Baker
Louis Armstrong	Pierre Cardin	Henry Fonda
Maria Callas	Sylvester Stalone	Edwin Aldrin
Fidel Castro	Agatha Christie	Betty Grable
Bruce Springsteen	Billie Jean King	Walt Disney
Michael Caine	Rudolph Valentino	

THE ESSENTIAL YOU

With the Moon in the sign of the balance, you will find yourself constantly weighing up everything and everyone you come across, and invariably finding that you simply cannot make up your mind either way! Others see you as an indecisive fence-sitter. In reality, you simply want to please everyone and be for them what they want you to be. Harmony is essential to your wellbeing. Peace, beauty and tranquillity is what you strive to achieve, for ugliness and discord upset you profoundly. Elegant, charming, suave and sophisticated, you are a genuine class act.

Lifestyle

THE LIBRA MOON AT HOME

All Libran-Moon natives have a sharply honed sense of aesthetics and a beautiful home environment takes priority over

comfort. Design is a strong feature, with furnishings and interiors that are stylish and elegant. A home that might be featured in *Vogue* is what you aspire to achieve.

YOU AND YOUR FAMILY

Characteristically, people who are born with the Moon in this sign belong to families who are creatively talented in some way – either well read or musically or artistically inclined. The mother tends to be very feminine, an attractive and indulgent personality who takes a great interest in the life and career of her Libra-Moon son or daughter. As a parent, you instil good manners in your children, and encourage their musical or artistic skills.

AT WORK

It is important that the environment in which you work is graceful and aesthetically pleasing. If it is, then you will be able to function at your most creative. You dislike stress and conflict, so any discord between yourself and your colleagues will have an adverse effect on your output. Since you are people-oriented, you tend to excel in teamwork rather than working in an individual capacity. The world of the Arts appeals to you but so, too, does the diplomatic service or any occupation where counselling, negotiating or mediation is required.

MONEY MATTERS

Because you have an eye for quality and expensive tastes in general, you need a substantial amount of money simply to survive. You would prefer to inherit it or win it on the lottery but, if you must work for it yourself, you will try your best to find an occupation that brings the least stress for the maximum gain.

HEALTH NOTES

Your system simply cannot tolerate too much conflict and you may succumb to glandular or kidney infections when under stress.

CHILDREN BORN WITH THE MOON IN LIBRA

These infants are the sweetest babies with the most delightful manners. They soon learn that their smiles and charming ways are a winning formula for achieving their own ends. You might think that butter simply wouldn't melt in their mouths! With such an engaging personality, Libra-Moon children become consummate psychologists from a very young age and soon learn to handle people with apparent ease.

YOUR SUN AND MOON SIGN COMBINATION CHART

Moon in Libra

This shows just how well your outward persona (Sun sign) and inner personality (Moon sign) are integrated.

Your Sun in	Combination keynotes	Star rating
Aries	Impatient	★★
Taurus	Loves an easy life	★★★★
Gemini	Witty but superficial	★★★★★
Cancer	Gracious	★★★
Leo	Extravagant	★★★★
Virgo	Analytical	★★★
Libra	Indecisive	★
Scorpio	Sophisticated	★★★
Sagittarius	Conciliatory	★★★
Capricorn	Status-conscious	★★
Aquarius	Fascinating	★★★★★
Pisces	Easy-going	★★★

★ *Highly subjective*   ★★ *At odds with yourself*   ★★★ *Need to work towards achieving inner balance*

★★★★ *In harmony*   ★★★★★ *Strongly integrated*

Your Partner's Moon in	HOW YOU RELATE TO YOUR PARTNER
	Your Moon in Libra
	When it comes to making decisions, you like to take your time in order to consider all the parameters. Your Aries-Moon partner, however, demands instant action. Despite your differences, there is a lot you can learn from each other.
Aries	
Taurus	Shared creative tastes offer excellent prospects for a successful combination. You and your Taurus-Moon partner will forge an artistic and highly sensual relationship together.
Gemini	Definitely on the same emotional wavelength. Gemini-Moon combined with a Libra-Moon make one of the best matches in the Zodiac. This is a potentially brilliant relationship.
Cancer	Your Cancer-Moon partner needs a lot of cuddling but you, on the other hand, prefer to keep your distance since you dislike too much physical contact. Altogether, then, an uphill struggle.
Leo	With a Leo-Moon and a Libra-Moon in the same house, it has to be five-star living all the way. This is certainly a fun-loving combination, but the relationship will only work with give and take on both sides.
Virgo	Verbal communications between you will be very satisfying with long conversations and debates well into the night. But when it comes to passion, you each look for different things.

Relating to Others

YOUR EMOTIONAL PATTERN

Charming, affable and easy-going, you're always prepared to please. This is because harmony and a peaceful existence are quintessentially important to your emotional wellbeing. And because, in relationships, any ill-feeling or the merest hint of an argument upsets you to the core, you immediately become conciliatory and do your best to find a compromise, so long as it leads to an easy life.

People with this moon placement are able to intellectualize their emotions and so, although immensely sociable and friendly, they can also be cool and aloof. With the right partner, they make delightful companions – chatty, amusing and graciously entertaining. But many may also be described as fair-weather friends, cordial for as long as everything goes well, but quick to distance themselves in times of difficulty.

In truth, you go through life in love with love itself. You idealize a world of honour and gallantry, of fair damsels and courtly knights. It is not so much fiery passion that moves you – it is romance that you seek. For natives of a Libran Moon are essentially romantic creatures who wish to live their lives in a permanently euphoric state of being. Alas, euphoria is by nature tenuous and, when the initial romantic magic of a new relationship inevitably settles into the humdrum realities of everyday life, then Libra-Moon subjects tend to feel total disillusionment.

As a member of this sign you probably know that you have exquisite tastes and, when it comes to choosing a partner, looks and presentation will be high on your list. So your ideal partner must be attractive, well-

groomed and well dressed. Nothing turns you off faster than coarseness, boorish behaviour or poor hygiene. But good manners, refinement, a noble bearing, and the promise of keeping the romance alive, will be the first steps towards winning your heart.

✳ ☆ ✳ ☆ ✳ ☆ ✳ ☆ ✳ ☆ ✳ ☆

In terms of medical astrology, the anatomical areas that are governed by the Zodiacal sign of Libra are the kidneys. If you were born with the Moon in this sign, then you may find that you have a slightly greater than normal tendency towards infections and discomfort in these areas or problems connected with the urinary system in general.

Astro Moon

69

Chapter 6

HOW YOU RELATE TO YOUR PARTNER

Your Partner's Moon in	Your Moon in Libra
Libra	A splendid meeting of minds, both with highly sophisticated tastes. But since you are both indecisive, with two Libra-Moons under the same roof, how would decisions ever get made?
Scorpio	An interesting match in which each can learn a great deal from his or her partner. However, a Scorpio-Moon needs more devotion than a Libra-Moon is prepared, or even able, to offer.
Sagittarius	You both like your freedom so that is something you have in common. A little knowledge of when to share and when to leave well alone will go a long way in this relationship.
Capricorn	Your Moon tends towards indolence and your partner's Moon is dedicated to hard work. You are light-hearted while Capricorn-Moons can be stern moralists. There are too many fundamental differences here.
Aquarius	Fun, friendship, understanding. You share so many characteristics and have such a wide variety of interests in common that life will be led in peaceful co-existence. A terrific combination.
Pisces	Both creative, both lovers of beauty, both needy of harmony and tranquillity. Sex can be sweet and gentle between you, but ultimately you will each blame the other for faults of your own respective making.

Moon in Scorpio

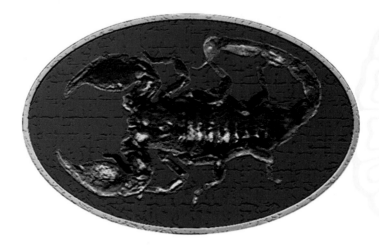

Astro Moon

Chapter 6

70 Key Character Points

Your instinctive response is:
penetrating and intense

Your best characteristics are:
shrewdness and an ability to focus exclusively on the task in hand

Your negative qualities are:
jealousy and irritability

You dislike:
disloyalty in any form

You need to:
feel in control of your environment and of the people you are with

You must:
learn to take yourself less seriously

THE ESSENTIAL YOU

Cool, sexy, mysterious, mean and broody – these are a few of the adjectives that describe an individual born with the Moon in Scorpio.

A born survivor, you are blessed with tremendous strength of character, an ability to focus your total attention upon a task and a tenacity of purpose that will not be deflected until your objective has been reached.

With these kinds of indomitable qualities, you tend to be a formidable personality to deal with. A master or mistress of control, you usually like to take charge of a situation – and always play your cards close to your chest.

PEOPLE WHO SHARE YOUR MOON SIGN

Claudia Cardinale	Charlie Chaplin	Elizabeth Taylor
Fred Zinneman	Warren Beatty	John Wayne
Prince Andrew	Stanley Kubrick	John Logie Baird
Maria Montessori	Raquel Welch	Louis Malle
Dave Brubeck	J P Getty	Steven Spielberg
Gerard Depardieu	Rod Stewart	John Steinbeck
Alfred Hitchcock	James Dean	Douglas Fairbanks Jr

Lifestyle

THE SCORPIO MOON AT HOME

Traditionalist at heart, you go for honest-to-goodness quality and comfort when it comes to furniture and fittings. Antique is usually preferable to modern and darker, richer colours chosen rather than lighter hues. Since Scorpio is a water sign, living by a river or overlooking the sea would be a great draw.

YOU AND YOUR FAMILY

Your admiration of feisty women probably stems from your early memories of your mother who, if she is typical of a Scorpio-Moon parent, may well have been either strong or manipulative, or both. You are likely to be loyal and supportive to your brothers and sisters and feel a close kinship with them. As parents, members of this Moon sign are usually loving but strict.

AT WORK

Scorpio-Moon individuals are unlikely ever to find themselves on skid row, since they have an uncanny sixth sense that leads them to employment of one sort or another. If you belong to this sign, you will operate more successfully as a boss rather than an employee for, in most situations, you like to be the one who gives the orders. With your intuitive abilities and investigative mind, psychological or psychiatric work will appeal. Surgery, the police force, or research of any kind will also attract.

Unwind by:

taking part in a karate class

> ### YOUR SUN AND MOON SIGN COMBINATION CHART
>
> ## Moon in Scorpio
>
> This shows just how well your outward persona (Sun sign) and inner personality (Moon sign) are integrated.
>
> | Your Sun in | Combination keynotes | Star rating |
> |---|---|---|
> | Aries | Athletic | ★★★ |
> | Taurus | Stubborn | ★★ |
> | Gemini | Sharp and perceptive | ★★★ |
> | Cancer | Deeply emotional | ★★★★★ |
> | Leo | Fiercely loyal | ★★★ |
> | Virgo | Vocational instinct | ★★★ |
> | Libra | Animal magnetism | ★★ |
> | Scorpio | Obsessional | ★ |
> | Sagittarius | Idealistic | ★★ |
> | Capricorn | Single-minded | ★★★ |
> | Aquarius | Insightful | ★★ |
> | Pisces | Psychologically aware | ★★★★★ |
>
> ★ Highly subjective   ★★ At odds with yourself   ★★★ Need to work towards achieving inner balance
> ★★★★ In harmony   ★★★★★ Strongly integrated

MONEY MATTERS

You are a canny investor, intuitively picking the policy or saving scheme that will yield the highest dividends.

HEALTH NOTES

Problems with the reproductive organs can sometimes be the weak link in the Scorpio-Moon system.

CHILDREN BORN WITH THE MOON IN SCORPIO

According to an old saying – when one Scorpio dies, another one is born. A baby whose chart shows the Moon in Scorpio, then, may well be born into a family that has recently lost one of its members.

The household of a Scorpio baby seems to revolve around him or her, more than with any other sign. Children with the Moon in Scorpio have big egos and make their demands known from the very beginning of their lives. They simply have to be noticed.

Relating to Others

YOUR EMOTIONAL PATTERN

Intense is the appropriate adjective to describe the emotions of a Scorpio-Moon subject. You may well appear glassy smooth on the surface, but your feelings will run in virtually unfathomable, labyrinthine channels, down to your very core. So deep, in fact, that others find you quite enigmatic. But this is precisely what gives you the air of mystery that makes you so fascinating and magnetically alluring. Indeed, members of the opposite sex fall over themselves to get close enough to you in an attempt to unlock your secrets.

Interestingly, though, while you yourself tend to be secretive, you have an innate ability to see through others, which makes you a brilliant psychologist and master of the art of subtle manipulation.

With your razor-sharp intuitive capacity, you can spot an untruth, a sycophant or a fraud a mile away. For, in your books, sincerity is what counts. Life for you is either black or white – with very little room for grey areas in between. You either take to someone on first meeting, or you dislike them on sight. Few people get a second chance.

Forever riding an emotional roller coaster, you know the heights of joy and the depths of misery. Sex is very important in your scheme of things and it is a deep, meaningful rela-

tionship that you seek to achieve with your chosen partner in life.

You cannot resist a challenge, so your ideal life partner needs to be spunky and passionate, prepared to give as good as he or she gets. To this relationship you pledge total commitment. You are prepared to give one hundred per cent loyalty, but you also demand one hundred per cent in return. When you are completely sure of your ground, then

you prove honest, supportive and deeply caring. A constant and faithful companion, you give your heart and soul willingly and totally to the one you love.

✳ ☆ ✳ ☆ ✳ ☆ ✳ ☆ ✳ ☆ ✳ ☆

Those born with the Moon in Scorpio may have a susceptibility to problems affecting their reproductive or excretory organs. That is because these are anatomical areas that are traditionally associated with this sign.

Your Moon in Scorpio

Aries
If you can curb your jealous impulses and respect your partner's need for personal freedom, the rewards, in terms of your shared passion, will more than make up for your differences.

Taurus
Your Moon is in a Water sign, that of your partner is in Earth. Earth and water mixed can produce a muddy swamp. Alternatively, they can form the basis of creation. The choice is yours.

Gemini
Your Scorpio-Moon is jealous and possessive whereas your partner's Gemini-Moon demands freedom. Consequently, this makes for a highly volatile situation.

Cancer
Intense feelings and deep love will underlie this union, despite occasional moods and temperamental outbursts. Passion will be plentiful and sex will be both satisfying and rewarding.

Leo
Though emotionally very different types, there is a powerful magnetic attraction that draws the two of you together. Sexually sultry, your union will sizzle and smoulder on.

Virgo
Potentially, a relationship together could be a scorcher in more ways than one. In reality, however, Scorpio-Moons are physically demanding, while Virgo-Moons can be prudish. So sex can be a problem here.

Libra
An interesting match in which each can learn a great deal from his or her partner. However, a Scorpio-Moon needs more devotion than a Libra-Moon is prepared, or even able, to offer.

Scorpio
Deep, and with a tendency to introspection, two Scorpio-Moons in the same house would produce a relationship that is crackling with tension – and where neither partner is willing, or able, to diffuse the situation.

Sagittarius
Your Moon is possessive and demands complete devotion. Your partner's Sagittarius-Moon needs freedom and a looser framework. You will constantly be chasing different goals.

Capricorn
There is great attraction between you that augurs well for a lasting union. However, both of you are dedicated in your own way but in different directions. You must try to find a common path.

Aquarius
Your Scorpio-Moon is insistent. Your partner's Aquarius-Moon is cold and distant. There is little agreement between you and this can lead to tension and discord.

Pisces
Emotionally, you two make an ideal match. Able to experience life's highs and lows with the same heart, you are magnetically drawn to each other. A brilliant liaison.

Moon in Sagittarius

74 Key Character Points

Your instinctive response is:
open and friendly

Your best characteristics are:
enthusiasm and far-sightedness

Your negative qualities are:
irresponsibility and tactlessness

You dislike:
being confined

You need:
freedom – to say and do what
comes naturally to you

You must:
learn to curb your restlessness

THE ESSENTIAL YOU

Being born with the Moon in the sign
of Sagittarius means that you are blessed
with a cheerful nature and a good-
humoured, happy-go-lucky disposition.
You are optimistic and enthusiastic,
eager to experience everything that life
has in store. Perhaps that is why you
are so restless, always looking for new
challenges and adventures. Fortunately,
you are adaptable and will bend according to the situation or company you find
yourself in. Though you may appear
superficial you are, in fact, deeply
philosophical, and your understanding
and wisdom in life is without equal.

PEOPLE WHO SHARE YOUR MOON SIGN

Bob Hope	Garry Kasparov	Ravi Shankar
Howard Hughes	Judy Garland	Barry Manilow
Herman Melville	Arthur Koestler	Bob Geldof
Christopher Reeve	Billy Graham	Pablo Picasso
Joan Sutherland	Danny DeVito	Randy Newman
Umberto Eco	Mary Tyler Moore	Yoko Ono
Billy Crystal	Albert Einstein	Rupert Murdoch

Lifestyle

THE SAGITTARIUS MOON AT HOME

Sagittarian-Moon natives are not by
nature the most domesticated of
people, so your home will permanently

have that relaxed and lived-in look about it. If you have a preference it will be for modern rather than antique. There is every chance that you will set up home in a different country to your native land, perhaps in a university town, or close to a cathedral.

You and Your Family

The Moon in Sagittarius is somehow associated with foreign lands, so perhaps you have mixed or immigrant parentage, or parents who travelled abroad extensively when you were young. Certainly, your parents had strong views on education and brought you up to be confident and independent. You see your family members as a united group, a team with each member pulling in the same direction. When it comes to your own children, you are more like a friend to them than a parent.

At Work

If your company allows you to work flexi-time, you will be in your element, getting all your tasks completed in double-quick time. Otherwise, since you buck against a rigid nine-to-five regime, and because you tend to be a law unto yourself, perhaps you would be better off self-employed, so that you can choose when and how you work. You're a born teacher, lecturer or demonstrator, would make a brilliant sports person, or would delight in the travel industry.

Unwind by:

throwing an informal party for all of your friends

Money Matters

Carefree by nature, the Moon-in-Sagittarius individual can also be carefree about money. As long as you have enough to see you through the next adventure that you have lined up, that is fine by you.

Health Notes

Being overweight can present a problem with this sign, particularly after middle-age and especially around the hip and thigh area!

Children Born with the Moon in Sagittarius

Youngsters of this sign are curious and adventurous. They seem to take an interest in anything and everything that moves. Interestingly, they are often born into easy-going families, of parents who are connected with clerical, religious or academic institutions. They are outgoing children, full of sunshine, who love the outdoors and tend to excel at sports and foreign languages.

YOUR SUN AND MOON SIGN COMBINATION CHART

Moon in Sagittarius

This shows just how well your outward persona (Sun sign) and inner personality (Moon sign) are integrated.

Your Sun in	Combination keynotes	Star rating
Aries	A born explorer	★★★★★
Taurus	Research interests	★★★★
Gemini	Constantly restless	★★
Cancer	Divided	★★
Leo	Sunny-natured	★★★★★
Virgo	Philosophical	★★
Libra	Sociable	★★★★
Scorpio	Investigative mind	★★
Sagittarius	Nomadic	★
Capricorn	Successful	★★★
Aquarius	Inspirational	★★★★
Pisces	Drawn to foreign lands	★★

★ *Highly subjective*   ★★ *At odds with yourself*   ★★★ *Need to work towards achieving inner balance*

★★★★ *In harmony*   ★★★★★ *Strongly integrated*

Relating to Others

YOUR EMOTIONAL PATTERN

"Don't fence me in" is the cry of the Moon-in-Sagittarius sign. Belonging to this group, then, means that you value your freedom more than just about any other aspect of life. So, when it comes to romantic relationships, you have a habit of becoming restless the moment you feel you are getting in too deeply. For a start, you dislike clingy or over-dependent partners. Not especially the jealous type yourself, you resent anyone who is jealous of you or who tries to tie you down. In the company of such people, you become off-hand and insensitive to their feelings.

As a lover, you are spontaneous and passionate, but you must learn to give others space to develop their own feelings in their own time. If you do tie the knot, it should be to a partner who is as emotionally uncomplicated as you are yourself but also someone who passionately shares your beliefs and philosophical views. However, Sagittarius-Moon natives can actually live quite happily without an intense love relationship in their lives – but only as long as they have a wide network of supportive friends around them.

Honest as the livelong day, you are emotionally open and frank. Little embarrasses you, least of all talking about your most intimate feelings or experiences, and you are constantly surprised to find that others are not as candid or as forthright as yourself in these matters. Consequently, you have a tendency to put your foot in it, or to embarrass those less thick-skinned than yourself with insensitive questions or tactless disclosures.

But, full of bonhomie, cheerful and carefree, you have the knack of

Your Partner's Moon in	HOW YOU RELATE TO YOUR PARTNER
	Your Moon in Sagittarius
Aries	Both adventurous and highly charged, both seeking challenge and distant horizons, this partnership offers excellent prospects and very few dull moments – in or out of bed.
Taurus	As a Taurus-Moon individual, your partner needs a sense of permanence and stability under his or her feet. But your Sagittarian-Moon hates to be tied down. There is little in common between you, it appears.
Gemini	Despite the fact that Sagittarian-Moons are at the opposite end of the spectrum to Gemini-Moons, this combination has been known to work very nicely.
Cancer	With different attitudes and disparate ambitions, you and your partner are unlikely to want the same things in life. At the end of the day, neither finds the other truly understanding.
Leo	What a fiery, dynamic duo you two make! This has all the ingredients of a powerful love affair. With your shared interests and similar ways of experiencing the world, you are bound to go far together.
Virgo	Virgo-Moons like to feel that they have their feet on terra firma, but Sagittarius-Moons dislike being pinned down. You are both too self-sufficient in your own ways to expect this relationship to work in the long-term.

Your Partner's Moon in	*Your Moon in Sagittarius*
Libra	You both like your freedom, so that is something you have in common. A little knowledge of when to share and when to leave well alone will go a long way in this relationship.
Scorpio	Your partner's Scorpio-Moon is possessive and demands complete devotion. You need freedom and a looser framework in which to relate. You will both constantly be chasing different goals.
Sagittarius	An understanding and richly philosophical relationship. You will know how to get the most out of life and even the most insignificant experience together will prove deeply rewarding.
Capricorn	You might as well face it, Capricorn-Moons and Sagittarian-Moons live on completely different planets. Making this relationship work can be an uphill struggle.
Aquarius	Your Moon signs have a lot in common, not least that you both recognize the other's need for space. In many ways, though, this is likely to be a highly unconventional pairing, and perhaps that is precisely what gives this partnership its momentum.
Pisces	Not the easiest of relationships for the reason that your Sagittarian-Moon is so freedom-loving whereas your partner's Pisces-Moon is clingy and dependent.

infecting everyone you meet with your own enthusiasm and optimism, which means that you make friends wherever you go. You are an adventurer *par excellence* and are at your happiest when you are, literally or metaphorically, on the road.

✳ ☆ ✳ ☆ ✳ ☆ ✳ ☆ ✳ ☆ ✳ ☆

Anatomically, Sagittarius is said to rule the thighs, the hips and the liver. If you were born with the Moon in this sign, then you probably have a taste for rich foods and high living — all of which is likely not just to affect the liver, but also to pile on the weight around the hip and thigh regions, too!

Moon in Capricorn

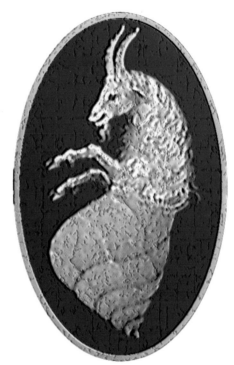

78   Key Character Points

Your instinctive response is:
cautious and reserved

Your best characteristics are:
industriousness and a strong sense
of responsibility

Your negative qualities are:
a certain snobbishness and
emotional detachment

You dislike:
childish behaviour

You need:
status, position and recognition
for your efforts

You must:
learn to moderate your cynicism

THE ESSENTIAL YOU

Efficient, down-to-earth and hard-working, you take a serious, mature attitude
to life. Other people sometimes interpret
your ultra-cautious nature incorrectly, as
pessimistic. Ambition is a positive spur
and you put in long hours to achieve the
position and status to which you aspire.
Your staying power and willingness to
work your way up the ladder mean that,
sooner or later, you will gain the power,
respect and recognition you seek.

Lifestyle

THE CAPRICORN MOON AT HOME

Traditional and formal are your tastes
in furniture and architecture. Preferring

PEOPLE WHO SHARE YOUR MOON SIGN

Stephen Sondheim

Yehudi Menuhin

Tammy Wynette

John Glenn Jr

Dorothy Parker

Johnny Carson

Kim Basinger

Franco Zeffirelli

Cher

James Stewart

Jane Russell

Yves Saint Laurent

Arnold Schwarzenegger

Arthur C Clarke

Mary Quant

to keep your environment simple, you do not appreciate ornate furniture or over-embellished interiors. People with this Moon placement tend to be house-proud, so at home there is a place for everything, and everything is in its place.

YOU AND YOUR FAMILY

Capricorn-Moon subjects often take after their fathers. Their mothers are likely to have been forceful individuals, never overtly affectionate, but achievement-motivated and ambitious for their children. Indeed, this is something you carry through to your own offspring, for you dearly want to see them succeed in life. You expect them to knuckle down and work as hard as you do. If they don't, you are quick to show your disapproval.

AT WORK

Perhaps the hardest-working and most industrious Moon sign, you excel in efficiency and organizational skills. You are practical and logical, using your initiative to get things done. Colleagues and employers soon learn that you are steady, reliable, responsible and always prepared to go the extra mile. You work such long hours that you are in danger of becoming a workaholic. The financial sector, civic or corporate management and local politics would suit your talents well.

Unwind by:

watching a really funny movie

MONEY MATTERS

You work hard and save your money. You have frugal tastes so your money stays

in the bank and grows steadily. Capricorn-Moon natives have been known to make fortunes by dint of their industriousness.

HEALTH NOTES

Natives of this Moon sign have a wiry constitution, so although they may look lean and spare they tend to be long-lived. The bones and joints may give them problems in later life, however – particularly rheumatism or arthritis, and especially in the knees.

CHILDREN BORN WITH THE MOON IN CAPRICORN

These children are born with an old head on young shoulders, which is just as well since, for whatever reason, they have to grow up fast. Sometimes, this placement can indicate that the parents are elderly and the child feels responsible for the family from an early age. Family life tends to be restricted and children of this sign often suffer from a lack of demonstrative affection, which may mar their own ability to form loving relationships in later life.

YOUR SUN AND MOON SIGN COMBINATION CHART

Moon in Capricorn

This shows just how well your outward persona (Sun sign) and inner personality (Moon sign) are integrated.

Your Sun in	Combination keynotes	Star rating
Aries	Determined	★★★★
Taurus	Very sound	★★★★★
Gemini	Well-organized	★★★
Cancer	Home-oriented	★★
Leo	A born leader	★★★★
Virgo	Methodical	★★★★★
Libra	Class-conscious	★★
Scorpio	Powerful	★★★★
Sagittarius	Charitable	★★
Capricorn	Workaholic	★
Aquarius	One step ahead	★★★
Pisces	Self-effacing	★★

★ *Highly subjective*   ★★ *At odds with yourself*   ★★★ *Need to work towards achieving inner balance*

★★★★ *In harmony*   ★★★★★ *Strongly integrated*

Relating to Others

YOUR EMOTIONAL PATTERN

If you were born with the Moon in Capricorn, you are a cool customer and you come across as distant and aloof. You're not given to overt displays of feeling, don't care for too much body contact, and sloppy sentimentality turns you off completely. But, although your head rules your heart, you do have a generous nature and, when it comes to relationships, you are practical and mature.

Never the sort to play silly games or to go in for one-night stands, no one could ever accuse you of being a flighty lover. On the contrary, you take your responsibilities seriously and, once you have given your word, you will remain faithful and true. Before embarking on that solemn commitment you will have thought through the consequences very carefully, for you are emotionally cautious and never rush into a relationship.

Customs and social conventions must be observed in your world. Although maintaining proprieties may indeed inhibit the free flow of spontaneous emotion, you feel that there is a correct way to go about things and you like to think that you follow the right path and thereby do your duty. If you didn't, you would worry dreadfully about what other people might think of you.

And then, of course, there is the question of status and position. These are fundamentally important to a Capricorn-Moon individual. Either you are busy climbing your own ladder of success, or you will want a partner with drive and ambition to root for, encourage – or push, if need be.

Sometimes you try to convince yourself that, as long as you are financially secure and in a good occupation with a prestigious position in life, love and affection are not really necessary. But, when you sit down and think about it, you soon come to the conclusion that life is pretty bleak without someone special to share all your troubles and your triumphs.

✳ ☆ ✳ ☆ ✳ ☆ ✳ ☆ ✳ ☆ ✳ ☆

Watch out for bone and joint problems if you were born with the Moon in this sign, since those are the areas that come under Capricorn's rule.

Your Moon in Capricorn

Your Partner's Moon in	
Aries	The chances of this combination lasting will be greatly improved if you and your partner happen to be in business together, since you will be able to channel your considerable, but disparate, passions into the success of your company.
Taurus	There is a wonderful meeting of hearts between these two Moon signs, which bodes extremely well for a compatible and lasting relationship together. Top marks for a solid and stable union.
Gemini	There is very little meeting of minds and hearts between Gemini-Moons and Capricorn-Moons. As a result, you and your partner would irritate each other, and trying to stay together could prove an uphill struggle.
Cancer	Despite the fact that your Moons are in opposite signs, this combination has all the makings of a highly successful partnership. All in all, a splendid match.
Leo	Not the easiest of pairings, since your partner's extravagance would affront your ideas about domestic budgeting and your Capricorn-Moon would not hesitate to puncture your partner's Leo-Moon pride.
Virgo	With both Moons in Earth signs, you each know exactly what the other wants and needs. This, therefore, is a splendid combination with excellent chances for durability and success.
Libra	Your Moon is dedicated to hard work, while your partner's Moon tends towards indolence. Libra-Moons are light-hearted. You can be a stern moralist. There are too many fundamental differences here.
Scorpio	There is great attraction between you that augurs well for a lasting union. However, both of you are dedicated in your own way but in different directions. You must try to find a common path.
Sagittarius	You might as well face it, Capricorn-Moons and Sagittarian-Moons live on completely different planets. Making this relationship work will call on all your resources, and more besides.
Capricorn	A strong match since both of you experience the world in the same way and share similar ambitions. You are both heavily work-oriented, which will bring success and rewards, especially so if you are in business together.
Aquarius	There are undeniable differences between you, yet Aquarius-Moon can lift your spirits and you can help to ground your partner.
Pisces	Problems, problems, problems. Capricorn-Moons may be described as rock-hard, while Pisces-Moons are soft as putty. This equation simply does not add up.

Moon in Aquarius

82 Key Character Points

Your instinctive response is:
cool but friendly

Your best characteristics are:
sincerity and humanitarian zeal

Your negative qualities are:
eccentricity and a tendency to
deny your feelings

You dislike:
maintaining the status quo

You need:
a mission in life

You must:
learn to give yourself emotionally
to those you love

THE ESSENTIAL YOU

Having the Moon in the sign of Aquarius
means that you are endowed with extra-
ordinary flair and originality. With your
far-sightedness, you have a rather unusual
imagination and often come up with ideas
that others consider odd or eccentric.
Odd though they may seem now, these
are the very ideas that in ten or twenty
years' time become accepted standards.
Driven by humanitarian instincts to
improve the world, you enjoy immersing
yourself in issues of global importance.

Lifestyle

THE AQUARIUS MOON AT HOME
Ultra-modern is the Aquarius-Moon
preference when it comes to the home

PEOPLE WHO SHARE YOUR MOON SIGN

Diana, Princess of Wales
Michelle Pfeiffer
Fidel Castro
Carl Lewis
Iris Murdoch
Jesse Owens
Tennessee Williams

Sophia Loren
Orson Welles
Muhammed Ali
Mary Baker Eddy
Henry Ford
George Gershwin
Margaret Atwood

John Lennon
Jean-Paul Sartre
Woody Allen
Leslie Caron
H G Wells
John Le Carré

and domestic environment. Here, there will be experimental shapes or colour schemes and the whole look will be quite different to other houses in the street. Housework is not your forte, your attitude being that there are too many other interests in life to waste time on cleaning up.

YOU AND YOUR FAMILY

Family life in your household is likely to be as unconventional as your Aquarian-Moon character. For example, you may have called your parents by their Christian names. Or perhaps there was a wide age difference between your parents, or is now between you and your partner. Or possibly your father had an unusual occupation – an astronaut, an inventor, a professor, or a genius of some sort.

AT WORK

Scientific work is a natural occupation for you, but a job that is not of the usual run-of-the-mill variety tends to draw your interest. You might join the media as a correspondent or go into film-making. Your creativity and far-sightedness would certainly pay off in the fashion industry or in dealing in the futures market. And because you are brilliant at logical thinking and delight in giving advice, belonging to an advisory team or think-tank would suit you well. But it will be the charitable organizations, or working for the good of the community, that will appeal to you most.

Unwind by:

playing chess, Scrabble or other board games with your friends

MONEY MATTERS

Money *per se* holds no great fascination for you and if you do invest, you will be highly discriminating, choosing to put your money only into those companies with a proven ecological or ethical track-record.

HEALTH NOTES

Ankles, shins and calves are the vulnerable areas for Aquarius-Moons. Circulatory problems, such as high blood pressure, may develop later in life.

CHILDREN BORN WITH THE MOON IN AQUARIUS

A child born with this Moon placement may seem like the cuckoo in the nest. It may be that he or she does not physically resemble any other family member, or that his or her tastes, preferences or behaviour will be markedly different to the rest. These youngsters develop into very bright or exceptionally gifted children who, because of their friendly nature and love of people, should never be isolated, but left to work as part of a team.

YOUR SUN AND MOON SIGN COMBINATION CHART

Moon in Aquarius

This shows just how well your outward persona (Sun sign) and inner personality (Moon sign) are integrated.

Your Sun in	Combination keynotes	Star rating
Aries	Controversial	★★★
Taurus	Provident	★★★
Gemini	Electric	★★★★★
Cancer	Compassionate	★★
Leo	Impulsive	★★
Virgo	Tender-hearted	★★
Libra	Easy-going	★★★★★
Scorpio	Insightful	★★
Sagittarius	Original	★★★★
Capricorn	Far-seeing	★★
Aquarius	Eccentric	★
Pisces	Flights of fancy	★★

★ *Highly subjective* ★★ *At odds with yourself* ★★★ *Need to work towards achieving inner balance*
★★★★ *In harmony* ★★★★★ *Strongly integrated*

Your Partner's Moon in	HOW YOU RELATE TO YOUR PARTNER
	Your Moon in Aquarius With the Moon in this sign, you will find it easy to respect your partner's need for independence and personal freedom. In return, your Aries-Moon partner will appreciate your need for privacy. In this partnership there is enough tolerance and understanding to make it work.
Aries	With the Moon in this sign, you will find it easy to respect your partner's need for independence and personal freedom. In return, your Aries-Moon partner will appreciate your need for privacy. In this partnership there is enough tolerance and understanding to make it work.
Taurus	An Aquarian Moon has little in common with a Taurus Moon, since each has different needs and wants different things from life. Consequently, there is no real meeting ground here.
Gemini	A splendidly amicable relationship where each partner is cool and independent, yet both see eye-to-eye. An easy pairing with every chance of long-term success.
Cancer	Aquarius-Moons and Cancer-Moons are emotionally poles apart – one is distant and remote, the other is clinging and dependent. Such differences are difficult to reconcile.
Leo	In many ways chalk and cheese, this combination has been known to work surprisingly successfully. Though you come from opposite ends of the spectrum, yet there is much to unite you.
Virgo	Your Aquarius-Moon relishes the unpredictable. Your partner's Virgo-Moon delights in being punctilious. Unless you both find a compromise, the odds would seem to be stacked against you.

Relating to Others

YOUR EMOTIONAL PATTERN

Being born with the Moon in this sign does not encourage you to forge deep attachments. In fact, because you are such a gregarious person, you prefer a large network of friends and acquaintances rather than a serious all-encompassing one-to-one type of relationship. You are very open about your feelings, and truly gen-

* ☆ * ☆ * ☆ * ☆ * ☆ * ☆ *

The Aquarian-Moon weak spots are the cardio-vascular system, the ankles and the shins.

uine in your sentiments, but curiously surprised when you find that others are not quite as dispassionate when it comes to matters of the heart as you are yourself.

The problem, if there is one, lies in your views and attitudes about human emotions which, like your progressive intellectual ideas, may be described as radical or advanced.

You possess an innate tolerance and open-mindedness, and so your approach to relationships is somewhat unconventional in comparison to the norm. For example, open marriages or *ménage à trois*, both of which many people find totally unacceptable, seem to be quite normal to you. It is precisely this kind of unorthodox character trait that makes others often see you as being unemotional and detached.

The Moon in this placement, as in Gemini and Libra, the other two Air signs, shows that you are a multi-faceted character – a chameleon who changes shape and colour according to your environment and the company. You live in the present. What you were last month, yesterday – even half-an-hour ago – was then. Now is now and that is all that counts. For the Aquarius-Moon person, it is always the moment that is to be experienced.

With this philosophy, then, it is not surprising that your friends and partners find you unpredictable, as you suddenly and for no apparent reason change your mind or your feelings, turning yesterday's belief on its head in favour of today's ideology. And this is exactly what makes you so fascinating, so original and so exciting to be with. One thing is certain – life can never be dull if it is shared with a partner who has an Aquarian Moon.

Your Partner's Moon in	HOW YOU RELATE TO YOUR PARTNER
	Your Moon in Aquarius
Libra	Fun, friendship, understanding – you share so many characteristics and have such a wide variety of interests in common that life will be led in peaceful co-existence. A terrific combination.
Scorpio	Your partner's Scorpio-Moon is insistent. Your Aquarius-Moon is cold and distant. There is little agreement between you and this can lead to tension and discord.
Sagittarius	Your Moon signs have a lot in common, not least that you both recognize the other's need for space. In many ways, though, this is likely to be a highly unconventional pairing, and perhaps that is precisely what gives your partnership its momentum.
Capricorn	There are undeniable differences between you, yet Capricorn-Moon can ground you while you can help to lift your partner's spirits. This is, however, a sobering relationship for both concerned.
Aquarius	An unconventional couple with an unorthodox attitude to life and relationships. Of all the signs, an Aquarius-Moon individual is likely to marry later in life rather than earlier.
Pisces	Aquarius-Moon coupled with Pisces-Moon is likely to produce a somewhat turbulent union. Each, however, has immense curiosity about what makes the other tick and the mystery will draw the two of you together.

Moon in Pisces

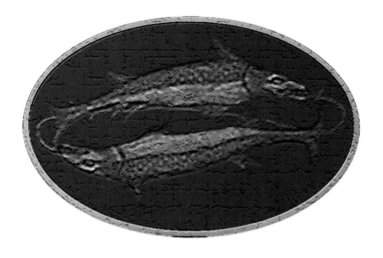

Key Character Points

Your instinctive response is:
gentle and sympathetic

Your best characteristics are:
creative talent and an ability to
empathize with others

Your negative qualities are:
moodiness and a tendency to
play the victim

You dislike:
aggression in any form

You need:
understanding and support

You must:
learn to live in the real world

PEOPLE WHO SHARE YOUR MOON SIGN

Paul Newman
Hermann Hesse
Elvis Presley
Norma Shearer
Grace Kelly
J R R Tolkein
Enrico Caruso

Hilary Clinton
Robin Williams
Robert De Niro
Frank Sinatra
Martin Scorcese
Ava Gardner

Allen Ginsberg
Michael Jackson
P D James
Marie Stopes
Charles Schultz
Sacha Distel

THE ESSENTIAL YOU

People who are born with the Moon in Pisces are tender flowers that need careful nurturing and protection. Belonging to this sign means that you are trusting and somewhat naive. Dreamy, romantic and compassionate, you live your life in the clouds, fantasizing a fairytale world that is as far removed from the harsh realities of everyday life as you can make it. The Moon in this placement works on your emotions, making you ultra-sensitive by sending overwhelming tidal waves of feeling through your heart. To hurt or offend others is your greatest fear. To find love and serenity is your dearest wish.

Lifestyle

THE PISCEAN MOON AT HOME

With the strong creative talents that are bound up with your Moon sign,

your home will be tastefully decorated and artistically inspired. Love of music and an appreciation of the Arts will be in evidence. You are drawn to water and ideally should try to live by a river or near the sea.

YOU AND YOUR FAMILY

For some reason you may not have been as close to your mother as you think a parent and child should be. There may have been difficulties, disappointments or rejections in your early life and, since it is crucial for you to feel strongly bonded to a family group, this apparent lack of understanding or acceptance would have bruised your tender sensitivities and diminished your self-confidence. To your own family you are selflessly loving, and happiest when you are sharing everything you have with those you love.

AT WORK

Employees with the Moon in Pisces make invaluable team members, always eager to help and to please their colleagues. As one of these, you positively flower in a supportive group of people. A creative environment is essential for you, and so work in the music industry, the fashion business or in the Arts would be ideal. Alternatively, you are also drawn to counselling, psychology or psychotherapy. Fringe medicine or alternative therapies also suit your talents.

Unwind by:

meditating or taking a walk

YOUR SUN AND MOON SIGN COMBINATION CHART

Moon in Pisces

This shows just how well your outward persona (Sun sign) and inner personality (Moon sign) are integrated.

Your Sun in	Combination keynotes	Star rating
Aries	Resilient	★★
Taurus	Creatively talented	★★★
Gemini	Story-teller	★★★
Cancer	Nurturing instinct	★★★★★
Leo	Romantic	★★★
Virgo	Perceptive	★★
Libra	Dreamy	★★★★
Scorpio	Psychoanalytical	★★★★★
Sagittarius	Far-ranging	★★★
Capricorn	Reserved	★★
Aquarius	Committed	★★
Pisces	Vulnerable	★

★ *Highly subjective*   ★★ *At odds with yourself*   ★★★ *Need to work towards achieving inner balance*

★★★★ *In harmony*   ★★★★★ *Strongly integrated*

MONEY MATTERS

The least money-conscious of all the Moon signs, when you have any cash you tend to give it away to those you think are more deserving than yourself. A partner who will wisely take your finances in hand for you would be greatly appreciated.

HEALTH NOTES

In one way or another, the feet are frequently a source of problems for the Pisces-Moon individual.

CHILDREN BORN WITH THE MOON IN PISCES

The Moon in Pisces produces sweet and gentle babies who are easily pleased and no trouble to rear. They grow into children with a passive nature and a fertile imagination, able to create a fantasy world into which they withdraw whenever they are upset. Often shy and sensitive, they tend to daydream in class. Tougher kids may find them "drippy" and consequently may tease or bully them. They excel in writing stories and in art.

Relating to Others

YOUR EMOTIONAL PATTERN

Sensitive, emotional and sentimental, you are the most romantic of all the signs. Moreover, you have a tender heart that can easily get hurt and this gives you an instinctive understanding of the suffering of others. And, because you are so gentle and compassionate, you make a caring partner, always ready to listen and to lend a helping hand. With your kind nature and dreamy, idealistic approach to relationships, you can be influenced all too easily by other stronger, and sometimes less scrupulous, individuals, who may take advantage of your tender heart.

Criticism and harsh words deeply wound you and crush your spirit. Quarrels and aggressive behaviour of any kind literally make you feel ill. If you are caught in the crossfire of conflict, for example a row in the family, your natural reaction would be to run away, find a job to do in another room perhaps, or go for a long drive, and hope that the storm will have blown itself out by the time you return.

It is possible that others will interpret your withdrawal as pure petulance and accuse you of going into "one of your sulks". In reality, disengaging yourself from the scene of battle is simply your natural defence mechanism, somewhat similar to burying your head in the sand – if you don't see it, it can't possibly be happening, so all is right again with your world. For you desperately want a world that is nice and pleasant, where people live in peace and harmony with each other, where there is no cruelty or hunger or suffering, but only love and compassion and empathy for one another.

These are the qualities that you yourself are prepared to give and these are the same qualities that you need a partner to offer to you. In addition, someone who will know how to boost your ego and encourage you to believe in yourself would be ideal.

* ☆ * ☆ * ☆ * ☆ * ☆ * ☆

Because Pisces is the sign of the Zodiac that rules alcohol and narcotic substances, those born with the Moon in this sign must take care not to "turn to the bottle" in an attempt to escape from their problems or from the stresses of everyday life. The feet, too, are governed by this sign and Moon-Pisceans have either dainty, ballerina-type feet, or are forever tripping over themselves when they walk.

Your Partner's Moon in	HOW YOU RELATE TO YOUR PARTNER
	## Your Moon in Pisces
Aries	Your tender feelings get short shrift in this relationship, since you find an Aries-Moon partner abrasive and impatient. Passions are certainly steamy between you, but you could end up the one who gets seriously burnt.
Taurus	With these two Moon placements there are potentially good spin-offs from one to the other. You two, therefore, could be very good for each other.
Gemini	A Pisces-Moon is perhaps the most emotionally clinging of the Moon signs. A Gemini-Moon is the most elusive. Neither has a true grasp of the other's feelings.
Cancer	Moons in Pisces and Cancer produce gentle, caring people with a loving and affectionate nature, so there will be shared feelings and understanding here. This is an ideal match.
Leo	Although on the surface this might appear a strange combination, yet there is a great deal of romance and enchantment between you and your Leo-Moon partner that will bind you together.
Virgo	There is no doubt that friendship between you and your Pisces-Moon companion is a sure bet. But when it comes to a more intimate relationship, you may find that each soon loses patience with the other.
Libra	Both creative, both lovers of beauty, both needy of harmony and tranquillity. Sex can be sweet and gentle between you, but ultimately you will each blame the other for faults of your own respective making.
Scorpio	Emotionally, you two make an ideal match. Able to experience life's highs and lows with the same heart, you are magnetically drawn to each other. A brilliant liaison.
Sagittarius	Not the easiest of relationships because your Pisces-Moon is clingy and dependent whereas your partner's Sagittarian-Moon is freedom-loving.
Capricorn	Problems, problems, problems. Capricorn-Moons may be described as rock-hard while Pisces-moons are soft as putty. This equation simply does not add up.
Aquarius	Aquarius-Moon coupled with Pisces-Moon is likely to produce a somewhat turbulent union. Each, however, has immense curiosity about what makes the other tick and the mystery will draw you together.
Pisces	A dreamy, idealistic and blissful romance. In reality, you lack the necessary worldly practicality that is essential to keep body and soul together.

CHAPTER 7
SUCCESS IN BUSINESS

As any good comedian or stock-broker knows only too well, timing is of the essence. Being on the right spot at exactly the right moment can make all the difference between success and failure. This applies to all areas of our lives, but it is especially true in the world of business. It really pays to know just when to schedule meetings in order to reach an amicable consensus; when to begin projects to ensure a really satisfactory completion; when to sign contracts, target publicity campaigns, ask for a raise or go for promotion, apply for a new job, set up on one's own, expand the business, seek a bank loan, employ and dismiss staff – and so on.

STAYING AHEAD OF THE GAME

The key to really successful timing can be found in the movements of the Moon, as its daily cycles influence the tide of events, affect moods and expectations, and generally alter the whole tempo of life.

To make sure that you really stay ahead of the game, you must learn to adapt to and work with the shifting requirements that are imposed by the changing lunar phases.

SOME GOLDEN RULES OF GOOD TIMING

In general, any new ventures launched during the two weeks in which the Moon is increasing are more likely to meet with success than those begun after the Full Moon. If you try to put a new scheme into motion under a waning Moon, the wheels will grind very slowly indeed, and the project is likely to fizzle out before it even begins to gather steam.

On the other hand, the period from Full to New Moon is propitious for anything to do with bringing matters to a close. This might include such matters as:

- slimming down operations
- shedding staff
- clearing up
- researching new lines
- investigating competitors

Keeping abreast of the changing lunar movements, and making sure that you schedule your activities according to the favourable cyclical influences of the Moon can bring success in business. Use the tables and advice in this book to tune into your own personal rhythms.

New Moon Day

Think of the day on which the New Moon falls as a Dynamic Day, or D-day for short. This is the point in the month when the Moon begins to grow again, redoubling her light and reflecting new creative energy on all worldly things. This is a time to move up a gear and plan our aspirations for the future – personal and business ones. Write down five to ten key objectives, register them consciously and then work to bring them to fruition – in the short term, over the next four weeks or, in the longer term, over the next few months.

1 Generate ideas and begin all new projects from the day after the New Moon up until the day before the next Full Moon.

2 The two weeks following the New Moon are periods of expansion and high-profile activities. Use them to promote yourself, your work or your company.

3 Make plans, set objectives and start the ball rolling on the day of the New Moon.

4 Evaluate and reassess your agenda and business plans after the Full Moon.

5 It is unwise to seek work, apply for a new position or put a new product on the market in the two weeks between the Full Moon and the next New Moon.

New Moon to First Quarter

- initiate new deals
- draw up contracts
- sign documents and agreements
- catch up on correspondence
- make new contacts
- apply for promotion or seek a new job
- introduce new ideas/submit proposals
- announce take-over bids
- enter into partnerships
- set projects in motion
- sue for damages
- start new construction work
- arrange important board meetings
- stand for election
- elect new members
- interview people, draw up shortlists, hire staff
- publish or broadcast favourable performance figures

First Quarter to Full Moon

- launch advertising ventures
- pursue all high-profile activities, such as promoting the company's image
- seek legal or financial advice
- lend money
- inform workforce of pay rises or bonus schemes
- announce mergers

Day of the Full Moon

- switch gear, and assess progress
- concentrate on bringing existing projects to fruition over the next two weeks
- if necessary, plan to eliminate all time-consuming and unproductive procedures

Full Moon to Third Quarter

- undertake all investigative, undercover work or projects of a secret nature
- concentrate on doing useful research
- explore new markets
- undertake profile studies of customers or clients
- prepare budgets and costings
- stock-take

Third Quarter to New Moon

- stand down or resign
- downsize
- demote or dismiss staff
- inform workforce of pay-cuts
- restructure
- delegate
- dissolve partnerships
- take out a loan
- fight a lawsuit
- publish or broadcast poor performance figures
- call a strike
- clean, paint or refurbish work premises
- clear decks
- tie up loose ends
- prepare to implement new projects during the next phase of the Moon

the markets. Some are long-term cycles affecting world economies over a period of several years. The lunar cycle may not be as dramatic, but it has a very definite effect on a monthly basis.

It appears that a down-turn occurs both at the time of the New Moon and at the Full Moon, while a significant rise may be expected eight and nine days after the New Moon. Perhaps keeping notes, comparing a few statistics, or plotting monthly graphs may bear this out and help decision-making when it comes to investments and trading.

HEEDING THE SIGNS

In addition, there seems to be some evidence that whichever sign the Moon is in at these sensitive times may also affect market trends, as each sign has its own unique "nature". Use the tables at the end of the book to discover what sign the Moon is in at any given time, and then consult the box headed "Signs of the Times" to learn how to work with this important influence.

Working with the Times

Those who keep an eye on the money markets may be interested to know of a powerful cycle of highs and lows that is linked to the lunar phases. There are, of course, other cycles, such as the Jupiter-Saturn planetary combination, which also have important triggering effects on the rise and fall of

✳ ☆ ✳ ☆ ✳ ☆ ✳ ☆

Knowing when to take risks, when to play safe, when to start new enterprises... astrologers believe that there is a link between the monthly lunar cycle and the ebb and flow of business fortune. It may literally pay to move with the rhythms of the Moon.

SIGNS OF THE TIMES

Moon in Aries

CONDUCIVE TO: Trading, buying, selling, making decisions on the spur of the moment, implementing tough measures, taking advantage of situations, launching new schemes, setting up new businesses (especially those of a risky or pioneering nature)

AVOID: Going in with all guns blazing, acting on impulse, skipping over the essentials

BEWARE: Other people's bad tempers

Important days for activities concerning: The automobile industries, mechanical trades, sports, pioneering enterprises

Moon in Taurus

CONDUCIVE TO: Making investments, leasing or renting property, taking on new staff, decorating/refurbishing business premises, showing empathy to one's colleagues

AVOID: A tendency to sit back, digging in your heels, missing good opportunities

BEWARE: Other people's inflexibility

Important days for activities concerning: The building industries, home furnishings, interior designs, farming, agriculture, horticulture, garden design, confectionery trade

Moon in Gemini

CONDUCIVE TO: Trade, buying, selling, making business trips, generating new ideas, correspondence, decorating, reorganizing/refurbishing business premises, introducing new machinery/ telecommunications equipment, giving presentations, crisis management

AVOID: Distractions from the main issue, a shallow appreciation of the situation, being underhand or economical with the truth, having too many irons in the fire

BEWARE: Con-men

Important days for activities concerning: The media, audio-visual equipment, communications industries, printing trade, newspapers and magazines, newsagents, postal services, schools, toy manufacturers

Moon in Cancer

CONDUCIVE TO: Signing documents, setting up a company crèche, bringing unsatisfactory conditions to an end

AVOID: Thinking too narrow mindedly, a reluctance to take risks, being over-sensitive to criticism, being influenced by other people's negative moods

BEWARE: People who think the world owes them a living

Important days for activities concerning: Domestic goods, property and real estate, furniture manufacturers, childcare products, marine and fishing industries

Moon in Leo

CONDUCIVE TO: Leasing or renting property, taking control of the situation, money deals, eliciting support, lucky breaks

AVOID: Overspending, a domineering attitude to your colleagues/workforce, forming intimate relationships with fellow workers

BEWARE: Other people's indiscretions

Important days for activities concerning: Luxury goods, designer brands, cosmetics industries, first-class travel, hotel trade, the theatre, children's goods, lotteries and gambling industries

Moon in Virgo

CONDUCIVE TO: Trade, buying, selling, business trips, reorganization, presenting detailed accounts, practical demonstrations, methodical reviews of mail-shots, stock-taking

AVOID: Missing the overall picture while worrying about details, being over-critical, making judgmental errors

BEWARE: Other people's fussiness

Important days for activities concerning: Hospitals, the medical profession, the veterinary services, the pharmaceutical industries, statisticians, precision-tools manufacturers, health-food shops, diet and fitness outlets, complementary health practitioners, caterers, pet-food manufacturers

SIGNS OF THE TIMES

Moon in Libra

CONDUCIVE TO: Decorating, refurbishing business premises, disclosing information, forging new business alliances, marketing, human or public relations, signing contracts, negotiations, settling disputes, going on a company outing, office parties

AVOID: Sitting on the fence, expecting others to take your share of the responsibility, making open enemies, any hint of underhandedness

BEWARE: Other people's indecisiveness

Important days for activities concerning: The diplomatic corps, the music and entertainment industry, the Arts, haute couture, bridal and wedding outfitters, advertising groups, public relations

Moon in Scorpio

CONDUCIVE TO: Signing documents, leasing or renting property, painting business premises, projecting confidence, solving problems, making discreet enquiries, stealing a march on competitors, making major deals while mental faculties are acute

AVOID: A reluctance to disclose all the facts, playing cards too close to one's chest, becoming too intense, operating a secret agenda, pretending to know more than one does

BEWARE: Other people's resentment

Important days for activities concerning: The police force, surgical procedures, research companies, the secret service, butchery trade, mining, investment management, funeral directors, mortuaries

Moon in Sagittarius

CONDUCIVE TO: Trade, promotions, advertising, important correspondence, travel, business meetings, lending or borrowing money, legal or judicial matters

AVOID: Becoming blind to detail, restlessness, financial irresponsibility, slap-dash work

BEWARE: Other people's carelessness

Important days for activities concerning: Publishing, the law, travel industries, foreign trade and communications, religious institutions, teaching, higher education

Moon in Capricorn

CONDUCIVE TO: Getting down to brass tacks, working overtime, high finances, rearranging the filing system, drawing up new schedules, administration, asking for promotion, setting up a new business, entertaining the boss

AVOID: An inflexible attitude, over-working, depression, a lack of compassion towards your colleagues/workforce

BEWARE: Other people's ruthless ambition

Important days for activities concerning: Banking and financial services, real estate, the local council, political parties, the head of state, royalty, superstars

Moon in Aquarius

CONDUCIVE TO: Leasing or renting property, improving working conditions, money transfers, decorating/refurbishing business premises, eliciting cooperation from colleagues

AVOID: Favouring the group at the expense of the individual, taking an overly detached point of view, going off at a tangent

BEWARE: Interruptions

Important days for activities concerning: The power industries, scientific research institutions, trade unions, new inventions, manufacturers of electronic or hi-tech equipment, clubs, groups and societies, social services

Moon in Pisces

CONDUCIVE TO: Signing documents, drawing up financial agreements, sending out mail-shots, making any necessary repairs to equipment, stock-taking

AVOID: Looking at your prospects through rose-tinted spectacles, being too easily influenced, illogical reasoning, self-doubts

BEWARE: Other people's unrealistic expectations, behind-the-scenes machinations

Important days for activities concerning: Film and television, petrochemical industries, oil refineries, the brewery trade, shipping, chiropody, shoe manufacturers

Company Profiles

No matter how big or small the company, whether it is well established or just being set up, drawing up its own astrological chart would be of enormous benefit in highlighting the company's progress. Of greatest importance to any business is the significance of the Moon, as the factors she represents will yield especially invaluable insights – not only about the day-to-day running of the business, but also about its future prospects and standing in the commercial world. For a start, company fortunes tend to run in cycles: the 7th/8th, 14th/15th, 21st/22nd, 28th/29th years being

significant either in terms of an up-turn or down-turn in yearly figures, expansion, contraction, introduction of new lines and so on. Note that these intervals correspond to lunar timing. Recognizing these patterns in the affairs of the company means that products and new developments can be targeted to take advantage of the forthcoming trends.

THE PUBLIC VIEW

Apart from the company's progress, the Moon in the chart will also, and most importantly, represent the public, including how the company is perceived in the outside world and how

✳ ☆ ✳ ☆ ✳ ☆ ✳ ☆ ✳ ☆ ✳ ☆

One basic rule of good business never changes with the passing years — signing contracts and finalizing deals at particularly auspicious times will increase the chances of lasting success. More and more companies are now in favour of undertaking astrological profiling. This can help to facilitate the most effective decision-making, investment planning, trading practices and personnel recruitment.

the markets will respond to its products. Consequently, studying the position and aspects that the Moon makes within the chart will give a fair indication of the company's fate in the years to come.

CHAPTER 8

MIND, BODY & HEALTH

Have you noticed how some days you wake up feeling so full of positive energy that you could climb a mountain? On other days, though, all you want to do is curl up and sleep. If you start to take note, you will find that these moods come and go on a cyclical basis. This pattern can often be matched to the Moon phases, and also to the particular astrological sign through which the Moon is travelling.

What happens is that the lunar phases and sign placements interact to affect our minds and bodies. As the Moon moves signs every two and a quarter days, so the nature of the influences changes, which also alters our mood – our perception of our situation.

YOUR HEALTH AND THE MOON

From the New Moon to the Full Moon is a time for new initiatives. Full Moon is the time for reaping rewards from our hard labours. With the waning Moon we should review endeavours and correct mistakes. Through the dark of the Moon it is advantageous to meditate, research, draw inner strength and lay plans in preparation for the new energies that appear with the emergence of the New Moon.

From New Moon to Full Moon
- A productive time when efforts will grow visibly
- Begin new projects
- Put ideas in motion
- Get medical treatment
- Have beauty treatments
- Have your hair cut if you want fast regrowth
- Become engaged/decide to live together/get married
- Make long-term relationship plans

First Quarter Moon
If you are trying to locate a lost phone number or hoping to meet someone whose address you've mislaid, look for these things around the Moon's First Quarters and they should simply fall into your lap.

Full Moon
- Feelings are heightened
- Matters appear larger than life
- Delay all decisions until another day
- Have your hair cut if you want it to grow back thicker

From Full Moon to New Moon
- Pluck eyebrows
- Have hair cut if you want to slow its growth
- Have hair dyed
- Use depilatory treatments
- Dental work
- Begin health regime
- Settle disputes with friends and family

Last Quarter Moon
- Get rid of clutter and everything that is causing an obstruction
- Throw out anything (or anyone) you no longer want or need
- Rest and recuperate
- Good time for self-analysis

Mental and Physical Health

MOON MADNESS

That the Moon influences our state of mind has been recognized throughout history. Medical staff in mental institutions have been especially convinced of this phenomenon and attempted suicides, psychotic behaviour and admissions to special care units tend to increase around Full Moon. The link between madness and the Moon has even been incorporated into several languages – the Italian phrase, *avere la luna*, which means "to be angry", translates literally as "having the moon".

SURGERY AND THE FULL MOON

If possible, avoid surgery around the Full Moon. Studies have revealed that blood flows more freely at this time of the month and is slower to clot. In fact, carrying out operations on Full Moon days has been banned by medical authorities in certain parts of the world. Since blood flow is more sluggish around the Last Quarter and New Moon times, these phases are more conducive to the healing process following surgery because the likelihood of haemorrhaging is reduced. The same advice applies to any dental work that involves extractions.

ILLNESS AND THE LUNAR CYCLE

If you fall sick between New Moon and Full Moon, your illness will normally be worse and take longer to shake off than illness contracted during the waning period (Full Moon to New Moon).

Energy levels and enthusiasm vary throughout the month. Taking up new dietary regimes and matching any fitness programmes to the lunar cycle can enhance their effectiveness on your health – both on a mental and a physical level.

INTOXICATING EFFECTS

Have you ever wondered why the same amount of alcohol sometimes has a greater effect on you than at other times? This may be because the strength of alcohol is intensified on the day of the Full Moon.

BODY IMAGE

Take advantage of the enhancing influences of the Moon in Taurus, Leo or Libra and have beauty treatments, facial makeovers or massages. These are also excellent times to change your image, hairstyle and wardrobe.

A health regime that involves "shedding" in some way – such as losing weight, getting rid of physical or emotional clutter, or giving up smoking or chocolate, for example – is more likely to be successful if it is begun when the Moon is decreasing, so plan to start after the Full Moon. It also helps if this coincides with the Moon being in the signs of Aries, Gemini, Leo, Virgo, Sagittarius or Aquarius.

Marriages Made in Heaven?

It would be ridiculous to expect people to arrange to meet their prospective partners, or even to choose to fall in love, only when the planetary patterns are auspicious. If we all did that, relationships would be pretty thin on the ground.

On the other hand, we do give considerable forethought and planning time to the arrangements of a wedding, so why not also give some thought, when wedding plans are being made, to the movements of the Moon? Try to arrange the ceremony for a day when the influences are especially beneficial to the ongoing contentment and stability of a relationship.

GOOD VIBRATIONS

In general, setting up home together or getting married are best begun during an increasing Moon period – that is, from New Moon to the day before the next Full Moon. The good auspices at this time will help the relationship to develop and prosper.

Avoid the days around the Full Moon when increased tension is likely to strain the occasion and throw a shadow of volatility and restlessness over the union. The waning Moon period should also be avoided, as this brings with it a decrease in fortune and diminishing prospects.

✷ ☆ ✷ ☆ ✷ ☆ ✷ ☆ ✷ ☆ ✷ ☆ ✷ ☆

Arranging the wedding date to coincide with an auspicious Moon can increase the chances of a lasting union and enduring love.

GOOD DAYS FOR WEDDING BELLS

If you want to understand the nature of the union itself, then you should examine the qualities of the Moon sign in operation at the time of the wedding. Read on...

The Earth signs –
Taurus, Virgo, Capricorn

Permanence, endurance and security underlie marriages begun when the Moon is in one of the Earth signs. Under Taurus the couple will be staunch and persevere together through thick and thin. With a Virgo rulership, the couple will be conscientious and hard working, but expect some critical nit-picking, too. A Capricorn Moon denotes an ambitious pair who are solid, stable and looked upon as pillars of society.

The Air signs –
Gemini, Libra, Aquarius

Tying the knot under one of the Air signs endows a bright and breezy character to the relationship, but perhaps one that is not renowned for its permanence. If any fickleness can be curbed, then marriage under a Gemini Moon can be amusing and light-hearted. An elegant and sophisticated union can be expected with the Libra Moon – a sign that, in fact, rules marriages and partnerships in general. Friendship will characterize the Aquarius Moon marriage, although each individual will insist firmly on acting independently of the other.

The Fire Signs –
Aries, Leo, Sagittarius

Passion typifies marriages made when the Moon is in a Fire sign. Desire will be impulsive with an Aries Moon at the helm but the ardour may con-

sume itself as rapidly as it began. The auspices for married life are excellent under the romantic and fun-loving Leo Moon. There is room for spiritual growth when the Moon is in Sagittarius but this couple will resent the least hint of being tied down.

The Water Signs –
Cancer, Scorpio, Pisces

The Water signs are fundamentally nurturing and with the Moon placed here, the sensual and strongly procreative urges of these signs will also be brought out. A Cancer Moon is one of the most auspicious placements for marriage. Under the sign of Scorpio, jealousy and possessiveness may mar the union. With a Pisces Moon, on the other hand, there will be tenderness and empathy in abundance but, unless addressed, co-dependency may cause problems.

End of the affair

Separation and divorce are, sadly, a fact of life these days. Unhappy though these events may be, if the split is inevitable, then choosing an appropriate time to end the relationship officially can ensure that parting occurs with the least amount of acrimony and rancour. Trying to end the relationship during a waxing Moon will simply drag out the proceedings and increase bad feelings. The Last Quarter, however, is generally thought to ease endings of all kinds and, with the prospect of the New Moon in sight, adds hope for fresh beginnings to come.

Staying in Tune

As the Moon enters each new sign, the characteristics associated with that sign are "triggered", allowing their influences to colour our states of mind and health. Certain activities will harmonize with the prevailing energies; others will prove counter-productive.

As the Moon travels through all the signs in turn each month, a little understanding of these characteristics and their effects means that we can tune in to the changing influences and requirements of each day. We can channel our activities in harmony with the flow, recognizing which tasks will bring satisfaction, which habits we should curb, which part of our body is susceptible and which behaviour must be avoided.

Taureans might enjoy giving a massage to someone close during the waning Moon phase.

Aries	RECOMMENDED ACTIVITIES DURING THE WAXING MOON PHASE	RECOMMENDED ACTIVITIES DURING THE WANING MOON PHASE	THINGS TO AVOID	HEALTH TRENDS TO WATCH
	• Set yourself a new challenge • Take up a martial art or self-defence discipline • Begin a new exercise regime	• Get your hair cut • Have an eye test • See the dentist	• Rashness • Driving too fast • Rushing a job • Wanting to get your way at all costs	• Headaches • Scalds and burns • Cuts • Accidents

	RECOMMENDED ACTIVITIES DURING THE WAXING MOON PHASE	RECOMMENDED ACTIVITIES DURING THE WANING MOON PHASE	THINGS TO AVOID	HEALTH TRENDS TO WATCH
Taurus	• Cook a new recipe • Go to the theatre • Make some new cushion covers • Start a savings scheme • Take out a new insurance policy • Work on the garden	• Plan a new colour scheme for your bedroom • Put your finances on a firmer footing • Give your lover a massage • Have a relaxing aromatherapy bath • Paint • Play music	• Eating too much • Wanting things you do not have • Being over-possessive	• Sore throat • Laryngitis
Gemini	• Write letters to your friends • Phone up your brother or sister • Take a computer course • Join a debating society • Make a start on that book you've always wanted to write	• Play a board game with your children • Go to the library • Buy books and writing materials • Put your feet up and read a magazine • Go for a drive in the country	• Being too easily distracted • Beginning one job before finishing another	• Nervous tension • Agitation • Restlessness
Cancer	• Visit your parents • Join an upholstery class • Paint your lounge • Move house • Look up your ancestry • Cook your family's favourite meal	• Take a walk along a river or sea-shore • Go swimming • Rearrange your furniture • Take a trip down memory lane • Plant a shrub or a tree	• Meddling in other people's affairs • Being over-clingy	• Worry • Moodiness • Stomach upsets • Skin problems
Leo	• Take the afternoon off and spend it with your partner • Make love • Be creative – paint, write, sew, sculpt, go to the theatre/concert/opera • Go to the races/gambling casino • Buy someone a present	• Take the children to the cinema • Tell those you love that you love them • Watch a funny pro-gramme on television • Hang a gilt-framed mirror in your hallway • Be conscious of your own happiness • Sunbathe	• Feelings of insignificance • Resentment • Imagining that no one appreciates you	• Backache • Circulatory problems

Cook up a dish tonight.

Take some creative time out.

	RECOMMENDED ACTIVITIES DURING THE WAXING MOON PHASE	RECOMMENDED ACTIVITIES DURING THE WANING MOON PHASE	THINGS TO AVOID	HEALTH TRENDS TO WATCH
Virgo	• Start to eat more healthily • Read up on alternative medicines/therapies • Join a health club • Seek medical diagnoses and treatments • Make new plans • Give your pet an extra cuddle	• Review your daily routine • Cut out bad habits • Have a clear-out • Go through your wardrobe and pack/give away anything you no longer wear	• Fussing over detail • Being over-critical • Fads	• Irritability • Gastric or dietary upsets
Libra	• Get married • Invite friends round • Go to a concert • Buy a new tape or CD • Send your partner red roses • Buy an exquisite item for the house – it needn't be expensive but it must be lovely • Go on a romantic weekend with your partner	• Take your lover out to an intimate restaurant for dinner • Create a space where you can go for peace and relaxation • Go to a museum/art gallery • Make an ikebana flower arrangement	• Feelings of being unloved • Loneliness • Stress	• Kidney ailments • Biochemical imbalances
Scorpio	• Join a psychology course • Go for a boat ride • Look for items that you have mislaid • Take up a new therapy • Call up a debt • Go on a murder-mystery weekend • Visit an astrologer • Learn about hypnosis	• Seek answers to questions that have been on your mind • Read a thriller • Psychoanalyse yourself • Clear out the cellar • Watch a spy movie • Solve a puzzle	• Jealousy • Spite • Wanting to take control of people and situations • Brooding	• Problems with the reproductive organs • Haemorrhoids

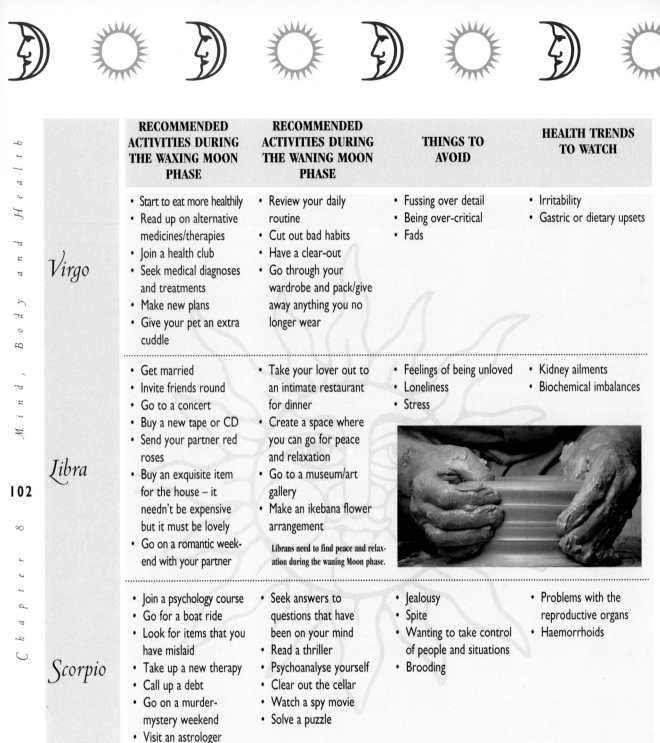

Librans need to find peace and relaxation during the waning Moon phase.

Many Happy Returns!

Each month, when the Moon returns to your own Moon sign, it is like a little birthday – a marker that sets the tone for the four weeks to come. How you are feeling at that time will find echoes throughout the coming month. Ideally, it would be best to know the exact degree your Moon was in at the very moment of your birth, but that requires a natal chart drawn up by an astrologer. Failing that, knowing the Zodiacal sign in which the Moon was placed when you were born will give a good enough approximation to indicate the trends that will affect you in the month to come. If you have got this far in the book and still don't know your Moon sign, turn to the tables at the end.

	RECOMMENDED ACTIVITIES DURING THE WAXING MOON PHASE	RECOMMENDED ACTIVITIES DURING THE WANING MOON PHASE	THINGS TO AVOID	HEALTH TRENDS TO WATCH
Sagittarius	• Enrol at a college • Set off on your holidays/travels • Arrange a camping weekend • Contact friends/family abroad • Ride a horse • Attend a lecture on philosophy	• Read a travel book • Contemplate, meditate or pray • Go to church • Take the dog for a walk in the country • Write up a list of your future aspirations	• Boredom • Taking unnecessary risks • Over-indulgence	• Liverishness • Putting on weight Indulge the Sagittarian passion for horseriding.
Capricorn	• Join the local political party • Spring-clean the house • Climb a mountain • Invite your boss to lunch • Get down to some serious work • Start a new business • Buy a smart business suit	• Write up a list of the ten things you want to achieve in your lifetime • Talk to your partner about your ambitions • Count the money in your piggy-bank • Go on an economy drive • Tell your lover how you feel about him/her	• Worrying about money, position or status • All work and no play	• Toothache • Skin abrasions • Problems of the joints – especially the knees
Aquarius	• Paint your kitchen units electric blue • Invent something the world needs and doesn't yet have • Organize a surprise party for a friend's birthday • Join a club • Buy a computer • Learn a new dance	• Rearrange the furniture before you go to bed • Offer your help at the local school/hospital • Meet friends for lunch	• Breaking the rules • Rebelling just for the sheer hell of it • Handing in your notice	• Ankle sprains • Circulatory disorders
Pisces	• Write a romantic story • Go swimming • Drink champagne in the bath • Compose a piece of music • Take your partner to a dance • Paint a scene in watercolours	• Have reflexology treatment • Write down your dreams • Snuggle up to your lover • Have an early night • Listen to your favourite music	• Falling in love with the first person you meet • Changing your mind • Feeling inadequate	• Physical and mental sensitivity • Problems with the feet

Mind, Body and Health

CHAPTER 9

HOME HINTS

Around the House

To keep your home at its best, coordinate your domestic activities with the appropriate lunar phases, or take advantage of the trends that come into force as the Moon travels through the different signs.

SPRING-CLEANING

Tackle major cleaning jobs after the Full Moon. The few days following the Last Quarter are excellent for thorough clear-outs.

BAKING

If you bake your own bread, you might notice that dough tends to rise higher during the two weeks of the increasing Moon (from New to Full) than in the second half of the lunar cycle.

BREWING

Many home-brewers observe strict rules for when to bottle their wines and beers. There are two specific times in the lunar cycle that are especially recommended: on the day of the Full Moon and on the day of the Last Quarter. Ideally, the Moon should also be in one of the water signs – Cancer, Scorpio or Pisces.

DESIGN AND DIY

Paint your house on the days around the Last Quarter and preferably when the Moon is in Taurus, Leo or Aquarius. Avoid both the New Moon and times when the Moon is in Cancer, Scorpio or Pisces – Water signs that may slow the drying process. Interior design, including purchasing materials, fares well under a waxing Moon, especially one in Taurus, Cancer, Leo, Libra and Aquarius. Times when the Moon is in Taurus or Cancer are ideal for working on anything associated with interiors and soft furnishings, especially furniture and upholstery. If DIY is involved, schedule your work for when the Moon is in Capricorn. Get electrical equipment fixed when the Moon is in Aquarius.

SMART MOVES

Seek and/or buy your new house when the Moon is in the "home" sign of Cancer. Buying it when the Moon is in Taurus will give you a sense of security, while the Moon in Leo will bring love and laughter into your home. Aquarius will ensure amicable relationships and a house that is always full of friends. For moving house, choose the period between the New Moon and the day before the Full Moon, with the Moon in Taurus, Leo, Scorpio or Aquarius. If you are building a house, begin to lay the foundations when the Moon is in Taurus, Leo or Aquarius, preferably on the day of the Full Moon.

ENTERTAINING

Whether you are throwing a huge party or having a couple of friends over for supper, try checking the planetary favours first:

The Moon in Aries

Ensure you provide some spills and thrills – lay on some games or go out for a champagne picnic – to make it a memorable occasion.

The Moon in Taurus

Provide a prodigious amount of food with several different desserts. Make sure everyone has somewhere to sit – comfort is an absolute must.

The Moon in Gemini

Parties go with a really sociable swing – especially surprise ones.

The Moon in Cancer

Go for traditional family get-togethers.

The Moon in Leo

Luxury and opulence are very much the key words here. Black tie will be essential for any social occasion that you organize tonight.

The Moon in Virgo

Healthy eating and the Virgo Moon go hand-in-hand, so make it a garden party with energy-packed salads and fresh fruits.

The Moon in Libra

Elegance is the hallmark here, so think quality rather than quantity, and pay attention to presentation. Play soft music and drift into cultured conversation with your guests.

The Moon in Scorpio

The Scorpio Moon is a seductive moon, so there is bound to be a frisson of sexual tension to the occasion, even when you don't expect it.

The Moon in Sagittarius

Informality is the key – create a relaxed, convivial atmosphere, add lots to eat and drink and then just sit back and watch the company mellow.

The Moon in Capricorn

Capricorn is the sign of status, authority and success, so invite the boss round or book a table at the very best restaurant in town. Formal functions are also highly recommended.

The Moon in Aquarius

Think up something totally different and imaginative to turn the occasion into a real experience under the Aquarian moon. A fireworks party might be ideal, or else rig up some disco lights and music and dance the night away.

The Moon in Pisces

Illusion is the name of the game when the Moon is in dreamy Pisces – how about a fancy-dress party or a masked ball?

YOUR LUNAR SHOPPING GUIDE

The Moon in Aries

SHOPPING TIP: Excellent for shopping because energies and enthusiasm are at a peak

BUY: Sports clothes and gear ☆ Hats ☆ Sunglasses ☆ Spectacles ☆ Tools ☆ Anything made of metal ☆ Cars ☆ DIY materials ☆ Anything red

AVOID: Buying on impulse

TIMELY ADVICE: Have your hair done

The Moon in Taurus

SHOPPING TIP: You'll want value for money with every purchase you make

BUY: Anything practical ☆ Consumer durables ☆ Luxury goods ☆ Cosmetics ☆ Chocolates and other delicacies ☆ Flowers ☆ Plants and garden furniture/equipment ☆ Seating ☆ Beds and bedding

AVOID: Gimmicky goods

TIMELY ADVICE: Open a new investment account

The Moon in Gemini

SHOPPING TIP: An excellent couple of days for window-shopping and buzzing around from store to store

BUY: Computers ☆ Gadgets ☆ Gimmicky goods ☆ Writing materials ☆ Books ☆ Telephones and other communications equipment ☆ Toys ☆ Dictionaries and encyclopaedias

AVOID: Long or far-flung shopping expeditions

TIMELY advice: Buy your car under this sign

The Moon in Cancer

SHOPPING TIP: Excellent for monthly essential shopping, buying for the home and for those you love

BUY: Food and other general provisions to replenish your store cupboards ☆ Kitchen equipment ☆ Presents and greetings cards ☆ Household knick-knacks ☆ China ☆ Linen and lace ☆ Souvenirs ☆ Antiques ☆ Boats ☆ Anything white or silver

AVOID: Shopping anywhere near your place of work

TIMELY ADVICE: Look for and/or buy a house

The Moon in Leo

SHOPPING TIP: Make sure you save up for this shopping expedition – you will be in an extravagant mood

BUY: Jewellery ☆ Luxury goods ☆ Silk lingerie ☆ Children's clothes ☆ Presents for your youngsters ☆ Theatre tickets ☆ Leisure wear ☆ Items for your hobbies and spare-time activities ☆ Champagne ☆ Caviar ☆ Anything made of gold

AVOID: Buying essential groceries

TIMELY ADVICE: Place a bet or buy a lottery ticket

The Moon in Virgo

SHOPPING TIP: You will have a keen eye for detail

BUY: Anything you need for the medicine cupboard ☆ Diaries ☆ Personal organizers ☆ Organic foods ☆ Vitamin and mineral supplements ☆ Cleaning materials ☆ Toiletries ☆ A subscription to the local health club ☆ A surprise treat for your employees ☆ Your bills for local services

AVOID: Anything that does not have a practical purpose

TIMELY ADVICE: Look into health insurance policies

The Moon in Libra

SHOPPING TIP: You may have problems making up your mind, so take a friend along to help you choose

BUY: Haute couture ☆ Anything beautiful, expensive or elegant ☆ Accessories ☆ Embellishments or decorations for the house ☆ Presents for your partner ☆ Concert tickets ☆ Tapes or CDs ☆ Perfume ☆ Flower arrangements ☆ Party food

AVOID: Shopping down-market or in a run-down area

TIMELY ADVICE: Book a table for a romantic dinner *à deux*

The Moon in Scorpio

SHOPPING TIP: You will be sharp and shrewd – unlikely to be taken in by sales patter

BUY: Crime or murder mystery novels ☆ Rich wines ☆ A pack of Tarot cards ☆ Exotic spices ☆ Sexy underwear ☆ Photographic equipment ☆ Perfumes or after-shave lotions ☆ Red roses for your lover ☆ A last will and testament form ☆ A new set of kitchen knives

AVOID: Deviating from your shopping list

TIMELY ADVICE: Make an appointment for a de-stressing massage

The Moon in Sagittarius

SHOPPING TIP: A brilliant time for a shopping spree as you won't mind parting with money and you'll be delighted with all the bargains you find

BUY: Imported goods ☆ Casual clothes ☆ Travel books ☆ Binoculars ☆ A compass ☆ Hiking boots ☆ Camping equipment ☆ Maps and atlases ☆ Presents for your in-laws ☆ Relics or religious items ☆ Anything secondhand

AVOID: Shopping in your own locality

TIMELY ADVICE: Book your holiday flight now

The Moon in Capricorn

SHOPPING TIP: Not the best time to shop as there could be all kinds of problems

BUY: Practical household items ☆ Good-quality clothes ☆ Consumer durables ☆ Professional tools ☆ Items for elderly relatives ☆ Office equipment ☆ Uniforms ☆ Hardware ☆ DIY materials

AVOID: Making frivolous purchases – you will regret having parted with your money

TIMELY ADVICE: Buy a burglar alarm now

The Moon in Aquarius

SHOPPING TIP: You're drawn to the weird and wonderful, so choose to shop in unusual stores

BUY: Lighting ☆ Electrical appliances ☆ Scientific instruments ☆ A book on meditation ☆ The latest kitchen gadget ☆ Anything electric blue ☆ A chandelier ☆ Aromatherapy oils ☆ Cards and gifts for your friends

AVOID: Shopping in a rush – you need time to browse

TIMELY ADVICE: Join a club

The Moon in Pisces

SHOPPING TIP: Plan to shop in short bursts, with several breaks for coffee or snacks – when the Moon is in Pisces, our feet can give us problems

BUY: Cosmetics ☆ Alcoholic drinks ☆ Tapes or CDs ☆ Shoes and hosiery ☆ A book about dreams ☆ Artist's materials ☆ Paintings ☆ Crystal glasses, decanters or bowls ☆ Romantic fiction ☆ Bedding ☆ Swimwear

AVOID: Major purchases – you are too suggestible and easily swayed by slick sales talk

TIMELY ADVICE: Treat yourself to a reflexology session

Shopping Tips

Juggling our busy lives, as we all do today, means that few of us can choose when to buy the essential things we need, but you might like to take note of the favourable lunar phases when it comes to making more important purchases.

THE DAY OF THE NEW MOON THROUGH TO THE FIRST QUARTER

Choose this period for researching products, window-shopping, seeking advice and either picking up or sending off for samples. You will find there is plenty of energy about at this time, people are sharp and willing to help and you will amass all the information you need in double-quick time.

FROM THE FIRST QUARTER TO THE LAST QUARTER

A favourable time to firm up decisions and make your important purchases. However, avoid any major financial outlay on the day before, or the day of, the Full Moon – you may be more than usually prone to impulse-buying. An excellent period for shopping is from the day after the Full Moon to the Last Quarter – you will make well-thought-out decisions and are more likely to get value for money.

FROM THE LAST QUARTER TO THE NEW MOON

An unsatisfactory time for shopping because energies are flagging all round – your judgement may not be at its

* ☆ * ☆ * ☆ * ☆ * ☆ * ☆

Whenever you need to make any major purchases, either for personal goods or for household items, try to synchronize your shopping trips with the favourable influences of the Moon. Doing this is much more likely to ensure totally satisfying results.

sharpest, shop assistants won't be at their most helpful, shopping generally will be difficult and goods unappealing. You might consider catalogue- or Internet-shopping as less problematic options.

In the Garden

When it comes to your garden, it may seem difficult trying to abide by lunar lore, and yet the success of using planetary influences has been recognized for thousands of years, backed up by extensive trials throughout Europe and America. Once the principles are grasped, look forward to healthy plants that are large, beautiful and disease-free, without recourse to chemicals – truly organic gardening.

Quick Tips

ANNUALS

Begin planting the day after the New Moon and up to the day before the First Quarter, when the Moon is in a fertile or semi-fertile sign. This will help plants to make short, shallow-lying roots and to establish themselves speedily.

BIENNIALS AND PERENNIALS

Begin planting the day after Full Moon and end on the day before the Last Quarter, when the Moon is in a fertile or semi-fertile sign. This will help plants to establish themselves slowly and to develop long, strong roots.

WEEDING

Weeding and hoeing are best done between the Last Quarter and the New Moon, when the Moon is in a barren sign. Avoid times when the Moon is in a fruitful sign – your weeding efforts won't last for very long.

SOIL CULTIVATION

Digging, plowing or tilling the soil should be carried out with the decreasing Moon and when the Moon is in a barren sign, or the weeds will spring up again all too quickly.

TRANSPLANTING

Always transplant when the Moon is increasing, between the New and Full Moons and during a fertile Moon sign.

GRAFTING

Grafts take best when the sap is rising and therefore when the Moon is waxing (from New to Full).

MOWING

Mow with the waxing moon to produce thick, lush regrowth. To slow growth, mow during the decreasing Moon.

COLLECTING SEED

Gathering seed is best done at Full Moon and preferably when the Moon is in the Fire or Air signs of Aries, Leo, Sagittarius, Gemini or Aquarius.

HARVESTING

Harvest fruit and vegetables during the waning period of the Moon, from Full Moon to New Moon, and preferably during the barren or semi-barren Fire or Air signs of Aries, Leo, Sagittarius, Gemini or Aquarius.

EIGHT RULES FOR SUCCESSFUL LUNAR GARDENING

1 Always plant or sow at the right season for the plant concerned (eg, annuals are planted in the spring of the year in which they will flower or fruit)

2 Pay attention to the situation preferred by each plant (free-draining soil, shady site etc)

3 Sow plants that crop above the ground during the waxing Moon

4 Sow plants that crop under the ground (such as roots and tubers) during the waning Moon

5 Sow annuals during the waxing Moon. Annuals need to establish roots quickly but these need only be shallow, spreading just below the surface. Planting at this time encourages this type of root growth and shallow-rooted annuals will also be easier to pull out in the Autumn, once they have finished flowering.

6 Plant biennials during the waning Moon. Biennials and perennials, such as shrubs and trees, need to concentrate their energies in producing a sturdy, wide-spreading root system, so they do better when planted during the waning Moon period, giving them a long, "quiet" period in which to establish themselves.

7 Never undertake any sowing or transplanting on New Moon, Full Moon and Quarter Moon days

8 Co-ordinate the Lunar Phases with the Astrological Signs through which the Moon is passing (*see pages 110–111*)

The Nature of the Signs

The 12 signs are grouped according to their fruitfulness. The barren or semi-barren signs are not good for growth, but are positively advantageous when it comes to weeding, pruning, destroying pests and other jobs concerned with soil management, control and elimination. Note that references to the fertility or barrenness of a sign applies strictly to agricultural procedures – not to individuals born under these signs.

THE FERTILE SIGNS
Cancer, Scorpio, Pisces
THE SEMI-FERTILE SIGNS
Taurus, Libra, Capricorn
THE SEMI-BARREN SIGNS
Aries, Sagittarius, Aquarius
THE BARREN SIGNS
Gemini, Leo, Virgo

109

CHOOSING THE RIGHT SIGN/MOON PHASE

When the Moon is in Aries
Nature: semi-barren

- Excellent time to weed when the Moon is in this sign and in a decreasing phase
- Plant pungent-flavoured vegetables such as garlic just before the Moon leaves this sign
- Cultivate the soil
- Mow

When the Moon is in Taurus
Nature: semi-fertile

- Best time for planting bulbs and sowing plants that crop under the ground, when the Moon is decreasing. Begin the day after Full Moon until the day before the Last Quarter
- Sow annuals, leafy vegetables and pastel-coloured flowering plants when the Moon is in this sign and in a waxing phase
- Do not plant ivies and other vines

When the Moon is in Gemini
Nature: barren

- Good time to weed, prune and destroy pests and diseases when the Moon is in this sign and between the Last Quarter and New Moon
- Cultivate the land
- Do not plant, sow or transplant

When the Moon is in Cancer
Nature: fertile

- Sow plants and flowers for hardiness and abundance when the Moon is in Cancer and during a waxing phase, from the day after New Moon to the day before Full Moon
- Best time to plant watery vegetables and fruits, such as melons and cucumbers, under this sign and during the increasing Moon
- Plant all mosses
- Water the garden well

Chapter 9 *Home Hints* 110

CHOOSING THE RIGHT SIGN/MOON PHASE

When the Moon is in Leo
Nature: barren

- Do not plant, sow or transplant under this sign
- Excellent for digging up weeds, using systemic weed-killers and destroying pests and diseases, especially during decreasing Moon phases
- Prune

When the Moon is in Virgo
Nature: barren

- Not recommended for sowing, planting or transplanting
- Prune and destroy weeds, pests and diseases
- Cultivate the soil

When the Moon is in Libra
Nature: semi-fertile

- Plant flowers for fragrance, beauty and rich colours when the Moon is in Libra and in a waxing phase, from the day after the New Moon to the day before the Full Moon
- Do not plant vegetables under this lunar sign
- Plant vines, climbers and creepers

When the Moon is in Scorpio
Nature: fertile

- Excellent sign for sowing, planting and transplanting fruit, flowers and vegetables that crop above the ground, during the Moon's increasing phases between the day after New Moon up to the day before Full Moon

- Plants grown under this sign will be healthy, robust and long-stemmed, producing a mass of off-shoots and seedlings
- Plant vines, climbers and creepers

When the Moon is in Sagittarius
Nature: semi-barren

- Plant only pungent-tasting fruit or vegetables during a waxing period and just before the Moon leaves this sign
- Cultivate the soil
- Mow

When the Moon is in Capricorn
Nature: semi-fertile

- Useful sign, although not the best, for general sowing and planting. Beneficial for producing hardiness and resistance to drought conditions

- Desirable for plants that crop under the ground
- Do not weed under this Moon sign

When the Moon is in Aquarius
Nature: semi-barren

- Cultivate the land
- Do not plant, sow, transplant or weed
- Mow

When the Moon is in Pisces
Nature: fertile

- Excellent for promoting good root growth and for all general planting during the increasing phase, between the day after New Moon until the day before Full Moon
- Sow compact, low-growing plants with pastel-coloured flowers
- Not recommended for ivies or vines

Make Your Own Moon Garden

According to ancient astrological lore, each plant comes under the dominion of one of the planets and it is the Moon that takes rulership over all white-flowering plants and silvery-coloured foliage. Try creating your own homage to the White Goddess, either by designing a whole Moon garden, or by planting up a small corner, a tiny terrace or even a window box in her honour.

To create your Moon garden, choose only white or creamy white flowering plants – many of these, such as Madonna lilies, jasmine, nicotiana and stocks, have a glorious scent. Emphasize the whiteness by interspersing or edging with the soft grey, green and silver foliage of, for example, artemisia or quilted-leaved hostas. And don't forget to introduce water, for not only will this add an extra dimension to your garden and provide an environment for water lilies, which are also lunar-ruled, but it too is governed by the Moon.

THE CHANGING SEASONS

With a little care and imagination, your Moon garden will flower prolifically, giving changing interest from one season into the next, and providing you with an abundance of frothy blossom that will fill the air with fragrance. Moreover, you will create for yourself a place of peace and tranquillity, a haven that will reflect on Earth the beauty and serenity of the Goddess herself.

MOON GARDEN MAGIC

Here are some ideas for plants, herbs and vegetables, including annuals and perennials, to choose for your Moon garden.

Flowers
Water lilies • White Poppies • Daisies • Snowdrops • Madonna lilies • White Phlox • Lily of the valley • All white Roses • Lotus • Nicotiana • White night-scented Stocks • White Saxifrage • Lunaria

Climbing plants
Convolvulus (often called the Moon flower – sacred to the Moon and bringing luck to its owner) • Honeysuckle • Summer Jasmine • Passion Flower

Shrubs
Deutzia • White Hydrangea • Hebe (white) • Lilac (white) • Buddleia (white) • Philadelphus

Trees
Weeping Willow • Ash • Aspens • Olive • Palm • Maple • Magnolia • Elder

Fruits and Vegetables
Melons • Cucumbers • Squashes • Watermelon • Onions • Watercress • Lettuce

Herbs
Hyssop • Rosemary (dew of the sea) • Lemon balm • Chamomile • Thyme

Silvery-leaved plants
Artemesia • Hostas • Senecio • Stachys • Lychnis • Sedum

CHAPTER 10

MOON LORE

The Moon has been woven into the myths and folk traditions of every civilization through the ages. Superstitions abound, many of which are still practised to this day – often despite our better reasoning, but still observed as if by compulsion. For the most part, these beliefs involve little rituals that are thought to transform our luck – or at least prevent misfortune descending on us.

112

NEW MOON SUPERSTITIONS

The energies of the New Moon are felt especially potently, so more superstitions are based around this phase than any other. For example, children were taught never to point to the New Moon as this was considered discourteous and guaranteed bad luck for the whole of the month to come. Nor was it deemed propitious to look at the New Moon through glass, or, even worse, reflected in a mirror, for the first glimpse of the new crescent should be made outside, in the open air. More bad luck was believed to descend on those who fell asleep with the Moon shining on their faces, for this was thought to cause nightmares, or even induce madness.

However, to bow or curtsey to the New Moon was highly recommended,

✳ ☆ ✳ ☆ ✳ ☆ ✳ ☆ ✳ ☆ ✳ ☆

To ensure good fortune, look at the New Moon over your right shoulder.

and ensured that a wish would be granted. In some countries, bowing several times was strongly advised. So, too, was turning a silver coin over in one's pocket at the sight of the New Moon – said to increase one's wealth.

CHILDBIRTH AND CHILDREN

Much of the folklore involving the Moon revolves around knowledge of cosmic movements and planetary patterns and the effects that these have

on all living things, both physically and behaviourally. Since conception and birth were seen as being linked to the phases of the Moon, it is not surprising that a good many old wives' tales involving children and childbirth have lunar knowledge at their core.

One such piece of wisdom advises expectant mothers to drink raspberry leaf tea to reduce the pain of giving birth. This is a proven tip that many midwives find works well as the chemical constituents of the leaf help to relax the muscles during labour. However, a word of caution here – raspberry leaf tea must not be taken during the early months of pregnancy as, in some cases, it can induce abortion. What is interesting about this ancient knowledge is, of course, that raspberries are traditionally ruled by the Moon.

Another piece of ancient lore is that a child develops certain characteristics according to the day on which he or she was born. The logic underlying this is that each day is said to be ruled by a particular planet, and the planet of the day stamps its own attributes upon those born under its sway. These characteristics have been captured in a famous rhyme:

> ☆
>
> MONDAY'S CHILD IS FAIR OF FACE,
> TUESDAY'S CHILD IS FULL OF GRACE,
> WEDNESDAY'S CHILD IS FULL OF WOE,
> THURSDAY'S CHILD HAS FAR TO GO,
> FRIDAY'S CHILD IS LOVING AND GIVING,
> SATURDAY'S CHILD WORKS HARD FOR ITS LIVING,
> BUT THE CHILD THAT IS BORN ON THE SABBATH DAY,
> IS BLITHE AND BONNY, GOOD AND GAY.
>
> ☆

THE PALE FACE OF THE MOON

Traditionally, it is the Moon that has rulership over Monday – *lundi* in French and *lunedi* in Italian take their root from *luna*, the Latin word for Moon. Astrologically, the Moon is said to confer upon all her subjects a round pale-skinned face, and it is this milky white complexion that is referred to in the first line of the verse shown above. It is interesting to note that another version substitutes "Monday's child is full in the face" for the first line, thus capturing the other characteristic of roundness that is associated with the Moon's influence on facial features.

Another physiological characteristic associated with the Moon may be found on the hand. The Mount of Luna, located at the base of the palm, lies just above the wrist and in a direct line below the little finger. This area of the hand is associated with imagination, racial memories, sensitivity and psychic talents. When underdeveloped, imaginative potential is lacking and the person's nature may be cold and unresponsive. When overdeveloped, moodiness, oversensitivity and sometimes even mental instability may be marked in the personality, as may dreaminess and a flighty, inconstant disposition, just like the ever-changing faces of the Moon. Interestingly, too, markings in this area of the hand can give information about the reproductive organs or gynaecological system – yet again echoing the link between childbirth and the Moon.

SPELLS AND INVOCATIONS

Moon lore also plays a role in all kinds of magical practices, with specific rituals and invocations assigned to the different phases of the Moon. Candles are frequently used in these practices, chants or rhymes are recited and the Moon goddesses are invoked in order to grant a wish or to answer a prayer.

Herbs are said to increase their potency if picked at appropriate times during the Moon's cycle, while any potions will be more effective if taken at an appropriate time. Talismans made when the Moon is new bring good fortune when it waxes to fullness, and any visualization exercises performed at New Moon can produce profound changes in both our conscious minds and our lives in general.

WISHING ON THE MOON

Try this on the night of the New Moon. Sit in a quiet room, light a white candle and visualize something that you long to happen. It might be an improvement in your health, an ambition you want to realize, the return of a lost lover, a windfall or a lucky break. Hold the thought in your mind as you write it down on a sheet of white paper.

Now, fold the paper and slip it underneath a bowl of white flowers, which you have placed by a windowsill where it will pick up the rays of the Moon. Alternatively, if you hope to increase your wealth, slip a coin or a bank note under the vase on the night of the Full Moon. If the wish is to be granted, you should see signs of it materializing before the month is out. But remember, only use magic in a positive way and only for good. Negative wishes that are harmful to others may have serious and unexpected repercussions on the person who makes them. Such are the laws that pertain to the magic of the Moon.

A PARTING THOUGHT

The Dark of the Moon

As you gaze upon the Moon, consider this: had you been born and lived your entire life on the far side of the Moon, the fact that your world has such a profound influence on the lives of those who live on the Earth would not concern you one jot. Nor, as you stood in contemplation, looking at the face of the Sun, would you wonder about the nature of the planet around which your own life revolves. From your hot, arid wasteland, you could not imagine the blue skies that envelop our world, the lush vegetation that clothes our land, the sparkling waters that fill our great oceans. You would know nothing of these things for the simple reason that, from your vantage point, you could not see the Earth, and therefore could not even know that we exist.

As you gaze upon the Moon, ask yourself this: how much is there that we cannot fathom because, as yet, we do not recognize the existence of those things we cannot see?

Moon Charts

LUNAR PHASE TABLES FOR THE YEARS 1920–2020

Listing in order: Year Month Day Hour Minute Key: FM=Full Moon LQ=Last Quarter NM=New Moon FQ=First Quarter

1920 Jan 05	21 05	FM
1920 Jan 13	00 08	LQ
1920 Jan 21	05 27	NM
1920 Jan 28	15 38	FQ
1920 Feb 04	08 42	FM
1920 Feb 11	20 49	LQ
1920 Feb 19	21 34	NM
1920 Feb 26	23 49	FQ
1920 Mar 04	21 12	FM
1920 Mar 12	17 57	LQ
1920 Mar 20	10 55	NM
1920 Mar 27	06 45	FQ
1920 Apr 03	10 54	FM
1920 Apr 11	13 24	LQ
1920 Apr 18	21 43	NM
1920 Apr 25	13 27	FQ
1920 May 03	01 47	FM
1920 May 11	05 51	LQ
1920 May 18	06 25	NM
1920 May 24	21 07	FQ
1920 Jun 01	17 18	FM
1920 Jun 09	18 58	LQ
1920 Jun 16	13 41	NM
1920 Jun 23	06 49	FQ
1920 Jul 01	08 40	FM
1920 Jul 09	05 05	LQ
1920 Jul 15	20 24	NM
1920 Jul 22	19 20	FQ
1920 Jul 30	23 19	FM
1920 Aug 07	12 50	LQ
1920 Aug 14	03 43	NM
1920 Aug 21	10 51	FQ
1920 Aug 29	13 02	FM
1920 Sep 05	19 05	LQ
1920 Sep 12	12 51	NM
1920 Sep 20	04 55	FQ
1920 Sep 28	01 56	FM
1920 Oct 05	00 53	LQ
1920 Oct 12	00 50	NM
1920 Oct 20	00 28	FQ
1920 Oct 27	14 09	FM
1920 Nov 03	07 35	LQ
1920 Nov 10	16 05	NM
1920 Nov 18	20 12	FQ
1920 Nov 26	01 42	FM
1920 Dec 02	16 29	LQ
1920 Dec 10	10 04	NM
1920 Dec 18	14 40	FQ
1920 Dec 25	12 38	FM
1921 Jan 01	04 34	LQ
1921 Jan 09	05 26	NM
1921 Jan 17	06 30	FQ
1921 Jan 23	23 07	FM
1921 Jan 30	20 02	LQ
1921 Feb 08	00 36	NM
1921 Feb 15	18 53	FQ
1921 Feb 22	09 32	FM
1921 Mar 01	14 03	LQ
1921 Mar 09	18 09	NM
1921 Mar 17	03 49	FQ
1921 Mar 23	20 18	FM
1921 Mar 31	09 13	LQ
1921 Apr 08	09 05	NM
1921 Apr 15	10 11	FQ
1921 Apr 22	07 49	FM
1921 Apr 30	04 08	LQ
1921 May 07	21 01	NM
1921 May 14	15 24	FQ
1921 May 21	20 15	FM
1921 May 29	21 44	LQ
1921 Jun 06	06 14	NM
1921 Jun 12	20 59	FQ
1921 Jun 20	09 41	FM
1921 Jun 28	13 17	LQ
1921 Jul 05	13 36	NM
1921 Jul 12	04 15	FQ
1921 Jul 20	00 07	FM
1921 Jul 28	02 20	LQ
1921 Aug 03	20 17	NM
1921 Aug 10	14 13	FQ
1921 Aug 18	15 28	FM
1921 Aug 26	12 51	LQ
1921 Sep 02	03 33	NM
1921 Sep 09	03 29	FQ
1921 Sep 17	07 20	FM
1921 Sep 24	21 17	LQ
1921 Oct 01	12 26	NM
1921 Oct 08	20 11	FQ
1921 Oct 16	22 59	FM
1921 Oct 24	04 31	LQ
1921 Oct 30	23 38	NM
1921 Nov 07	15 53	FQ
1921 Nov 15	13 39	FM
1921 Nov 22	11 41	LQ
1921 Nov 29	13 25	NM
1921 Dec 07	13 19	FQ
1921 Dec 15	02 50	FM
1921 Dec 21	19 54	LQ
1921 Dec 29	05 39	NM
1922 Jan 06	10 23	FQ
1922 Jan 13	14 36	FM
1922 Jan 20	06 00	LQ
1922 Jan 27	23 48	NM
1922 Feb 05	04 52	FQ
1922 Feb 12	01 17	FM
1922 Feb 18	18 18	LQ
1922 Feb 26	18 47	NM
1922 Mar 06	19 21	FQ
1922 Mar 13	11 14	FM
1922 Mar 20	08 43	LQ
1922 Mar 28	13 03	NM
1922 Apr 05	05 45	FQ
1922 Apr 11	20 43	FM
1922 Apr 19	00 53	LQ
1922 Apr 27	05 03	NM
1922 May 04	12 55	FQ
1922 May 11	06 06	FM
1922 May 18	18 17	LQ
1922 May 26	18 04	NM
1922 Jun 02	18 10	FQ
1922 Jun 09	15 58	FM
1922 Jun 17	12 03	LQ
1922 Jun 25	04 19	NM
1922 Jul 01	22 51	FQ
1922 Jul 09	03 07	FM
1922 Jul 17	05 11	LQ
1922 Jul 24	12 47	NM
1922 Jul 31	04 21	FQ
1922 Aug 07	16 18	FM
1922 Aug 15	20 45	LQ
1922 Aug 22	20 34	NM
1922 Aug 29	11 55	FQ
1922 Sep 06	07 47	FM
1922 Sep 14	10 20	LQ
1922 Sep 21	04 38	NM
1922 Sep 27	22 40	FQ
1922 Oct 06	00 58	FM
1922 Oct 13	21 55	LQ
1922 Oct 20	13 40	NM
1922 Oct 27	13 26	FQ
1922 Nov 04	18 36	FM
1922 Nov 12	07 52	LQ
1922 Nov 19	00 06	NM
1922 Nov 26	08 15	FQ
1922 Dec 04	11 23	FM
1922 Dec 11	16 40	LQ
1922 Dec 18	12 20	NM
1922 Dec 26	05 53	FQ
1923 Jan 03	02 33	FM
1923 Jan 10	00 54	LQ
1923 Jan 17	02 41	NM
1923 Jan 25	03 59	FQ
1923 Feb 01	15 53	FM
1923 Feb 08	09 16	LQ
1923 Feb 15	19 07	NM
1923 Feb 24	00 06	FQ
1923 Mar 03	03 23	FM
1923 Mar 09	18 31	LQ
1923 Mar 17	12 51	NM
1923 Mar 25	16 41	FQ
1923 Apr 01	13 10	FM
1923 Apr 08	05 22	LQ
1923 Apr 16	06 28	NM
1923 Apr 24	05 20	FQ
1923 Apr 30	21 30	FM
1923 May 07	18 18	LQ
1923 May 15	22 38	NM
1923 May 23	14 25	FQ
1923 May 30	05 07	FM
1923 Jun 06	09 19	LQ
1923 Jun 14	12 42	NM
1923 Jun 21	20 46	FQ
1923 Jun 28	13 04	FM
1923 Jul 06	01 56	LQ
1923 Jul 14	00 45	NM
1923 Jul 21	01 32	FQ
1923 Jul 27	22 32	FM
1923 Aug 04	19 22	LQ
1923 Aug 12	11 16	NM
1923 Aug 19	06 07	FQ
1923 Aug 26	10 29	FM
1923 Sep 03	12 47	LQ
1923 Sep 10	20 52	NM
1923 Sep 17	12 04	FQ
1923 Sep 25	01 16	FM
1923 Oct 03	05 29	LQ
1923 Oct 10	06 05	NM
1923 Oct 16	20 53	FQ
1923 Oct 24	18 26	FM
1923 Nov 01	20 49	LQ
1923 Nov 08	15 27	NM
1923 Nov 15	09 41	FQ
1923 Nov 23	12 58	FM
1923 Dec 01	10 09	LQ
1923 Dec 08	01 30	NM
1923 Dec 15	02 38	FQ
1923 Dec 23	07 33	FM
1923 Dec 30	21 07	LQ
1924 Jan 06	12 48	NM
1924 Jan 13	22 44	FQ
1924 Jan 22	00 57	FM
1924 Jan 29	05 53	LQ
1924 Feb 05	01 38	NM
1924 Feb 12	20 09	FQ
1924 Feb 20	16 07	FM
1924 Feb 27	13 15	LQ
1924 Mar 05	15 58	NM
1924 Mar 13	16 50	FQ
1924 Mar 21	04 30	FM
1924 Mar 27	20 24	LQ
1924 Apr 04	07 17	NM
1924 Apr 12	11 12	FQ
1924 Apr 19	14 10	FM
1924 Apr 26	04 28	LQ
1924 May 03	23 00	NM
1924 May 12	02 14	FQ
1924 May 18	21 52	FM
1924 May 25	14 16	LQ
1924 Jun 02	14 34	NM
1924 Jun 10	13 37	FQ
1924 Jun 17	04 41	FM
1924 Jun 24	02 16	LQ
1924 Jul 02	05 35	NM
1924 Jul 09	21 46	FQ
1924 Jul 16	11 49	FM
1924 Jul 23	16 36	LQ
1924 Jul 31	19 42	NM
1924 Aug 08	03 41	FQ
1924 Aug 14	20 19	FM
1924 Aug 22	09 10	LQ
1924 Aug 30	08 37	NM
1924 Sep 06	08 45	FQ
1924 Sep 13	07 00	FM
1924 Sep 21	03 35	LQ
1924 Oct 05	14 30	FQ
1924 Oct 12	20 21	FM
1924 Oct 20	22 54	LQ
1924 Oct 28	06 57	NM
1924 Nov 03	22 18	FQ
1924 Nov 11	12 31	FM
1924 Nov 19	17 38	LQ
1924 Nov 26	17 15	NM
1924 Dec 03	09 10	FQ
1924 Dec 11	07 03	FM
1924 Dec 19	10 11	LQ
1924 Dec 26	03 45	NM
1925 Jan 01	23 25	FQ
1925 Jan 10	02 47	FM
1925 Jan 17	23 33	LQ
1925 Jan 24	14 45	NM
1925 Jan 31	16 43	FQ
1925 Feb 08	21 49	FM
1925 Feb 16	09 41	LQ
1925 Feb 23	02 12	NM
1925 Mar 02	12 06	FQ
1925 Mar 10	14 21	FM
1925 Mar 17	17 21	LQ
1925 Mar 24	14 03	NM
1925 Apr 01	08 12	FQ
1925 Apr 09	03 33	FM
1925 Apr 15	23 40	LQ
1925 Apr 23	02 28	NM
1925 May 01	03 20	FQ
1925 May 08	13 42	FM
1925 May 15	05 46	LQ
1925 May 22	15 48	NM
1925 May 30	20 04	FQ
1925 Jun 06	21 48	FM
1925 Jun 13	12 44	LQ
1925 Jun 21	06 17	NM
1925 Jun 29	09 43	FQ
1925 Jul 06	04 54	FM
1925 Jul 12	21 34	LQ
1925 Jul 20	21 40	NM
1925 Jul 28	20 23	FQ
1925 Aug 04	11 59	FM
1925 Aug 11	09 11	LQ
1925 Aug 19	13 15	NM
1925 Aug 27	04 46	FQ
1925 Sep 02	19 53	FM
1925 Sep 10	00 11	LQ
1925 Sep 18	04 12	NM
1925 Sep 25	11 51	FQ
1925 Oct 02	05 23	FM
1925 Oct 09	18 34	LQ
1925 Oct 17	18 06	NM
1925 Oct 24	18 38	FQ
1925 Oct 31	17 16	FM
1925 Nov 08	15 13	LQ
1925 Nov 16	06 58	NM
1925 Nov 23	02 05	FQ
1925 Nov 30	08 11	FM
1925 Dec 08	12 11	LQ
1925 Dec 15	19 05	NM
1925 Dec 22	11 08	FQ
1925 Dec 30	02 01	FM
1926 Jan 07	07 22	LQ
1926 Jan 14	06 34	NM
1926 Jan 20	22 31	FQ
1926 Jan 28	21 35	FM
1926 Feb 05	23 25	LQ
1926 Feb 12	17 20	NM
1926 Feb 19	12 36	FQ
1926 Feb 27	16 51	FM
1926 Mar 07	11 49	LQ
1926 Mar 14	03 20	NM
1926 Mar 21	05 12	FQ
1926 Mar 29	10 00	FM
1926 Apr 05	20 50	LQ
1926 Apr 12	12 56	NM
1926 Apr 19	23 23	FQ
1926 Apr 28	00 16	FM
1926 May 05	03 13	LQ
1926 May 11	22 55	NM
1926 May 19	17 48	FQ
1926 May 27	11 49	FM
1926 Jun 03	08 09	LQ
1926 Jun 10	10 08	NM
1926 Jun 18	11 13	FQ
1926 Jun 25	21 13	FM
1926 Jul 02	13 02	LQ
1926 Jul 09	23 06	NM
1926 Jul 18	02 55	FQ
1926 Jul 25	05 13	FM
1926 Jul 31	19 25	LQ
1926 Aug 08	13 49	NM
1926 Aug 16	16 39	FQ
1926 Aug 23	12 38	FM
1926 Aug 30	04 40	LQ
1926 Sep 07	05 45	NM
1926 Sep 15	04 26	FQ
1926 Sep 21	20 19	FM
1926 Sep 28	17 48	LQ
1926 Oct 06	22 13	NM
1926 Oct 14	14 28	FQ
1926 Oct 21	05 15	FM
1926 Oct 28	10 57	LQ
1926 Nov 05	14 34	NM
1926 Nov 12	23 01	FQ
1926 Nov 19	16 21	FM
1926 Nov 27	07 15	LQ
1926 Dec 05	06 11	NM
1926 Dec 12	06 47	FQ
1926 Dec 19	06 09	FM
1926 Dec 27	04 59	LQ
1927 Jan 03	20 28	NM
1927 Jan 10	14 43	FQ
1927 Jan 17	22 27	FM
1927 Jan 26	02 05	LQ
1927 Feb 02	08 54	NM
1927 Feb 08	23 54	FQ
1927 Feb 16	16 18	FM
1927 Feb 24	20 42	LQ
1927 Mar 03	19 24	NM
1927 Mar 10	11 03	FQ
1927 Mar 18	10 24	FM
1927 Mar 26	11 35	LQ
1927 Apr 02	04 24	NM
1927 Apr 09	00 21	FQ
1927 Apr 17	03 35	FM
1927 Apr 24	22 21	LQ
1927 May 01	12 40	NM
1927 May 08	15 27	FQ
1927 May 16	19 03	FM
1927 May 24	05 34	LQ
1927 May 30	21 06	NM
1927 Jun 07	07 49	FQ
1927 Jun 15	08 19	FM
1927 Jun 22	10 29	LQ
1927 Jun 29	06 32	NM
1927 Jul 07	00 52	FQ
1927 Jul 14	19 22	FM
1927 Jul 21	14 43	LQ
1927 Jul 28	17 36	NM
1927 Aug 05	18 05	FQ
1927 Aug 13	04 37	FM
1927 Aug 19	19 54	LQ
1927 Aug 27	06 45	NM
1927 Sep 04	10 44	FQ
1927 Sep 11	12 54	FM
1927 Sep 18	03 29	LQ
1927 Sep 25	22 11	NM
1927 Oct 04	02 01	FQ
1927 Oct 10	21 14	FM
1927 Oct 17	14 32	LQ
1927 Oct 25	15 37	NM
1927 Nov 02	15 16	FQ
1927 Nov 09	06 36	FM
1927 Nov 16	05 28	LQ
1927 Nov 24	10 09	NM
1927 Dec 02	02 15	FQ
1927 Dec 08	17 32	FM
1927 Dec 16	00 04	LQ
1927 Dec 24	04 13	NM
1927 Dec 31	11 22	FQ
1928 Jan 07	06 08	FM
1928 Jan 14	21 14	LQ
1928 Jan 22	20 19	NM
1928 Jan 29	19 25	FQ
1928 Feb 05	20 11	FM
1928 Feb 13	19 05	LQ
1928 Feb 21	09 41	NM
1928 Feb 28	03 21	FQ
1928 Mar 06	11 27	FM
1928 Mar 14	15 20	LQ
1928 Mar 21	20 29	NM
1928 Mar 28	11 54	FQ
1928 Apr 05	03 38	FM
1928 Apr 13	08 09	LQ
1928 Apr 20	05 25	NM
1928 Apr 26	21 42	FQ
1928 May 04	20 12	FM
1928 May 12	20 50	LQ
1928 May 19	13 14	NM
1928 May 26	09 11	FQ
1928 Jun 03	12 13	FM
1928 Jun 11	05 51	LQ
1928 Jun 17	20 42	NM
1928 Jun 24	22 47	FQ
1928 Jul 03	02 48	FM
1928 Jul 10	12 16	LQ
1928 Jul 17	04 35	NM
1928 Jul 24	14 38	FQ
1928 Aug 01	15 30	FM
1928 Aug 08	17 24	LQ
1928 Aug 15	13 48	NM
1928 Aug 23	08 21	FQ
1928 Aug 31	02 34	FM
1928 Sep 06	22 35	LQ
1928 Sep 14	01 20	NM
1928 Sep 22	02 58	FQ
1928 Sep 29	12 42	FM
1928 Oct 06	05 06	LQ
1928 Oct 13	15 56	NM
1928 Oct 21	21 06	FQ
1928 Oct 28	22 43	FM
1928 Nov 04	14 06	LQ
1928 Nov 12	09 35	NM
1928 Nov 20	13 36	FQ
1928 Nov 27	09 05	FM
1928 Dec 04	02 31	LQ
1928 Dec 12	05 06	NM
1928 Dec 20	03 43	FQ
1928 Dec 26	19 55	FM
1929 Jan 02	18 44	LQ
1929 Jan 11	00 28	NM
1929 Jan 18	15 15	FQ

Moon Charts

Moon Charts

116

1929 Jan 25	07 09	FM
1929 Feb 01	14 10	LQ
1929 Feb 09	17 55	NM
1929 Feb 17	00 22	FQ
1929 Feb 23	18 59	FM
1929 Mar 03	11 09	LQ
1929 Mar 11	08 37	NM
1929 Mar 18	07 41	FQ
1929 Mar 25	07 46	FM
1929 Apr 02	07 29	LQ
1929 Apr 09	20 32	NM
1929 Apr 16	14 09	FQ
1929 Apr 23	21 47	FM
1929 May 02	01 25	LQ
1929 May 09	06 07	NM
1929 May 15	20 56	FQ
1929 May 23	12 50	FM
1929 May 31	16 13	LQ
1929 Jun 07	13 56	NM
1929 Jun 14	05 14	FQ
1929 Jun 22	04 15	FM
1929 Jun 30	03 54	LQ
1929 Jul 06	20 47	NM
1929 Jul 13	16 05	FQ
1929 Jul 21	19 21	FM
1929 Jul 29	12 56	LQ
1929 Aug 05	03 40	NM
1929 Aug 12	06 01	FQ
1929 Aug 20	09 42	FM
1929 Aug 27	20 02	LQ
1929 Sep 03	11 47	NM
1929 Sep 10	22 57	FQ
1929 Sep 18	23 16	FM
1929 Sep 26	02 07	LQ
1929 Oct 02	22 19	NM
1929 Oct 10	18 05	FQ
1929 Oct 18	12 06	FM
1929 Oct 25	08 21	LQ
1929 Nov 01	12 01	NM
1929 Nov 09	14 10	FQ
1929 Nov 17	00 14	FM
1929 Nov 23	16 04	LQ
1929 Dec 01	04 48	NM
1929 Dec 09	09 42	FQ
1929 Dec 16	11 38	FM
1929 Dec 23	02 27	LQ
1929 Dec 30	23 42	NM
1930 Jan 08	03 11	FQ
1930 Jan 14	22 21	FM
1930 Jan 21	16 07	LQ
1930 Jan 29	19 07	NM
1930 Feb 06	17 26	FQ
1930 Feb 13	08 38	FM
1930 Feb 20	08 44	LQ
1930 Feb 28	13 33	NM
1930 Mar 08	04 00	FQ
1930 Mar 14	18 58	FM
1930 Mar 22	03 13	LQ
1930 Mar 30	05 46	NM
1930 Apr 06	11 25	FQ
1930 Apr 13	05 48	FM
1930 Apr 20	22 08	LQ
1930 Apr 28	19 08	NM
1930 May 05	16 53	FQ
1930 May 12	17 29	FM
1930 May 20	16 21	LQ
1930 May 28	05 37	NM
1930 Jun 03	21 56	FQ
1930 Jun 11	06 12	FM
1930 Jun 19	09 00	LQ
1930 Jun 26	13 47	NM
1930 Jul 03	04 03	FQ
1930 Jul 10	20 01	FM
1930 Jul 18	23 29	LQ
1930 Jul 25	20 42	NM
1930 Aug 01	12 26	FQ
1930 Aug 09	10 58	FM
1930 Aug 17	11 31	LQ
1930 Aug 24	03 37	NM
1930 Aug 30	23 57	FQ
1930 Sep 08	02 48	FM
1930 Sep 15	21 13	LQ
1930 Sep 22	11 41	NM
1930 Sep 29	14 58	FQ
1930 Oct 07	18 56	FM
1930 Oct 15	05 12	LQ
1930 Oct 21	21 48	NM
1930 Oct 29	09 22	FQ
1930 Nov 06	10 28	FM
1930 Nov 13	12 27	LQ
1930 Nov 20	10 21	NM
1930 Nov 28	06 18	FQ
1930 Dec 06	00 40	FM
1930 Dec 12	20 07	LQ
1930 Dec 20	01 24	NM
1930 Dec 28	03 59	FQ
1931 Jan 04	13 15	FM
1931 Jan 11	05 09	LQ
1931 Jan 18	18 35	NM
1931 Jan 27	00 05	FQ
1931 Feb 03	00 26	FM
1931 Feb 09	16 09	LQ
1931 Feb 17	13 11	NM
1931 Feb 25	16 42	FQ
1931 Mar 04	10 36	FM
1931 Mar 11	05 15	LQ
1931 Mar 19	07 51	NM
1931 Mar 27	05 04	FQ
1931 Apr 02	20 05	FM
1931 Apr 09	20 15	LQ
1931 Apr 18	01 00	NM
1931 Apr 25	13 40	FQ
1931 May 02	05 14	FM
1931 May 09	12 48	LQ
1931 May 17	15 28	NM
1931 May 24	19 39	FQ
1931 May 31	14 33	FM
1931 Jun 08	06 18	LQ
1931 Jun 16	03 02	NM
1931 Jun 23	00 23	FQ
1931 Jun 30	00 47	FM
1931 Jul 07	23 52	LQ
1931 Jul 15	12 20	NM
1931 Jul 22	05 16	FQ
1931 Jul 29	12 47	FM
1931 Aug 06	16 28	LQ
1931 Aug 13	20 27	NM
1931 Aug 20	11 36	FQ
1931 Aug 28	03 09	FM
1931 Sep 05	07 21	LQ
1931 Sep 12	04 26	NM
1931 Sep 18	20 37	FQ
1931 Sep 26	19 45	FM
1931 Oct 04	20 15	LQ
1931 Oct 11	13 06	NM
1931 Oct 18	09 20	FQ
1931 Oct 26	13 34	FM
1931 Nov 03	07 17	LQ
1931 Nov 09	22 55	NM
1931 Nov 17	02 13	FQ
1931 Nov 25	07 10	FM
1931 Dec 02	16 50	LQ
1931 Dec 09	10 16	NM
1931 Dec 16	22 43	FQ
1931 Dec 24	23 23	FM
1932 Jan 01	01 23	LQ
1932 Jan 07	23 29	NM
1932 Jan 15	20 55	FQ
1932 Jan 23	13 44	FM
1932 Jan 30	09 32	LQ
1932 Feb 06	14 45	NM
1932 Feb 14	18 16	FQ
1932 Feb 22	02 07	FM
1932 Feb 28	18 03	LQ
1932 Mar 07	07 44	NM
1932 Mar 15	12 41	FQ
1932 Mar 22	12 37	FM
1932 Mar 29	03 43	LQ
1932 Apr 06	01 21	NM
1932 Apr 14	03 15	FQ
1932 Apr 20	21 27	FM
1932 Apr 27	15 14	LQ
1932 May 05	18 11	NM
1932 May 13	14 02	FQ
1932 May 20	05 08	FM
1932 May 27	04 54	LQ
1932 Jun 04	09 16	NM
1932 Jun 11	21 39	FQ
1932 Jun 18	12 38	FM
1932 Jun 25	20 36	LQ
1932 Jul 03	22 20	NM
1932 Jul 11	03 07	FQ
1932 Jul 17	21 06	FM
1932 Jul 25	13 41	LQ
1932 Aug 02	09 42	NM
1932 Aug 09	07 40	FQ
1932 Aug 16	07 41	FM
1932 Aug 24	07 21	LQ
1932 Aug 31	19 55	NM
1932 Sep 07	12 49	FQ
1932 Sep 14	21 06	FM
1932 Sep 23	00 47	LQ
1932 Sep 30	05 30	NM
1932 Oct 06	20 05	FQ
1932 Oct 14	13 18	FM
1932 Oct 22	17 14	LQ
1932 Oct 29	14 56	NM
1932 Nov 05	06 50	FQ
1932 Nov 13	07 28	FM
1932 Nov 21	07 58	LQ
1932 Nov 28	00 43	NM
1932 Dec 04	21 45	FQ
1932 Dec 13	02 21	FM
1932 Dec 20	20 22	LQ
1932 Dec 27	11 22	NM
1933 Jan 03	16 24	FQ
1933 Jan 11	20 36	FM
1933 Jan 19	06 15	LQ
1933 Jan 25	23 20	NM
1933 Feb 02	13 16	FQ
1933 Feb 10	13 00	FM
1933 Feb 17	14 08	LQ
1933 Feb 24	12 44	NM
1933 Mar 04	10 23	FQ
1933 Mar 12	02 46	FM
1933 Mar 18	21 04	LQ
1933 Mar 26	03 20	NM
1933 Apr 03	05 56	FQ
1933 Apr 10	13 38	FM
1933 Apr 17	04 17	LQ
1933 Apr 24	18 38	NM
1933 May 02	22 39	FQ
1933 May 09	22 04	FM
1933 May 16	12 50	LQ
1933 May 24	10 07	NM
1933 Jun 01	11 53	FQ
1933 Jun 08	05 04	FM
1933 Jun 14	23 25	LQ
1933 Jun 23	01 22	NM
1933 Jun 30	21 40	FQ
1933 Jul 07	11 50	FM
1933 Jul 14	12 24	LQ
1933 Jul 22	16 03	NM
1933 Jul 30	04 44	FQ
1933 Aug 05	19 31	FM
1933 Aug 13	03 49	LQ
1933 Aug 21	05 48	NM
1933 Aug 28	10 13	FQ
1933 Sep 04	05 04	FM
1933 Sep 11	21 30	LQ
1933 Sep 19	18 21	NM
1933 Sep 26	15 36	FQ
1933 Oct 03	17 08	FM
1933 Oct 11	16 45	LQ
1933 Oct 19	05 45	NM
1933 Oct 25	22 21	FQ
1933 Nov 02	07 59	FM
1933 Nov 10	12 18	LQ
1933 Nov 17	16 24	NM
1933 Nov 24	07 38	FQ
1933 Dec 02	01 31	FM
1933 Dec 10	06 24	LQ
1933 Dec 17	02 53	NM
1933 Dec 23	20 09	FQ
1933 Dec 31	20 54	FM
1934 Jan 08	21 36	LQ
1934 Jan 15	13 37	NM
1934 Jan 22	11 50	FQ
1934 Jan 30	16 31	FM
1934 Feb 07	09 22	LQ
1934 Feb 14	00 43	NM
1934 Feb 21	06 05	FQ
1934 Mar 01	10 26	FM
1934 Mar 08	18 06	LQ
1934 Mar 15	12 08	NM
1934 Mar 23	01 44	FQ
1934 Mar 31	01 14	FM
1934 Apr 07	00 48	LQ
1934 Apr 13	23 57	NM
1934 Apr 21	21 20	FQ
1934 Apr 29	12 45	FM
1934 May 06	06 41	LQ
1934 May 13	12 30	NM
1934 May 21	15 20	FQ
1934 May 28	21 41	FM
1934 Jun 04	12 53	LQ
1934 Jun 12	02 11	NM
1934 Jun 20	06 37	FQ
1934 Jun 27	05 08	FM
1934 Jul 03	20 28	LQ
1934 Jul 11	17 06	NM
1934 Jul 19	18 53	FQ
1934 Jul 26	12 08	FM
1934 Aug 02	06 27	LQ
1934 Aug 10	08 46	NM
1934 Aug 18	04 33	FQ
1934 Aug 24	19 37	FM
1934 Aug 31	19 40	LQ
1934 Sep 09	00 20	NM
1934 Sep 16	12 26	FQ
1934 Sep 23	04 19	FM
1934 Sep 30	12 29	LQ
1934 Oct 08	15 05	NM
1934 Oct 15	19 29	FQ
1934 Oct 22	15 01	FM
1934 Oct 30	08 22	LQ
1934 Nov 07	04 44	NM
1934 Nov 14	02 39	FQ
1934 Nov 21	04 26	FM
1934 Nov 29	05 39	LQ
1934 Dec 06	17 25	NM
1934 Dec 13	10 51	FQ
1934 Dec 20	20 53	FM
1934 Dec 29	02 08	LQ
1935 Jan 05	05 20	NM
1935 Jan 11	20 55	FQ
1935 Jan 19	15 44	FM
1935 Jan 27	19 59	LQ
1935 Feb 03	16 27	NM
1935 Feb 10	09 25	FQ
1935 Feb 18	11 17	FM
1935 Feb 26	10 14	LQ
1935 Mar 05	02 40	NM
1935 Mar 12	00 30	FQ
1935 Mar 20	05 31	FM
1935 Mar 27	20 51	LQ
1935 Apr 03	12 10	NM
1935 Apr 10	17 42	FQ
1935 Apr 18	21 10	FM
1935 Apr 26	04 20	LQ
1935 May 02	21 36	NM
1935 May 10	11 54	FQ
1935 May 18	09 57	FM
1935 May 25	09 44	LQ
1935 Jun 01	07 52	NM
1935 Jun 09	05 49	FQ
1935 Jun 16	20 20	FM
1935 Jun 23	14 21	LQ
1935 Jun 30	19 44	NM
1935 Jul 08	22 28	FQ
1935 Jul 16	05 00	FM
1935 Jul 22	19 42	LQ
1935 Jul 30	09 32	NM
1935 Aug 07	13 23	FQ
1935 Aug 14	12 43	FM
1935 Aug 21	03 17	LQ
1935 Aug 29	01 00	NM
1935 Sep 06	02 26	FQ
1935 Sep 12	20 18	FM
1935 Sep 19	14 23	LQ
1935 Sep 27	17 29	NM
1935 Oct 05	13 39	FQ
1935 Oct 12	04 39	FM
1935 Oct 19	05 36	LQ
1935 Oct 27	10 15	NM
1935 Nov 03	23 12	FQ
1935 Nov 10	14 42	FM
1935 Nov 18	00 36	LQ
1935 Nov 26	02 36	NM
1935 Dec 03	07 28	FQ
1935 Dec 10	03 10	FM
1935 Dec 17	21 57	LQ
1935 Dec 25	17 49	NM
1936 Jan 01	15 15	FQ
1936 Jan 08	18 15	FM
1936 Jan 16	19 41	LQ
1936 Jan 24	07 18	NM
1936 Jan 30	23 35	FQ
1936 Feb 07	11 19	FM
1936 Feb 15	15 45	LQ
1936 Feb 22	18 42	NM
1936 Feb 29	09 28	FQ
1936 Mar 08	05 14	FM
1936 Mar 16	08 35	LQ
1936 Mar 23	04 13	NM
1936 Mar 29	21 22	FQ
1936 Apr 06	22 46	FM
1936 Apr 14	21 21	LQ
1936 Apr 21	12 32	NM
1936 Apr 28	11 16	FQ
1936 May 06	15 01	FM
1936 May 14	06 12	LQ
1936 May 20	20 34	NM
1936 May 28	02 46	FQ
1936 Jun 05	05 22	FM
1936 Jun 12	12 05	LQ
1936 Jun 19	05 14	NM
1936 Jun 26	19 23	FQ
1936 Jul 04	17 34	FM
1936 Jul 11	16 28	LQ
1936 Jul 18	15 19	NM
1936 Jul 26	12 36	FQ
1936 Aug 03	03 47	FM
1936 Aug 09	20 59	LQ
1936 Aug 17	03 21	NM
1936 Aug 25	05 49	FQ
1936 Sep 01	12 37	FM
1936 Sep 08	03 14	LQ
1936 Sep 15	17 41	NM
1936 Sep 23	22 12	FQ
1936 Sep 30	21 01	FM
1936 Oct 07	12 28	LQ
1936 Oct 15	10 20	NM
1936 Oct 23	12 54	FQ
1936 Oct 30	05 57	FM
1936 Nov 06	01 29	LQ
1936 Nov 14	04 42	NM
1936 Nov 22	01 19	FQ
1936 Nov 28	16 12	FM
1936 Dec 05	18 20	LQ
1936 Dec 13	23 25	NM
1936 Dec 21	11 30	FQ
1936 Dec 28	04 00	FM
1937 Jan 04	14 22	LQ
1937 Jan 12	16 47	NM
1937 Jan 19	20 02	FQ
1937 Jan 26	17 15	FM
1937 Feb 03	12 04	LQ
1937 Feb 11	07 34	NM
1937 Feb 18	03 49	FQ
1937 Feb 25	07 43	FM
1937 Mar 05	09 17	LQ
1937 Mar 12	19 32	NM
1937 Mar 19	11 46	FQ
1937 Mar 26	23 12	FM
1937 Apr 04	03 53	LQ
1937 Apr 11	05 10	NM
1937 Apr 17	20 34	FQ
1937 Apr 25	15 23	FM
1937 May 03	18 36	LQ
1937 May 10	13 17	NM
1937 May 17	06 49	FQ
1937 May 25	07 38	FM
1937 Jun 02	05 24	LQ
1937 Jun 08	20 43	NM
1937 Jun 15	19 03	FQ
1937 Jun 23	22 59	FM
1937 Jul 01	13 03	LQ
1937 Jul 08	04 12	NM
1937 Jul 15	09 36	FQ
1937 Jul 23	12 45	FM
1937 Jul 30	18 47	LQ
1937 Aug 06	12 37	NM
1937 Aug 14	02 28	FQ
1937 Aug 22	00 47	FM
1937 Aug 28	23 54	LQ
1937 Sep 04	22 53	NM
1937 Sep 12	20 57	FQ
1937 Sep 20	11 32	FM
1937 Sep 27	05 43	LQ
1937 Oct 04	11 58	NM
1937 Oct 12	15 47	FQ
1937 Oct 19	21 47	FM
1937 Oct 26	13 26	LQ
1937 Nov 03	04 16	NM
1937 Nov 11	09 33	FQ
1937 Nov 18	08 09	FM
1937 Nov 25	00 04	LQ
1937 Dec 02	23 11	NM
1937 Dec 11	01 12	FQ
1937 Dec 17	18 52	FM
1937 Dec 24	14 20	LQ
1938 Jan 01	18 58	NM
1938 Jan 09	14 13	FQ
1938 Jan 16	05 53	FM
1938 Jan 23	08 09	LQ
1938 Jan 31	13 35	NM
1938 Feb 08	00 32	FQ
1938 Feb 14	17 14	FM
1938 Feb 22	04 24	LQ
1938 Mar 02	05 40	NM
1938 Mar 09	08 35	FQ
1938 Mar 16	05 15	FM
1938 Mar 24	01 06	LQ
1938 Mar 31	18 52	NM
1938 Apr 07	15 10	FQ
1938 Apr 14	18 21	FM
1938 Apr 22	20 14	LQ
1938 Apr 30	05 28	NM
1938 May 06	21 24	FQ
1938 May 14	08 39	FM
1938 May 22	12 36	LQ
1938 May 29	13 59	NM
1938 Jun 05	04 32	FQ
1938 Jun 12	23 47	FM
1938 Jun 21	01 52	LQ
1938 Jun 27	21 10	NM
1938 Jul 04	13 47	FQ
1938 Jul 12	15 04	FM
1938 Jul 20	12 19	LQ
1938 Jul 27	03 53	NM
1938 Aug 03	02 00	FQ
1938 Aug 11	05 57	FM
1938 Aug 18	20 30	LQ
1938 Aug 25	11 17	NM
1938 Sep 01	17 28	FQ
1938 Sep 09	20 08	FM
1938 Sep 17	03 12	LQ
1938 Sep 23	20 34	NM
1938 Oct 01	11 45	FQ
1938 Oct 09	09 37	FM
1938 Oct 16	09 24	LQ
1938 Oct 23	08 42	NM
1938 Oct 31	07 45	FQ
1938 Nov 07	22 23	FM
1938 Nov 14	16 20	LQ
1938 Nov 22	00 05	NM
1938 Nov 30	03 59	FQ
1938 Dec 07	10 22	FM
1938 Dec 14	01 17	LQ
1938 Dec 21	18 07	NM
1938 Dec 29	22 53	FQ
1939 Jan 05	21 30	FM
1939 Jan 12	13 10	LQ
1939 Jan 20	13 26	NM
1939 Jan 28	15 00	FQ
1939 Feb 04	07 54	FM
1939 Feb 11	04 12	LQ
1939 Feb 19	08 28	NM
1939 Feb 27	03 26	FQ
1939 Mar 05	18 00	FM
1939 Mar 12	21 37	LQ
1939 Mar 21	01 49	NM
1939 Mar 28	12 16	FQ
1939 Apr 04	04 18	FM
1939 Apr 11	16 11	LQ
1939 Apr 19	16 35	NM
1939 Apr 26	18 25	FQ
1939 May 03	15 15	FM
1939 May 11	10 40	LQ

Moon Charts

1939 May 19	04 25	NM
1939 May 25	23 20	FQ
1939 Jun 02	03 11	FM
1939 Jun 10	04 07	LQ
1939 Jun 17	13 37	NM
1939 Jun 24	04 35	FQ
1939 Jul 01	16 16	FM
1939 Jul 09	19 49	LQ
1939 Jul 16	21 03	NM
1939 Jul 23	11 34	FQ
1939 Jul 31	06 37	FM
1939 Aug 08	09 18	LQ
1939 Aug 15	03 53	NM
1939 Aug 21	21 20	FQ
1939 Aug 29	22 09	FM
1939 Sep 06	20 24	LQ
1939 Sep 13	11 22	NM
1939 Sep 20	10 34	FQ
1939 Sep 28	14 27	FM
1939 Oct 06	05 27	LQ
1939 Oct 12	20 30	NM
1939 Oct 20	03 24	FQ
1939 Oct 28	06 42	FM
1939 Nov 04	13 12	LQ
1939 Nov 11	07 54	NM
1939 Nov 18	23 21	FQ
1939 Nov 26	21 54	FM
1939 Dec 03	20 40	LQ
1939 Dec 10	21 45	NM
1939 Dec 18	21 04	FQ
1939 Dec 26	11 28	FM
1940 Jan 02	04 56	LQ
1940 Jan 09	13 53	NM
1940 Jan 17	18 21	FQ
1940 Jan 24	23 22	FM
1940 Jan 31	14 47	LQ
1940 Feb 08	07 45	NM
1940 Feb 16	12 55	FQ
1940 Feb 23	09 55	FM
1940 Mar 01	02 35	LQ
1940 Mar 09	02 23	NM
1940 Mar 17	03 25	FQ
1940 Mar 23	19 33	FM
1940 Mar 30	16 20	LQ
1940 Apr 07	20 18	NM
1940 Apr 15	13 45	FQ
1940 Apr 22	04 37	FM
1940 Apr 29	07 49	LQ
1940 May 07	12 07	NM
1940 May 14	20 51	FQ
1940 May 21	13 33	FM
1940 May 29	00 40	LQ
1940 Jun 06	01 05	NM
1940 Jun 13	01 59	FQ
1940 Jun 19	23 02	FM
1940 Jun 27	18 13	LQ
1940 Jul 05	11 28	NM
1940 Jul 12	06 35	FQ
1940 Jul 19	09 55	FM
1940 Jul 27	11 29	LQ
1940 Aug 03	20 09	NM
1940 Aug 10	12 00	FQ
1940 Aug 17	23 02	FM
1940 Aug 26	03 33	LQ
1940 Sep 02	04 15	NM
1940 Sep 08	19 32	FQ
1940 Sep 16	14 41	FM
1940 Sep 24	17 47	LQ
1940 Oct 01	12 41	NM
1940 Oct 08	06 18	FQ
1940 Oct 16	08 15	FM
1940 Oct 24	06 04	LQ
1940 Oct 30	22 03	NM
1940 Nov 06	21 08	FQ
1940 Nov 15	02 23	FM
1940 Nov 22	16 36	LQ
1940 Nov 29	08 42	NM
1940 Dec 06	16 01	FQ
1940 Dec 14	19 38	FM
1940 Dec 22	01 45	LQ
1940 Dec 28	20 56	NM
1941 Jan 05	13 40	FQ
1941 Jan 13	11 04	FM
1941 Jan 20	10 01	LQ
1941 Jan 27	11 03	NM
1941 Feb 04	11 42	FQ
1941 Feb 12	00 26	FM
1941 Feb 18	18 07	LQ
1941 Feb 26	03 02	NM
1941 Mar 06	07 42	FQ
1941 Mar 13	11 47	FM
1941 Mar 20	02 51	LQ
1941 Mar 27	20 14	NM
1941 Apr 05	00 12	FQ
1941 Apr 11	21 15	FM
1941 Apr 18	13 03	LQ
1941 Apr 26	13 23	NM
1941 May 04	12 48	FQ
1941 May 11	05 15	FM
1941 May 18	01 17	LQ
1941 May 26	05 18	NM
1941 Jun 02	21 56	FQ
1941 Jun 09	12 34	FM
1941 Jun 16	15 45	LQ
1941 Jun 24	19 22	NM
1941 Jul 02	04 24	FQ
1941 Jul 08	20 17	FM
1941 Jul 16	08 07	LQ
1941 Jul 24	07 39	NM
1941 Jul 31	09 19	FQ
1941 Aug 07	05 38	FM
1941 Aug 15	01 40	LQ
1941 Aug 22	18 34	NM
1941 Aug 29	14 04	FQ
1941 Sep 05	17 36	FM
1941 Sep 13	19 31	LQ
1941 Sep 21	04 38	NM
1941 Sep 27	20 09	FQ
1941 Oct 05	08 32	FM
1941 Oct 13	12 52	LQ
1941 Oct 20	14 20	NM
1941 Oct 27	05 04	FQ
1941 Nov 04	02 00	FM
1941 Nov 12	04 53	LQ
1941 Nov 19	00 03	NM
1941 Nov 25	17 52	FQ
1941 Dec 03	20 51	FM
1941 Dec 11	18 48	LQ
1941 Dec 18	10 18	NM
1941 Dec 25	10 43	FQ
1942 Jan 02	15 42	FM
1942 Jan 10	06 05	LQ
1942 Jan 16	21 32	NM
1942 Jan 24	06 36	FQ
1942 Feb 01	09 12	FM
1942 Feb 08	14 52	LQ
1942 Feb 15	10 02	NM
1942 Feb 23	03 40	FQ
1942 Mar 03	00 20	FM
1942 Mar 09	22 00	LQ
1942 Mar 16	23 50	NM
1942 Mar 25	00 01	FQ
1942 Apr 01	12 32	FM
1942 Apr 08	04 43	LQ
1942 Apr 15	14 33	NM
1942 Apr 23	18 10	FQ
1942 Apr 30	21 59	FM
1942 May 07	12 13	LQ
1942 May 15	05 45	NM
1942 May 23	09 11	FQ
1942 May 30	05 29	FM
1942 Jun 05	21 26	LQ
1942 Jun 13	21 02	NM
1942 Jun 21	20 44	FQ
1942 Jun 28	12 09	FM
1942 Jul 05	08 58	LQ
1942 Jul 13	12 03	NM
1942 Jul 21	05 13	FQ
1942 Jul 27	19 14	FM
1942 Aug 03	23 04	LQ
1942 Aug 12	02 28	NM
1942 Aug 19	11 30	FQ
1942 Aug 26	03 46	FM
1942 Sep 02	15 42	LQ
1942 Sep 10	15 53	NM
1942 Sep 17	16 57	FQ
1942 Sep 24	14 34	FM
1942 Oct 02	10 27	LQ
1942 Oct 10	04 06	NM
1942 Oct 16	22 58	FQ
1942 Oct 24	04 05	FM
1942 Nov 01	06 18	LQ
1942 Nov 08	15 19	NM
1942 Nov 15	06 57	FQ
1942 Nov 22	20 24	FM
1942 Dec 01	01 37	LQ
1942 Dec 08	01 59	NM
1942 Dec 14	17 47	FQ
1942 Dec 22	15 03	FM
1942 Dec 30	18 37	LQ
1943 Jan 06	12 37	NM
1943 Jan 13	07 49	FQ
1943 Jan 21	10 48	FM
1943 Jan 29	08 13	LQ
1943 Feb 04	23 29	NM
1943 Feb 12	00 40	FQ
1943 Feb 20	05 45	FM
1943 Feb 27	18 22	LQ
1943 Mar 06	10 34	NM
1943 Mar 13	19 30	FQ
1943 Mar 21	22 08	FM
1943 Mar 29	01 52	LQ
1943 Apr 04	21 53	NM
1943 Apr 12	15 04	FQ
1943 Apr 20	11 11	FM
1943 Apr 27	07 51	LQ
1943 May 04	09 43	NM
1943 May 12	09 52	FQ
1943 May 19	21 13	FM
1943 May 26	13 34	LQ
1943 Jun 02	22 33	NM
1943 Jun 11	02 35	FQ
1943 Jun 18	05 14	FM
1943 Jun 24	20 08	LQ
1943 Jul 02	12 44	NM
1943 Jul 10	16 29	FQ
1943 Jul 17	12 21	FM
1943 Jul 24	04 38	LQ
1943 Aug 01	04 06	NM
1943 Aug 09	03 36	FQ
1943 Aug 15	19 34	FM
1943 Aug 22	16 04	LQ
1943 Aug 30	19 59	NM
1943 Sep 07	12 33	FQ
1943 Sep 14	03 40	FM
1943 Sep 21	07 06	LQ
1943 Sep 29	11 29	NM
1943 Oct 06	20 10	FQ
1943 Oct 13	13 23	FM
1943 Oct 21	01 42	LQ
1943 Oct 29	01 59	NM
1943 Nov 05	03 22	FQ
1943 Nov 12	01 27	FM
1943 Nov 19	22 43	LQ
1943 Nov 27	15 23	NM
1943 Dec 04	11 03	FQ
1943 Dec 11	16 24	FM
1943 Dec 19	20 03	LQ
1943 Dec 27	03 50	NM
1944 Jan 02	20 04	FQ
1944 Jan 10	10 09	FM
1944 Jan 18	15 32	LQ
1944 Jan 25	15 24	NM
1944 Feb 01	07 08	FQ
1944 Feb 09	05 29	FM
1944 Feb 17	07 42	LQ
1944 Feb 24	01 59	NM
1944 Mar 01	20 40	FQ
1944 Mar 10	00 28	FM
1944 Mar 17	20 05	LQ
1944 Mar 24	11 36	NM
1944 Mar 31	12 34	FQ
1944 Apr 08	17 22	FM
1944 Apr 16	04 59	LQ
1944 Apr 22	20 43	NM
1944 Apr 30	06 06	FQ
1944 May 08	07 28	FM
1944 May 15	11 12	LQ
1944 May 22	06 12	NM
1944 May 30	00 06	FQ
1944 Jun 06	18 58	FM
1944 Jun 13	15 56	LQ
1944 Jun 20	17 00	NM
1944 Jun 28	17 27	FQ
1944 Jul 06	04 27	FM
1944 Jul 12	20 39	LQ
1944 Jul 20	05 42	NM
1944 Jul 28	09 23	FQ
1944 Aug 04	12 39	FM
1944 Aug 11	02 52	LQ
1944 Aug 18	20 25	NM
1944 Aug 26	23 39	FQ
1944 Sep 02	20 21	FM
1944 Sep 09	12 03	LQ
1944 Sep 17	12 37	NM
1944 Sep 25	12 07	FQ
1944 Oct 02	04 21	FM
1944 Oct 09	01 12	LQ
1944 Oct 17	05 35	NM
1944 Oct 24	22 48	FQ
1944 Oct 31	13 35	FM
1944 Nov 07	18 29	LQ
1944 Nov 15	22 29	NM
1944 Nov 23	07 53	FQ
1944 Nov 30	00 52	FM
1944 Dec 07	14 57	LQ
1944 Dec 15	14 35	NM
1944 Dec 22	15 54	FQ
1944 Dec 29	14 38	FM
1945 Jan 06	12 47	LQ
1945 Jan 14	05 07	NM
1945 Jan 20	23 48	FQ
1945 Jan 28	06 41	FM
1945 Feb 05	09 55	LQ
1945 Feb 12	17 33	NM
1945 Feb 19	08 38	FQ
1945 Feb 27	00 07	FM
1945 Mar 07	04 30	LQ
1945 Mar 14	03 51	NM
1945 Mar 20	19 11	FQ
1945 Mar 28	17 44	FM
1945 Apr 05	19 18	LQ
1945 Apr 12	12 29	NM
1945 Apr 19	07 46	FQ
1945 Apr 27	10 33	FM
1945 May 05	06 02	LQ
1945 May 11	20 21	NM
1945 May 18	22 12	FQ
1945 May 27	01 49	FM
1945 Jun 03	13 15	LQ
1945 Jun 10	04 26	NM
1945 Jun 17	14 05	FQ
1945 Jun 25	15 08	FM
1945 Jul 02	18 13	LQ
1945 Jul 09	13 35	NM
1945 Jul 17	07 01	FQ
1945 Jul 25	02 25	FM
1945 Jul 31	22 30	LQ
1945 Aug 08	00 32	NM
1945 Aug 16	00 27	FQ
1945 Aug 23	12 03	FM
1945 Aug 30	03 44	LQ
1945 Sep 06	13 44	NM
1945 Sep 14	17 38	FQ
1945 Sep 21	20 46	FM
1945 Sep 28	11 24	LQ
1945 Oct 06	05 22	NM
1945 Oct 14	09 38	FQ
1945 Oct 21	05 32	FM
1945 Oct 27	22 30	LQ
1945 Nov 04	23 11	NM
1945 Nov 12	23 34	FQ
1945 Nov 19	15 13	FM
1945 Nov 26	13 28	LQ
1945 Dec 04	18 07	NM
1945 Dec 12	11 05	FQ
1945 Dec 19	02 17	FM
1945 Dec 26	08 00	LQ
1946 Jan 03	12 30	NM
1946 Jan 10	20 27	FQ
1946 Jan 17	14 47	FM
1946 Jan 25	05 00	LQ
1946 Feb 02	04 43	NM
1946 Feb 09	04 28	FQ
1946 Feb 16	04 28	FM
1946 Feb 24	02 36	LQ
1946 Mar 03	18 01	NM
1946 Mar 10	12 03	FQ
1946 Mar 17	19 11	FM
1946 Mar 25	22 37	LQ
1946 Apr 02	04 37	NM
1946 Apr 08	20 04	FQ
1946 Apr 16	10 47	FM
1946 Apr 24	15 18	LQ
1946 May 01	13 16	NM
1946 May 08	05 13	FQ
1946 May 16	02 52	FM
1946 May 24	04 02	LQ
1946 May 30	20 49	NM
1946 Jun 06	16 06	FQ
1946 Jun 14	18 42	FM
1946 Jun 22	13 12	LQ
1946 Jun 29	04 06	NM
1946 Jul 06	05 15	FQ
1946 Jul 14	09 23	FM
1946 Jul 21	19 52	LQ
1946 Jul 28	11 54	NM
1946 Aug 04	20 55	FQ
1946 Aug 12	22 26	FM
1946 Aug 20	01 17	LQ
1946 Aug 26	21 07	NM
1946 Sep 03	14 49	FQ
1946 Sep 11	09 59	FM
1946 Sep 18	06 44	LQ
1946 Sep 25	08 45	NM
1946 Oct 03	09 53	FQ
1946 Oct 10	20 40	FM
1946 Oct 17	13 28	LQ
1946 Oct 24	23 32	NM
1946 Nov 02	04 40	FQ
1946 Nov 09	07 10	FM
1946 Nov 15	22 35	LQ
1946 Nov 23	17 24	NM
1946 Dec 01	21 48	FQ
1946 Dec 08	17 52	FM
1946 Dec 15	10 57	LQ
1946 Dec 23	13 06	NM
1946 Dec 31	12 23	FQ
1947 Jan 07	04 47	FM
1947 Jan 14	02 56	LQ
1947 Jan 22	08 34	NM
1947 Jan 30	00 07	FQ
1947 Feb 05	15 50	FM
1947 Feb 12	21 58	LQ
1947 Feb 21	02 00	NM
1947 Feb 28	09 12	FQ
1947 Mar 07	03 15	FM
1947 Mar 14	18 28	LQ
1947 Mar 22	16 34	NM
1947 Mar 29	16 15	FQ
1947 Apr 05	15 28	FM
1947 Apr 13	14 23	LQ
1947 Apr 21	04 19	NM
1947 Apr 27	22 18	FQ
1947 May 05	04 53	FM
1947 May 13	08 08	LQ
1947 May 20	13 44	NM
1947 May 27	04 36	FQ
1947 Jun 03	19 27	FM
1947 Jun 11	22 58	LQ
1947 Jun 18	21 26	NM
1947 Jun 25	12 25	FQ
1947 Jul 03	10 39	FM
1947 Jul 11	10 54	LQ
1947 Jul 18	04 15	NM
1947 Jul 24	22 54	FQ
1947 Aug 02	01 50	FM
1947 Aug 09	20 22	LQ
1947 Aug 16	11 12	NM
1947 Aug 23	12 40	FQ
1947 Aug 31	16 34	FM
1947 Sep 08	03 57	LQ
1947 Sep 14	19 28	NM
1947 Sep 22	05 42	FQ
1947 Sep 30	06 41	FM
1947 Oct 07	10 29	LQ
1947 Oct 14	06 10	NM
1947 Oct 22	01 11	FQ
1947 Oct 29	20 07	FM
1947 Nov 05	17 03	LQ
1947 Nov 12	20 01	NM
1947 Nov 20	21 44	FQ
1947 Nov 28	08 45	FM
1947 Dec 05	00 55	LQ
1947 Dec 12	12 53	NM
1947 Dec 20	17 44	FQ
1947 Dec 27	20 27	FM
1948 Jan 03	11 13	LQ
1948 Jan 11	07 45	NM
1948 Jan 19	11 32	FQ
1948 Jan 26	07 11	FM
1948 Feb 02	00 31	LQ
1948 Feb 10	03 02	NM
1948 Feb 18	01 55	FQ
1948 Feb 24	17 16	FM
1948 Mar 02	16 35	LQ
1948 Mar 10	21 15	NM
1948 Mar 18	12 27	FQ
1948 Mar 25	03 10	FM
1948 Apr 01	10 25	LQ
1948 Apr 09	13 17	NM
1948 Apr 16	19 42	FQ
1948 Apr 23	13 28	FM
1948 May 01	04 48	LQ
1948 May 09	02 30	NM
1948 May 16	00 55	FQ
1948 May 23	00 37	FM
1948 May 30	22 43	LQ
1948 Jun 07	12 55	NM
1948 Jun 14	05 40	FQ
1948 Jun 21	12 54	FM
1948 Jun 29	15 23	LQ
1948 Jul 06	21 09	NM
1948 Jul 13	11 30	FQ
1948 Jul 21	02 31	FM
1948 Jul 29	06 11	LQ
1948 Aug 05	04 13	NM
1948 Aug 11	19 40	FQ
1948 Aug 19	17 32	FM
1948 Aug 27	18 46	LQ
1948 Sep 03	11 21	NM
1948 Sep 10	07 05	FQ
1948 Sep 18	09 43	FM
1948 Sep 26	05 07	LQ
1948 Oct 02	19 42	NM
1948 Oct 09	22 10	FQ
1948 Oct 18	02 23	FM
1948 Oct 25	13 41	LQ
1948 Nov 01	06 03	NM
1948 Nov 08	16 46	FQ
1948 Nov 16	18 31	FM
1948 Nov 23	21 22	LQ
1948 Nov 30	18 44	NM
1948 Dec 08	13 57	FQ
1948 Dec 16	09 11	FM
1948 Dec 23	05 12	LQ
1948 Dec 30	09 45	NM
1949 Jan 07	11 51	FQ
1949 Jan 14	21 59	FM
1949 Jan 21	14 07	LQ
1949 Jan 29	02 42	NM
1949 Feb 06	08 05	FQ
1949 Feb 13	09 08	FM
1949 Feb 20	00 43	LQ
1949 Feb 27	20 55	NM
1949 Mar 08	00 42	FQ
1949 Mar 14	19 03	FM
1949 Mar 21	13 10	LQ
1949 Mar 29	15 11	NM
1949 Apr 06	13 01	FQ
1949 Apr 13	04 08	FM
1949 Apr 20	03 27	LQ
1949 Apr 28	08 02	NM
1949 May 05	21 33	FQ
1949 May 12	12 51	FM
1949 May 19	19 22	LQ
1949 May 27	22 24	NM
1949 Jun 04	03 27	FQ
1949 Jun 10	21 45	FM
1949 Jun 18	12 29	LQ
1949 Jun 26	10 02	NM
1949 Jul 03	08 08	FQ
1949 Jul 10	07 41	FM
1949 Jul 18	06 02	LQ
1949 Jul 25	19 33	NM
1949 Aug 01	12 57	FQ
1949 Aug 08	19 33	FM
1949 Aug 16	22 59	LQ
1949 Aug 24	03 59	NM
1949 Aug 30	19 16	FQ
1949 Sep 07	09 59	FM
1949 Sep 15	14 29	LQ
1949 Sep 22	12 21	NM

1949 Sep 29	04 18	FQ
1949 Oct 07	02 53	FM
1949 Oct 15	04 06	LQ
1949 Oct 21	21 23	NM
1949 Oct 28	17 04	FQ
1949 Nov 05	21 09	FM
1949 Nov 13	15 48	LQ
1949 Nov 20	07 29	NM
1949 Nov 27	10 01	FQ
1949 Dec 05	15 13	FM
1949 Dec 13	01 48	LQ
1949 Dec 19	18 56	NM
1949 Dec 27	06 31	FQ
1950 Jan 04	07 48	FM
1950 Jan 11	10 31	LQ
1950 Jan 18	08 00	NM
1950 Jan 26	04 39	FQ
1950 Feb 02	22 16	FM
1950 Feb 09	18 32	LQ
1950 Feb 16	22 53	NM
1950 Feb 25	01 52	FQ
1950 Mar 04	10 34	FM
1950 Mar 11	02 38	LQ
1950 Mar 18	15 20	NM
1950 Mar 26	20 10	FQ
1950 Apr 02	20 49	FM
1950 Apr 09	11 42	LQ
1950 Apr 17	08 25	NM
1950 Apr 25	10 40	FQ
1950 May 02	05 19	FM
1950 May 08	22 32	LQ
1950 May 17	00 54	NM
1950 May 24	21 28	FQ
1950 May 31	12 43	FM
1950 Jun 07	11 35	LQ
1950 Jun 15	15 53	NM
1950 Jun 23	05 13	FQ
1950 Jun 29	19 58	FM
1950 Jul 07	02 53	LQ
1950 Jul 15	05 05	NM
1950 Jul 22	10 50	FQ
1950 Jul 29	04 18	FM
1950 Aug 05	19 56	LQ
1950 Aug 13	16 48	NM
1950 Aug 20	15 35	FQ
1950 Aug 27	14 51	FM
1950 Sep 04	13 53	LQ
1950 Sep 12	03 29	NM
1950 Sep 18	20 54	FQ
1950 Sep 26	04 21	FM
1950 Oct 04	07 53	LQ
1950 Oct 11	13 34	NM
1950 Oct 18	04 18	FQ
1950 Oct 25	20 46	FM
1950 Nov 03	01 00	LQ
1950 Nov 09	23 25	NM
1950 Nov 16	15 06	FQ
1950 Nov 24	15 14	FM
1950 Dec 02	16 22	LQ
1950 Dec 09	09 28	NM
1950 Dec 16	05 56	FQ
1950 Dec 24	10 23	FM
1951 Jan 01	05 11	LQ
1951 Jan 07	20 10	NM
1951 Jan 15	00 23	FQ
1951 Jan 23	04 47	FM
1951 Jan 30	15 14	LQ
1951 Feb 06	07 54	NM
1951 Feb 13	20 55	FQ
1951 Feb 21	21 12	FM
1951 Feb 28	22 59	LQ
1951 Mar 07	20 51	NM
1951 Mar 15	17 40	FQ
1951 Mar 23	10 50	FM
1951 Mar 30	05 35	LQ
1951 Apr 06	10 52	NM
1951 Apr 14	12 56	FQ
1951 Apr 21	21 30	FM
1951 Apr 28	12 18	LQ
1951 May 06	01 36	NM
1951 May 14	05 32	FQ
1951 May 21	05 45	FM
1951 May 27	20 17	LQ
1951 Jun 04	16 40	NM
1951 Jun 12	18 52	FQ
1951 Jun 19	12 36	FM
1951 Jun 26	06 21	LQ
1951 Jul 04	07 48	NM
1951 Jul 12	04 56	FQ
1951 Jul 18	19 17	FM
1951 Jul 25	18 59	LQ
1951 Aug 02	22 39	NM
1951 Aug 10	12 22	FQ
1951 Aug 17	02 59	FM
1951 Aug 24	10 20	LQ
1951 Sep 01	12 50	NM
1951 Sep 08	18 16	FQ
1951 Sep 15	12 38	FM
1951 Sep 23	04 13	LQ
1951 Oct 01	01 57	NM
1951 Oct 08	00 00	FQ
1951 Oct 15	00 51	FM
1951 Oct 22	23 55	LQ
1951 Oct 30	13 55	NM
1951 Nov 06	06 59	FQ
1951 Nov 13	15 52	FM
1951 Nov 21	20 01	LQ
1951 Nov 29	01 00	NM
1951 Dec 05	16 20	FQ
1951 Dec 13	09 30	FM
1951 Dec 21	14 37	LQ
1951 Dec 28	11 43	NM
1952 Jan 04	04 42	FQ
1952 Jan 12	04 55	FM
1952 Jan 20	06 09	LQ
1952 Jan 26	22 26	NM
1952 Feb 02	20 01	FQ
1952 Feb 11	00 28	FM
1952 Feb 18	18 01	LQ
1952 Feb 25	09 16	NM
1952 Mar 03	13 43	FQ
1952 Mar 11	18 14	FM
1952 Mar 19	02 40	LQ
1952 Mar 25	20 13	NM
1952 Apr 02	08 48	FQ
1952 Apr 10	08 53	FM
1952 Apr 17	09 07	LQ
1952 Apr 24	07 27	NM
1952 May 02	03 58	FQ
1952 May 09	20 16	FM
1952 May 16	14 39	LQ
1952 May 23	19 28	NM
1952 May 31	21 46	FQ
1952 Jun 08	05 07	FM
1952 Jun 14	20 28	LQ
1952 Jun 22	08 45	NM
1952 Jun 30	13 11	FQ
1952 Jul 07	12 33	FM
1952 Jul 14	03 42	LQ
1952 Jul 21	23 31	NM
1952 Jul 30	01 51	FQ
1952 Aug 05	19 40	FM
1952 Aug 12	13 27	LQ
1952 Aug 20	15 20	NM
1952 Aug 28	12 03	FQ
1952 Sep 04	03 19	FM
1952 Sep 11	02 36	LQ
1952 Sep 19	07 22	NM
1952 Sep 26	20 31	FQ
1952 Oct 03	12 15	FM
1952 Oct 10	19 33	LQ
1952 Oct 18	22 42	NM
1952 Oct 26	04 04	FQ
1952 Nov 01	23 10	FM
1952 Nov 09	15 43	LQ
1952 Nov 17	12 56	NM
1952 Nov 24	11 34	FQ
1952 Dec 01	12 41	FM
1952 Dec 09	13 22	LQ
1952 Dec 17	02 02	NM
1952 Dec 23	19 52	FQ
1952 Dec 31	05 06	FM
1953 Jan 08	10 09	LQ
1953 Jan 15	14 08	NM
1953 Jan 22	05 43	FQ
1953 Jan 29	23 44	FM
1953 Feb 07	04 09	LQ
1953 Feb 14	01 10	NM
1953 Feb 20	17 44	FQ
1953 Feb 28	18 59	FM
1953 Mar 08	18 26	LQ
1953 Mar 15	11 05	NM
1953 Mar 22	08 11	FQ
1953 Mar 30	12 55	FM
1953 Apr 07	04 58	LQ
1953 Apr 13	20 09	NM
1953 Apr 21	00 40	FQ
1953 Apr 29	04 20	FM
1953 May 06	12 21	LQ
1953 May 13	05 06	NM
1953 May 20	18 20	FQ
1953 May 28	17 03	FM
1953 Jun 04	17 35	LQ
1953 Jun 11	14 55	NM
1953 Jun 19	12 01	FQ
1953 Jun 27	03 29	FM
1953 Jul 03	22 03	LQ
1953 Jul 11	02 28	NM
1953 Jul 19	04 47	FQ
1953 Jul 26	12 21	FM
1953 Aug 02	03 16	LQ
1953 Aug 09	16 10	NM
1953 Aug 17	20 08	FQ
1953 Aug 24	20 21	FM
1953 Aug 31	10 46	LQ
1953 Sep 08	07 48	NM
1953 Sep 16	09 49	FQ
1953 Sep 23	04 15	FM
1953 Sep 29	21 51	LQ
1953 Oct 08	00 40	NM
1953 Oct 15	21 44	FQ
1953 Oct 22	12 56	FM
1953 Oct 29	13 09	LQ
1953 Nov 06	17 58	NM
1953 Nov 14	07 52	FQ
1953 Nov 20	23 12	FM
1953 Nov 28	08 16	LQ
1953 Dec 06	10 48	NM
1953 Dec 13	16 30	FQ
1953 Dec 20	11 43	FM
1953 Dec 28	05 43	LQ
1954 Jan 05	02 21	NM
1954 Jan 12	00 22	FQ
1954 Jan 19	02 37	FM
1954 Jan 27	03 28	LQ
1954 Feb 03	15 55	NM
1954 Feb 10	08 29	FQ
1954 Feb 17	19 17	FM
1954 Feb 25	23 29	LQ
1954 Mar 05	03 11	NM
1954 Mar 11	17 52	FQ
1954 Mar 19	12 42	FM
1954 Mar 27	16 14	LQ
1954 Apr 03	12 25	NM
1954 Apr 10	05 05	FQ
1954 Apr 18	05 48	FM
1954 Apr 26	04 57	LQ
1954 May 02	20 22	NM
1954 May 09	18 17	FQ
1954 May 17	21 47	FM
1954 May 25	13 49	LQ
1954 Jun 01	04 03	NM
1954 Jun 08	09 14	FQ
1954 Jun 16	12 06	FM
1954 Jun 23	19 46	LQ
1954 Jun 30	12 26	NM
1954 Jul 08	01 33	FQ
1954 Jul 16	00 29	FM
1954 Jul 23	00 14	LQ
1954 Jul 29	22 20	NM
1954 Aug 06	18 51	FQ
1954 Aug 14	11 03	FM
1954 Aug 21	04 51	LQ
1954 Aug 28	10 21	NM
1954 Sep 05	12 28	FQ
1954 Sep 12	20 19	FM
1954 Sep 19	11 11	LQ
1954 Sep 27	00 50	NM
1954 Oct 05	05 31	FQ
1954 Oct 12	05 10	FM
1954 Oct 18	20 30	LQ
1954 Oct 26	17 47	NM
1954 Nov 03	20 55	FQ
1954 Nov 10	14 29	FM
1954 Nov 17	09 33	LQ
1954 Nov 25	12 30	NM
1954 Dec 03	09 56	FQ
1954 Dec 10	00 56	FM
1954 Dec 17	02 21	LQ
1954 Dec 25	07 33	NM
1955 Jan 01	20 29	FQ
1955 Jan 08	12 44	FM
1955 Jan 15	22 14	LQ
1955 Jan 24	01 07	NM
1955 Jan 31	05 05	FQ
1955 Feb 07	01 43	FM
1955 Feb 14	19 40	LQ
1955 Feb 22	15 54	NM
1955 Mar 01	12 40	FQ
1955 Mar 08	15 41	FM
1955 Mar 16	16 36	LQ
1955 Mar 24	03 42	NM
1955 Mar 30	20 10	FQ
1955 Apr 07	06 35	FM
1955 Apr 15	11 01	LQ
1955 Apr 22	13 06	NM
1955 Apr 29	04 23	FQ
1955 May 06	22 14	FM
1955 May 15	01 42	LQ
1955 May 21	20 58	NM
1955 May 28	14 01	FQ
1955 Jun 05	14 08	FM
1955 Jun 13	12 37	LQ
1955 Jun 20	04 12	NM
1955 Jun 27	01 44	FQ
1955 Jul 05	05 29	FM
1955 Jul 12	20 31	LQ
1955 Jul 19	11 34	NM
1955 Jul 26	16 00	FQ
1955 Aug 03	19 30	FM
1955 Aug 11	02 33	LQ
1955 Aug 17	19 58	NM
1955 Aug 25	08 52	FQ
1955 Sep 02	07 59	FM
1955 Sep 09	07 59	LQ
1955 Sep 16	06 19	NM
1955 Sep 24	03 41	FQ
1955 Oct 01	19 17	FM
1955 Oct 08	14 04	LQ
1955 Oct 15	19 32	NM
1955 Oct 23	23 05	FQ
1955 Oct 31	06 04	FM
1955 Nov 06	21 56	LQ
1955 Nov 14	12 01	NM
1955 Nov 22	17 29	FQ
1955 Nov 29	16 50	FM
1955 Dec 06	08 35	LQ
1955 Dec 14	07 07	NM
1955 Dec 22	09 39	FQ
1955 Dec 29	03 44	FM
1956 Jan 04	22 41	LQ
1956 Jan 13	03 01	NM
1956 Jan 20	22 58	FQ
1956 Jan 27	14 40	FM
1956 Feb 03	16 08	LQ
1956 Feb 11	21 38	NM
1956 Feb 19	09 21	FQ
1956 Feb 26	01 42	FM
1956 Mar 04	11 53	LQ
1956 Mar 12	13 37	NM
1956 Mar 19	17 14	FQ
1956 Mar 26	13 11	FM
1956 Apr 03	08 06	LQ
1956 Apr 11	02 39	NM
1956 Apr 17	23 28	FQ
1956 Apr 25	01 41	FM
1956 May 03	02 55	LQ
1956 May 10	13 04	NM
1956 May 17	05 15	FQ
1956 May 24	15 26	FM
1956 Jun 01	19 13	LQ
1956 Jun 08	21 29	NM
1956 Jun 15	11 56	FQ
1956 Jun 23	06 13	FM
1956 Jul 01	08 41	LQ
1956 Jul 08	04 37	NM
1956 Jul 14	20 47	FQ
1956 Jul 22	21 29	FM
1956 Jul 30	19 31	LQ
1956 Aug 06	11 25	NM
1956 Aug 13	08 45	FQ
1956 Aug 21	12 38	FM
1956 Aug 29	04 13	LQ
1956 Sep 04	18 57	NM
1956 Sep 12	00 13	FQ
1956 Sep 20	03 19	FM
1956 Sep 27	11 25	LQ
1956 Oct 04	04 25	NM
1956 Oct 11	18 44	FQ
1956 Oct 19	17 25	FM
1956 Oct 26	18 02	LQ
1956 Nov 02	16 44	NM
1956 Nov 10	15 09	FQ
1956 Nov 18	06 45	FM
1956 Nov 25	01 13	LQ
1956 Dec 02	08 12	NM
1956 Dec 10	11 51	FQ
1956 Dec 17	19 06	FM
1956 Dec 24	10 10	LQ
1957 Jan 01	02 14	NM
1957 Jan 09	07 06	FQ
1957 Jan 16	06 21	FM
1957 Jan 22	21 48	LQ
1957 Jan 30	21 25	NM
1957 Feb 07	23 23	FQ
1957 Feb 14	16 38	FM
1957 Feb 21	12 19	LQ
1957 Mar 01	16 12	NM
1957 Mar 09	11 50	FQ
1957 Mar 16	02 22	FM
1957 Mar 23	05 04	LQ
1957 Mar 31	09 19	NM
1957 Apr 07	20 33	FQ
1957 Apr 14	12 09	FM
1957 Apr 21	23 00	LQ
1957 Apr 29	23 54	NM
1957 May 07	02 29	FQ
1957 May 13	22 34	FM
1957 May 21	17 03	LQ
1957 May 29	11 39	NM
1957 Jun 05	07 10	FQ
1957 Jun 12	10 02	FM
1957 Jun 20	10 22	LQ
1957 Jun 27	20 53	NM
1957 Jul 04	12 09	FQ
1957 Jul 11	22 50	FM
1957 Jul 20	02 17	LQ
1957 Jul 27	04 28	NM
1957 Aug 02	18 55	FQ
1957 Aug 10	13 08	FM
1957 Aug 18	16 16	LQ
1957 Aug 25	11 32	NM
1957 Sep 01	04 35	FQ
1957 Sep 09	04 55	FM
1957 Sep 17	04 02	LQ
1957 Sep 23	19 18	NM
1957 Sep 30	17 49	FQ
1957 Oct 08	21 42	FM
1957 Oct 16	13 44	LQ
1957 Oct 23	04 43	NM
1957 Oct 30	10 48	FQ
1957 Nov 07	14 32	FM
1957 Nov 14	21 59	LQ
1957 Nov 21	16 19	NM
1957 Nov 29	06 58	FQ
1957 Dec 07	06 16	FM
1957 Dec 14	05 45	LQ
1957 Dec 21	06 12	NM
1957 Dec 29	04 52	FQ
1958 Jan 05	20 09	FM
1958 Jan 12	14 01	LQ
1958 Jan 19	22 08	NM
1958 Jan 28	02 16	FQ
1958 Feb 04	08 05	FM
1958 Feb 10	23 34	LQ
1958 Feb 18	15 38	NM
1958 Feb 26	20 52	FQ
1958 Mar 05	18 28	FM
1958 Mar 12	10 48	LQ
1958 Mar 20	09 50	NM
1958 Mar 28	11 19	FQ
1958 Apr 04	03 45	FM
1958 Apr 10	23 50	LQ
1958 Apr 19	03 23	NM
1958 Apr 26	21 36	FQ
1958 May 03	12 23	FM
1958 May 10	14 38	LQ
1958 May 18	19 00	NM
1958 May 26	04 38	FQ
1958 Jun 01	20 55	FM
1958 Jun 09	06 59	LQ
1958 Jun 17	07 59	NM
1958 Jun 24	09 45	FQ
1958 Jul 01	06 04	FM
1958 Jul 09	00 21	LQ
1958 Jul 16	18 33	NM
1958 Jul 23	14 19	FQ
1958 Jul 30	16 47	FM
1958 Aug 07	17 49	LQ
1958 Aug 15	03 33	NM
1958 Aug 21	19 45	FQ
1958 Aug 29	05 53	FM
1958 Sep 06	10 24	LQ
1958 Sep 13	12 02	NM
1958 Sep 20	03 17	FQ
1958 Sep 27	21 44	FM
1958 Oct 06	01 20	LQ
1958 Oct 12	20 52	NM
1958 Oct 19	14 07	FQ
1958 Oct 27	15 41	FM
1958 Nov 04	14 19	LQ
1958 Nov 11	06 34	NM
1958 Nov 18	04 59	FQ
1958 Nov 26	10 17	FM
1958 Dec 04	01 24	LQ
1958 Dec 10	17 23	NM
1958 Dec 17	23 52	FQ
1958 Dec 26	03 54	FM
1959 Jan 02	10 50	LQ
1959 Jan 09	05 34	NM
1959 Jan 16	21 27	FQ
1959 Jan 24	19 32	FM
1959 Jan 31	19 06	LQ
1959 Feb 07	19 22	NM
1959 Feb 15	19 20	FQ
1959 Feb 23	08 54	FM
1959 Mar 02	02 54	LQ
1959 Mar 09	10 51	NM
1959 Mar 17	15 10	FQ
1959 Mar 24	20 02	FM
1959 Mar 31	11 06	LQ
1959 Apr 08	03 29	NM
1959 Apr 16	07 33	FQ
1959 Apr 23	05 13	FM
1959 Apr 29	20 38	LQ
1959 May 07	20 11	NM
1959 May 15	20 09	FQ
1959 May 22	12 56	FM
1959 May 29	08 14	LQ
1959 Jun 06	11 53	NM
1959 Jun 14	05 23	FQ
1959 Jun 20	20 00	FM
1959 Jun 27	22 12	LQ
1959 Jul 06	02 00	NM
1959 Jul 13	12 01	FQ
1959 Jul 20	03 33	FM
1959 Jul 27	14 22	LQ
1959 Aug 04	14 34	NM
1959 Aug 11	17 10	FQ
1959 Aug 18	12 51	FM
1959 Aug 26	08 03	LQ
1959 Sep 03	01 56	NM
1959 Sep 09	22 07	FQ
1959 Sep 17	00 52	FM
1959 Sep 25	02 22	LQ
1959 Oct 02	12 31	NM
1959 Oct 09	04 22	FQ
1959 Oct 16	15 59	FM
1959 Oct 24	20 22	LQ
1959 Oct 31	22 41	NM
1959 Nov 07	13 24	FQ
1959 Nov 15	09 42	FM
1959 Nov 23	13 03	LQ
1959 Nov 30	08 46	NM
1959 Dec 07	02 12	FQ
1959 Dec 15	04 49	FM
1959 Dec 23	03 28	LQ
1959 Dec 29	19 09	NM
1960 Jan 05	18 53	FQ
1960 Jan 13	23 51	FM
1960 Jan 21	15 01	LQ

1960 Jan 28	06 15	NM
1960 Feb 04	14 26	FQ
1960 Feb 12	17 24	FM
1960 Feb 19	23 47	LQ
1960 Feb 26	18 23	NM
1960 Mar 05	11 06	FQ
1960 Mar 13	08 26	FM
1960 Mar 20	06 40	LQ
1960 Mar 27	07 37	NM
1960 Apr 04	07 04	FQ
1960 Apr 11	20 27	FM
1960 Apr 18	12 57	LQ
1960 Apr 25	21 44	NM
1960 May 04	01 00	FQ
1960 May 11	05 42	FM
1960 May 17	19 54	LQ
1960 May 25	12 26	NM
1960 Jun 02	16 01	FQ
1960 Jun 09	13 02	FM
1960 Jun 16	04 35	LQ
1960 Jun 24	03 27	NM
1960 Jul 02	03 48	FQ
1960 Jul 08	19 36	FM
1960 Jul 15	15 43	LQ
1960 Jul 23	18 31	NM
1960 Jul 31	12 38	FQ
1960 Aug 07	02 41	FM
1960 Aug 14	05 37	LQ
1960 Aug 22	09 15	NM
1960 Aug 29	19 22	FQ
1960 Sep 05	11 19	FM
1960 Sep 12	22 19	LQ
1960 Sep 20	23 12	NM
1960 Sep 28	01 13	FQ
1960 Oct 04	22 16	FM
1960 Oct 12	17 25	LQ
1960 Oct 20	12 02	NM
1960 Oct 27	07 34	FQ
1960 Nov 03	11 58	FM
1960 Nov 11	13 47	LQ
1960 Nov 18	23 46	NM
1960 Nov 25	15 42	FQ
1960 Dec 03	04 24	FM
1960 Dec 11	09 38	LQ
1960 Dec 18	10 47	NM
1960 Dec 25	02 30	FQ
1961 Jan 01	23 06	FM
1961 Jan 10	03 02	LQ
1961 Jan 16	21 30	NM
1961 Jan 23	16 13	FQ
1961 Jan 31	18 47	FM
1961 Feb 08	16 49	LQ
1961 Feb 15	08 10	NM
1961 Feb 22	08 34	FQ
1961 Mar 02	13 35	FM
1961 Mar 10	02 57	LQ
1961 Mar 16	18 51	NM
1961 Mar 24	02 48	FQ
1961 Apr 01	05 47	FM
1961 Apr 08	10 16	LQ
1961 Apr 15	05 37	NM
1961 Apr 22	21 49	FQ
1961 Apr 30	18 40	FM
1961 May 07	15 57	LQ
1961 May 14	16 54	NM
1961 May 22	16 18	FQ
1961 May 30	04 37	FM
1961 Jun 05	21 18	LQ
1961 Jun 13	05 16	NM
1961 Jun 21	09 01	FQ
1961 Jun 28	12 37	FM
1961 Jul 05	03 32	LQ
1961 Jul 12	19 11	NM
1961 Jul 20	23 13	FQ
1961 Jul 27	19 50	FM
1961 Aug 03	11 47	LQ
1961 Aug 11	10 36	NM
1961 Aug 19	10 51	FQ
1961 Aug 26	03 13	FM
1961 Sep 01	23 05	LQ
1961 Sep 10	02 49	NM
1961 Sep 17	20 23	FQ
1961 Sep 24	11 33	FM
1961 Oct 01	14 10	LQ
1961 Oct 09	18 52	NM
1961 Oct 17	04 34	FQ
1961 Oct 23	21 30	FM
1961 Oct 31	08 58	LQ
1961 Nov 08	09 58	NM
1961 Nov 15	12 12	FQ
1961 Nov 22	09 44	FM
1961 Nov 30	06 18	LQ
1961 Dec 07	23 52	NM
1961 Dec 14	20 05	FQ
1961 Dec 22	00 42	FM
1961 Dec 30	03 57	LQ
1962 Jan 06	12 35	NM
1962 Jan 13	05 01	FQ
1962 Jan 20	18 16	FM
1962 Jan 28	23 36	LQ
1962 Feb 05	00 10	NM
1962 Feb 11	15 43	FQ
1962 Feb 19	13 18	FM
1962 Feb 27	15 50	LQ
1962 Mar 06	10 31	NM
1962 Mar 13	04 38	FQ
1962 Mar 21	07 55	FM
1962 Mar 29	04 11	LQ
1962 Apr 04	19 45	NM
1962 Apr 11	19 50	FQ
1962 Apr 20	00 33	FM
1962 Apr 27	12 59	LQ
1962 May 04	04 25	NM
1962 May 11	12 44	FQ
1962 May 19	14 32	FM
1962 May 26	19 05	LQ
1962 Jun 02	13 27	NM
1962 Jun 10	06 21	FQ
1962 Jun 18	02 02	FM
1962 Jun 24	23 42	LQ
1962 Jul 01	23 52	NM
1962 Jul 09	23 39	FQ
1962 Jul 17	11 41	FM
1962 Jul 24	04 18	LQ
1962 Jul 31	12 24	NM
1962 Aug 08	15 55	FQ
1962 Aug 15	20 09	FM
1962 Aug 22	10 26	LQ
1962 Aug 30	03 09	NM
1962 Sep 07	06 44	FQ
1962 Sep 14	04 11	FM
1962 Sep 20	19 36	LQ
1962 Sep 28	19 39	NM
1962 Oct 06	19 54	FQ
1962 Oct 13	12 33	FM
1962 Oct 20	08 47	LQ
1962 Oct 28	13 05	NM
1962 Nov 05	07 15	FQ
1962 Nov 11	22 03	FM
1962 Nov 19	02 09	LQ
1962 Nov 27	06 29	NM
1962 Dec 04	16 48	FQ
1962 Dec 11	09 27	FM
1962 Dec 18	22 42	LQ
1962 Dec 26	22 59	NM
1963 Jan 03	01 02	FQ
1963 Jan 09	23 08	FM
1963 Jan 17	20 34	LQ
1963 Jan 25	13 42	NM
1963 Feb 01	08 50	FQ
1963 Feb 08	14 52	FM
1963 Feb 16	17 38	LQ
1963 Feb 24	02 06	NM
1963 Mar 02	17 17	FQ
1963 Mar 10	07 49	FM
1963 Mar 18	12 08	LQ
1963 Mar 25	12 10	NM
1963 Apr 01	03 15	FQ
1963 Apr 09	00 57	FM
1963 Apr 17	02 52	LQ
1963 Apr 23	20 28	NM
1963 Apr 30	15 08	FQ
1963 May 08	17 23	FM
1963 May 16	13 36	LQ
1963 May 23	04 00	NM
1963 May 30	04 55	FQ
1963 Jun 07	08 31	FM
1963 Jun 14	20 53	LQ
1963 Jun 21	11 46	NM
1963 Jun 28	20 23	FQ
1963 Jul 06	21 55	FM
1963 Jul 14	01 57	LQ
1963 Jul 20	20 43	NM
1963 Jul 28	13 13	FQ
1963 Aug 05	09 31	FM
1963 Aug 12	06 21	LQ
1963 Aug 19	07 34	NM
1963 Aug 27	06 54	FQ
1963 Sep 03	19 33	FM
1963 Sep 10	11 42	LQ
1963 Sep 17	20 51	NM
1963 Sep 26	00 38	FQ
1963 Oct 03	04 44	FM
1963 Oct 09	19 27	LQ
1963 Oct 17	12 43	NM
1963 Oct 25	17 20	FQ
1963 Nov 01	13 55	FM
1963 Nov 08	06 37	LQ
1963 Nov 16	06 50	NM
1963 Nov 24	07 56	FQ
1963 Nov 30	23 54	FM
1963 Dec 07	21 34	LQ
1963 Dec 16	02 06	NM
1963 Dec 23	19 54	FQ
1963 Dec 30	11 04	FM
1964 Jan 06	15 58	LQ
1964 Jan 14	20 43	NM
1964 Jan 22	05 29	FQ
1964 Jan 28	23 23	FM
1964 Feb 05	12 42	LQ
1964 Feb 13	13 01	NM
1964 Feb 20	13 24	FQ
1964 Feb 27	12 39	FM
1964 Mar 06	10 00	LQ
1964 Mar 14	02 14	NM
1964 Mar 20	20 39	FQ
1964 Mar 28	02 48	FM
1964 Apr 05	05 45	LQ
1964 Apr 12	12 37	NM
1964 Apr 19	04 09	FQ
1964 Apr 26	17 50	FM
1964 May 04	22 20	LQ
1964 May 11	21 02	NM
1964 May 18	12 42	FQ
1964 May 26	09 29	FM
1964 Jun 03	11 07	LQ
1964 Jun 10	04 22	NM
1964 Jun 16	23 02	FQ
1964 Jun 25	01 08	FM
1964 Jul 02	20 31	LQ
1964 Jul 09	11 31	NM
1964 Jul 16	11 47	FQ
1964 Jul 24	15 58	FM
1964 Aug 01	03 29	LQ
1964 Aug 07	19 17	NM
1964 Aug 15	03 19	FQ
1964 Aug 23	05 25	FM
1964 Aug 30	09 15	LQ
1964 Sep 06	04 34	NM
1964 Sep 13	21 24	FQ
1964 Sep 21	17 31	FM
1964 Sep 28	15 01	LQ
1964 Oct 05	16 20	NM
1964 Oct 13	16 56	FQ
1964 Oct 21	04 45	FM
1964 Oct 27	21 58	LQ
1964 Nov 04	07 16	NM
1964 Nov 12	12 20	FQ
1964 Nov 19	15 43	FM
1964 Nov 26	07 10	LQ
1964 Dec 04	01 18	NM
1964 Dec 12	06 01	FQ
1964 Dec 19	02 41	FM
1964 Dec 25	19 27	LQ
1965 Jan 02	21 07	NM
1965 Jan 10	20 59	FQ
1965 Jan 17	13 37	FM
1965 Jan 24	11 07	LQ
1965 Feb 01	16 35	NM
1965 Feb 09	08 53	FQ
1965 Feb 16	00 27	FM
1965 Feb 23	05 39	LQ
1965 Mar 03	09 56	NM
1965 Mar 10	17 52	FQ
1965 Mar 17	11 24	FM
1965 Mar 25	01 36	LQ
1965 Apr 02	00 20	NM
1965 Apr 09	00 40	FQ
1965 Apr 15	23 02	FM
1965 Apr 23	21 07	LQ
1965 May 01	11 56	NM
1965 May 08	06 19	FQ
1965 May 15	11 52	FM
1965 May 23	14 40	LQ
1965 May 30	21 12	NM
1965 Jun 06	12 11	FQ
1965 Jun 14	01 59	FM
1965 Jun 22	05 36	LQ
1965 Jun 29	04 52	NM
1965 Jul 05	19 36	FQ
1965 Jul 13	17 01	FM
1965 Jul 21	17 53	LQ
1965 Jul 28	11 45	NM
1965 Aug 04	05 47	FQ
1965 Aug 12	08 22	FM
1965 Aug 20	03 50	LQ
1965 Aug 26	18 50	NM
1965 Sep 02	19 27	FQ
1965 Sep 10	23 32	FM
1965 Sep 18	11 58	LQ
1965 Sep 25	03 18	NM
1965 Oct 02	12 37	FQ
1965 Oct 10	14 14	FM
1965 Oct 17	19 00	LQ
1965 Oct 24	14 11	NM
1965 Nov 01	08 26	FQ
1965 Nov 09	04 15	FM
1965 Nov 16	01 54	LQ
1965 Nov 23	04 10	NM
1965 Dec 01	05 24	FQ
1965 Dec 08	17 21	FM
1965 Dec 15	09 52	LQ
1965 Dec 22	21 03	NM
1965 Dec 31	01 46	FQ
1966 Jan 07	05 16	FM
1966 Jan 13	20 00	LQ
1966 Jan 21	15 46	NM
1966 Jan 29	19 48	FQ
1966 Feb 05	15 58	FM
1966 Feb 12	08 53	LQ
1966 Feb 20	10 49	NM
1966 Feb 28	10 15	FQ
1966 Mar 07	01 45	FM
1966 Mar 14	00 19	LQ
1966 Mar 22	04 46	NM
1966 Mar 29	20 43	FQ
1966 Apr 05	11 13	FM
1966 Apr 12	17 28	LQ
1966 Apr 20	20 35	NM
1966 Apr 28	03 49	FQ
1966 May 04	21 00	FM
1966 May 12	11 19	LQ
1966 May 20	09 42	NM
1966 May 27	08 50	FQ
1966 Jun 03	07 40	FM
1966 Jun 11	04 58	LQ
1966 Jun 18	20 09	NM
1966 Jun 25	13 22	FQ
1966 Jul 02	19 36	FM
1966 Jul 10	21 43	LQ
1966 Jul 18	04 30	NM
1966 Jul 24	19 00	FQ
1966 Aug 01	09 05	FM
1966 Aug 09	12 55	LQ
1966 Aug 16	11 48	NM
1966 Aug 23	03 02	FQ
1966 Aug 31	00 14	FM
1966 Sep 08	02 07	LQ
1966 Sep 14	19 13	NM
1966 Sep 21	14 25	FQ
1966 Sep 29	16 47	FM
1966 Oct 07	13 08	LQ
1966 Oct 14	03 51	NM
1966 Oct 21	05 34	FQ
1966 Oct 29	10 00	FM
1966 Nov 05	22 18	LQ
1966 Nov 12	14 26	NM
1966 Nov 20	00 20	FQ
1966 Nov 28	02 40	FM
1966 Dec 05	06 22	LQ
1966 Dec 12	03 13	NM
1966 Dec 19	21 41	FQ
1966 Dec 27	17 43	FM
1967 Jan 03	14 19	LQ
1967 Jan 10	18 06	NM
1967 Jan 18	19 41	FQ
1967 Jan 26	06 40	FM
1967 Feb 01	23 03	LQ
1967 Feb 09	10 44	NM
1967 Feb 17	15 56	FQ
1967 Feb 24	17 43	FM
1967 Mar 03	09 10	LQ
1967 Mar 11	04 30	NM
1967 Mar 19	08 31	FQ
1967 Mar 26	03 21	FM
1967 Apr 01	20 58	LQ
1967 Apr 09	22 20	NM
1967 Apr 17	20 48	FQ
1967 Apr 24	12 03	FM
1967 May 01	10 32	LQ
1967 May 09	14 55	NM
1967 May 17	05 18	FQ
1967 May 23	20 22	FM
1967 May 31	01 52	LQ
1967 Jun 08	05 13	NM
1967 Jun 15	11 12	FQ
1967 Jun 22	04 57	FM
1967 Jun 29	18 39	LQ
1967 Jul 07	17 00	NM
1967 Jul 14	15 53	FQ
1967 Jul 21	14 39	FM
1967 Jul 29	12 14	LQ
1967 Aug 06	02 48	NM
1967 Aug 12	20 44	FQ
1967 Aug 20	02 27	FM
1967 Aug 28	05 35	LQ
1967 Sep 04	11 37	NM
1967 Sep 11	03 06	FQ
1967 Sep 18	16 59	FM
1967 Sep 26	21 44	LQ
1967 Oct 03	20 24	NM
1967 Oct 10	12 11	FQ
1967 Oct 18	10 11	FM
1967 Oct 26	12 04	LQ
1967 Nov 02	05 48	NM
1967 Nov 09	01 00	FQ
1967 Nov 17	04 52	FM
1967 Nov 25	00 23	LQ
1967 Dec 01	16 10	NM
1967 Dec 08	17 57	FQ
1967 Dec 16	23 21	FM
1967 Dec 24	10 48	LQ
1967 Dec 31	03 38	NM
1968 Jan 07	14 23	FQ
1968 Jan 15	16 11	FM
1968 Jan 22	19 38	LQ
1968 Jan 29	16 29	NM
1968 Feb 06	12 20	FQ
1968 Feb 14	06 43	FM
1968 Feb 21	03 28	LQ
1968 Feb 28	06 55	NM
1968 Mar 07	09 20	FQ
1968 Mar 14	18 52	FM
1968 Mar 21	11 07	LQ
1968 Mar 28	22 48	NM
1968 Apr 06	03 27	FQ
1968 Apr 13	04 52	FM
1968 Apr 19	19 35	LQ
1968 Apr 27	15 21	NM
1968 May 05	17 54	FQ
1968 May 12	13 05	FM
1968 May 19	05 44	LQ
1968 May 27	07 30	NM
1968 Jun 04	04 47	FQ
1968 Jun 10	20 13	FM
1968 Jun 17	18 14	LQ
1968 Jun 25	22 24	NM
1968 Jul 03	12 42	FQ
1968 Jul 10	03 18	FM
1968 Jul 17	09 11	LQ
1968 Jul 25	11 49	NM
1968 Aug 01	18 34	FQ
1968 Aug 08	11 32	FM
1968 Aug 16	02 13	LQ
1968 Aug 23	23 57	NM
1968 Aug 30	23 34	FQ
1968 Sep 06	22 07	FM
1968 Sep 14	20 31	LQ
1968 Sep 22	11 08	NM
1968 Sep 29	05 06	FQ
1968 Oct 06	11 46	FM
1968 Oct 14	15 05	LQ
1968 Oct 21	21 44	NM
1968 Oct 28	12 40	FQ
1968 Nov 05	04 25	FM
1968 Nov 13	08 53	LQ
1968 Nov 20	08 01	NM
1968 Nov 26	23 30	FQ
1968 Dec 04	23 07	FM
1968 Dec 13	00 49	LQ
1968 Dec 19	18 18	NM
1968 Dec 26	14 14	FQ
1969 Jan 03	18 28	FM
1969 Jan 11	14 00	LQ
1969 Jan 18	04 59	NM
1969 Jan 25	08 23	FQ
1969 Feb 02	12 56	FM
1969 Feb 10	00 08	LQ
1969 Feb 16	16 25	NM
1969 Feb 24	04 30	FQ
1969 Mar 04	05 17	FM
1969 Mar 11	07 44	LQ
1969 Mar 18	04 51	NM
1969 Mar 26	00 48	FQ
1969 Apr 02	18 45	FM
1969 Apr 09	13 58	LQ
1969 Apr 16	18 16	NM
1969 Apr 24	19 44	FQ
1969 May 02	05 13	FM
1969 May 08	20 12	LQ
1969 May 16	08 26	NM
1969 May 24	12 15	FQ
1969 May 31	13 18	FM
1969 Jun 07	03 39	LQ
1969 Jun 14	23 09	NM
1969 Jun 23	01 44	FQ
1969 Jun 29	20 04	FM
1969 Jul 06	13 17	LQ
1969 Jul 14	14 11	NM
1969 Jul 22	12 09	FQ
1969 Jul 29	02 45	FM
1969 Aug 05	01 38	LQ
1969 Aug 13	05 16	NM
1969 Aug 20	20 03	FQ
1969 Aug 27	10 32	FM
1969 Sep 03	16 58	LQ
1969 Sep 11	19 56	NM
1969 Sep 19	02 24	FQ
1969 Sep 25	20 21	FM
1969 Oct 03	11 05	LQ
1969 Oct 11	09 39	NM
1969 Oct 18	08 32	FQ
1969 Oct 25	08 44	FM
1969 Nov 02	07 14	LQ
1969 Nov 09	22 11	NM
1969 Nov 16	15 45	FQ
1969 Nov 23	23 54	FM
1969 Dec 02	03 50	LQ
1969 Dec 09	09 42	NM
1969 Dec 16	01 09	FQ
1969 Dec 23	17 35	FM
1969 Dec 31	22 52	LQ
1970 Jan 07	20 35	NM
1970 Jan 14	13 18	FQ
1970 Jan 22	12 55	FM
1970 Jan 30	14 38	LQ
1970 Feb 06	07 13	NM
1970 Feb 13	04 10	FQ
1970 Feb 21	08 19	FM
1970 Mar 01	02 33	LQ
1970 Mar 07	17 42	NM
1970 Mar 14	21 16	FQ
1970 Mar 23	01 52	FM
1970 Mar 30	11 05	LQ
1970 Apr 06	04 09	NM
1970 Apr 13	15 44	FQ
1970 Apr 21	16 21	FM
1970 Apr 28	17 18	LQ
1970 May 05	14 51	NM
1970 May 13	10 26	FQ

Moon Charts Moon Charts
120

1970 May 21	03 38	FM
1970 May 27	22 32	LQ
1970 Jun 04	02 21	NM
1970 Jun 12	04 06	FQ
1970 Jun 19	12 27	FM
1970 Jun 26	04 01	LQ
1970 Jul 03	15 18	NM
1970 Jul 11	19 43	FQ
1970 Jul 18	19 58	FM
1970 Jul 25	11 00	LQ
1970 Aug 02	05 58	NM
1970 Aug 10	08 50	FQ
1970 Aug 17	03 15	FM
1970 Aug 23	20 34	LQ
1970 Aug 31	22 01	NM
1970 Sep 08	19 38	FQ
1970 Sep 15	11 09	FM
1970 Sep 22	09 42	LQ
1970 Sep 30	14 31	NM
1970 Oct 08	04 43	FQ
1970 Oct 14	20 21	FM
1970 Oct 22	02 47	LQ
1970 Oct 30	06 28	NM
1970 Nov 06	12 47	FQ
1970 Nov 13	07 28	FM
1970 Nov 20	23 13	LQ
1970 Nov 28	21 14	NM
1970 Dec 05	20 36	FQ
1970 Dec 12	21 03	FM
1970 Dec 20	21 09	LQ
1970 Dec 28	10 43	NM
1971 Jan 04	04 55	FQ
1971 Jan 11	13 20	FM
1971 Jan 19	18 08	LQ
1971 Jan 26	22 55	NM
1971 Feb 02	14 31	FQ
1971 Feb 10	07 41	FM
1971 Feb 18	12 14	LQ
1971 Feb 25	09 48	NM
1971 Mar 04	02 01	FQ
1971 Mar 12	02 34	FM
1971 Mar 20	02 30	LQ
1971 Mar 26	19 23	NM
1971 Apr 02	15 46	FQ
1971 Apr 10	20 10	FM
1971 Apr 18	12 58	LQ
1971 Apr 25	04 02	NM
1971 May 02	07 34	FQ
1971 May 10	11 24	FM
1971 May 17	20 15	LQ
1971 May 24	12 32	NM
1971 Jun 01	00 42	FQ
1971 Jun 09	00 04	FM
1971 Jun 16	01 24	LQ
1971 Jun 22	21 57	NM
1971 Jun 30	18 11	FQ
1971 Jul 08	10 37	FM
1971 Jul 15	05 47	LQ
1971 Jul 22	09 15	NM
1971 Jul 30	11 07	FQ
1971 Aug 06	19 42	FM
1971 Aug 13	10 55	LQ
1971 Aug 20	22 53	NM
1971 Aug 29	02 56	FQ
1971 Sep 05	04 02	FM
1971 Sep 11	18 23	LQ
1971 Sep 19	14 42	NM
1971 Sep 27	17 17	FQ
1971 Oct 04	12 19	FM
1971 Oct 11	05 29	LQ
1971 Oct 19	07 59	NM
1971 Oct 27	05 54	FQ
1971 Nov 02	21 19	FM
1971 Nov 09	20 51	LQ
1971 Nov 18	01 46	NM
1971 Nov 25	16 37	FQ
1971 Dec 02	07 48	FM
1971 Dec 09	16 02	LQ
1971 Dec 17	19 03	NM
1971 Dec 25	01 35	FQ
1971 Dec 31	20 20	FM
1972 Jan 08	13 31	LQ
1972 Jan 16	10 52	NM
1972 Jan 23	09 29	FQ
1972 Jan 30	10 58	FM
1972 Feb 07	11 11	LQ
1972 Feb 15	00 29	NM
1972 Feb 21	17 20	FQ
1972 Feb 29	03 12	FM
1972 Mar 08	07 05	LQ
1972 Mar 15	11 35	NM
1972 Mar 22	02 12	FQ
1972 Mar 29	20 05	FM
1972 Apr 06	23 44	LQ
1972 Apr 13	20 31	NM
1972 Apr 20	12 45	FQ
1972 Apr 28	12 44	FM
1972 May 06	12 26	LQ
1972 May 13	04 08	NM
1972 May 20	01 16	FQ
1972 May 28	04 28	FM
1972 Jun 04	21 22	LQ
1972 Jun 11	11 30	NM
1972 Jun 18	15 41	FQ
1972 Jun 26	18 46	FM
1972 Jul 04	03 25	LQ
1972 Jul 10	19 39	NM
1972 Jul 18	07 46	FQ
1972 Jul 26	07 24	FM
1972 Aug 02	08 02	LQ
1972 Aug 09	05 26	NM
1972 Aug 17	01 09	FQ
1972 Aug 24	18 22	FM
1972 Aug 31	12 48	LQ
1972 Sep 07	17 28	NM
1972 Sep 15	19 13	FQ
1972 Sep 23	04 07	FM
1972 Sep 29	19 16	LQ
1972 Oct 07	08 08	NM
1972 Oct 15	12 55	FQ
1972 Oct 22	13 25	FM
1972 Oct 29	04 41	LQ
1972 Nov 06	01 21	NM
1972 Nov 14	05 01	FQ
1972 Nov 20	23 06	FM
1972 Nov 27	17 45	LQ
1972 Dec 05	20 24	NM
1972 Dec 13	18 36	FQ
1972 Dec 20	09 45	FM
1972 Dec 27	10 27	LQ
1973 Jan 04	15 42	NM
1973 Jan 12	05 27	FQ
1973 Jan 18	21 28	FM
1973 Jan 26	06 05	LQ
1973 Feb 03	09 23	NM
1973 Feb 10	14 05	FQ
1973 Feb 17	10 07	FM
1973 Feb 25	03 10	LQ
1973 Mar 05	00 07	NM
1973 Mar 11	21 26	FQ
1973 Mar 18	23 33	FM
1973 Mar 26	23 46	LQ
1973 Apr 03	11 45	NM
1973 Apr 10	04 28	FQ
1973 Apr 17	13 51	FM
1973 Apr 25	17 59	LQ
1973 May 02	20 55	NM
1973 May 09	12 07	FQ
1973 May 17	04 58	FM
1973 May 25	08 40	LQ
1973 Jun 01	04 34	NM
1973 Jun 07	21 11	FQ
1973 Jun 15	20 35	FM
1973 Jun 23	19 45	LQ
1973 Jun 30	11 39	NM
1973 Jul 07	08 26	FQ
1973 Jul 15	11 56	FM
1973 Jul 23	03 58	LQ
1973 Jul 29	18 59	NM
1973 Aug 05	22 27	FQ
1973 Aug 14	02 17	FM
1973 Aug 21	10 22	LQ
1973 Aug 28	03 25	NM
1973 Sep 04	15 22	FQ
1973 Sep 12	15 16	FM
1973 Sep 19	16 11	LQ
1973 Sep 26	13 54	NM
1973 Oct 04	10 32	FQ
1973 Oct 12	03 09	FM
1973 Oct 18	22 33	LQ
1973 Oct 26	03 17	NM
1973 Nov 03	06 29	FQ
1973 Nov 10	14 27	FM
1973 Nov 17	06 34	LQ
1973 Nov 24	19 55	NM
1973 Dec 03	01 29	FQ
1973 Dec 10	01 35	FM
1973 Dec 16	17 13	LQ
1973 Dec 24	15 07	NM
1974 Jan 01	18 06	FQ
1974 Jan 08	12 36	FM
1974 Jan 15	07 04	LQ
1974 Jan 23	11 02	NM
1974 Jan 31	07 39	FQ
1974 Feb 06	23 24	FM
1974 Feb 14	00 04	LQ
1974 Feb 22	05 34	NM
1974 Mar 01	18 03	FQ
1974 Mar 08	10 03	FM
1974 Mar 15	19 15	LQ
1974 Mar 23	21 24	NM
1974 Mar 31	01 44	FQ
1974 Apr 06	21 00	FM
1974 Apr 14	14 57	LQ
1974 Apr 22	10 16	NM
1974 Apr 29	07 39	FQ
1974 May 06	08 55	FM
1974 May 14	09 29	LQ
1974 May 21	20 34	NM
1974 May 28	13 03	FQ
1974 Jun 04	22 10	FM
1974 Jun 13	01 45	LQ
1974 Jun 20	04 56	NM
1974 Jun 26	19 20	FQ
1974 Jul 04	12 40	FM
1974 Jul 12	15 28	LQ
1974 Jul 19	12 06	NM
1974 Jul 26	03 51	FQ
1974 Aug 03	03 57	FM
1974 Aug 11	02 46	LQ
1974 Aug 17	19 01	NM
1974 Aug 24	15 38	FQ
1974 Sep 01	19 25	FM
1974 Sep 09	12 01	LQ
1974 Sep 16	02 45	NM
1974 Sep 23	07 08	FQ
1974 Oct 01	10 38	FM
1974 Oct 08	19 46	LQ
1974 Oct 15	12 25	NM
1974 Oct 23	01 53	FQ
1974 Oct 31	01 19	FM
1974 Nov 07	02 47	LQ
1974 Nov 14	00 53	NM
1974 Nov 21	22 39	FQ
1974 Nov 29	15 10	FM
1974 Dec 06	10 10	LQ
1974 Dec 13	16 25	NM
1974 Dec 21	19 43	FQ
1974 Dec 29	03 51	FM
1975 Jan 04	19 04	LQ
1975 Jan 12	10 20	NM
1975 Jan 20	15 14	FQ
1975 Jan 27	15 09	FM
1975 Feb 03	06 23	LQ
1975 Feb 11	05 17	NM
1975 Feb 19	07 38	FQ
1975 Feb 26	01 14	FM
1975 Mar 04	20 20	LQ
1975 Mar 12	23 47	NM
1975 Mar 20	20 05	FQ
1975 Mar 27	10 36	FM
1975 Apr 03	12 25	LQ
1975 Apr 11	16 39	NM
1975 Apr 19	04 41	FQ
1975 Apr 25	19 55	FM
1975 May 03	05 44	LQ
1975 May 11	07 05	NM
1975 May 18	10 29	FQ
1975 May 25	05 51	FM
1975 Jun 01	23 22	LQ
1975 Jun 09	18 49	NM
1975 Jun 16	14 58	FQ
1975 Jun 23	16 54	FM
1975 Jul 01	16 37	LQ
1975 Jul 09	04 10	NM
1975 Jul 15	19 47	FQ
1975 Jul 23	05 28	FM
1975 Jul 31	08 48	LQ
1975 Aug 07	11 57	NM
1975 Aug 14	02 24	FQ
1975 Aug 21	19 48	FM
1975 Aug 29	23 20	LQ
1975 Sep 05	19 19	NM
1975 Sep 12	11 59	FQ
1975 Sep 20	11 50	FM
1975 Sep 28	11 46	LQ
1975 Oct 05	03 23	NM
1975 Oct 12	01 15	FQ
1975 Oct 20	05 06	FM
1975 Oct 27	22 07	LQ
1975 Nov 03	13 05	NM
1975 Nov 10	18 21	FQ
1975 Nov 18	22 28	FM
1975 Nov 26	06 52	LQ
1975 Dec 03	00 50	NM
1975 Dec 10	14 39	FQ
1975 Dec 18	14 39	FM
1975 Dec 25	14 52	LQ
1976 Jan 01	14 40	NM
1976 Jan 09	12 40	FQ
1976 Jan 17	04 47	FM
1976 Jan 23	23 04	LQ
1976 Jan 31	06 20	NM
1976 Feb 08	10 05	FQ
1976 Feb 15	16 43	FM
1976 Feb 22	08 16	LQ
1976 Feb 29	23 25	NM
1976 Mar 09	04 38	FQ
1976 Mar 16	02 53	FM
1976 Mar 22	18 54	LQ
1976 Mar 30	17 08	NM
1976 Apr 07	19 02	FQ
1976 Apr 14	11 49	FM
1976 Apr 21	07 14	LQ
1976 Apr 29	10 19	NM
1976 May 07	05 17	FQ
1976 May 13	20 04	FM
1976 May 20	21 22	LQ
1976 May 29	01 47	NM
1976 Jun 05	12 20	FQ
1976 Jun 12	04 15	FM
1976 Jun 19	13 15	LQ
1976 Jun 27	14 50	NM
1976 Jul 04	17 28	FQ
1976 Jul 11	13 09	FM
1976 Jul 19	06 29	LQ
1976 Jul 27	01 39	NM
1976 Aug 02	22 07	FQ
1976 Aug 09	23 44	FM
1976 Aug 18	00 13	LQ
1976 Aug 25	11 01	NM
1976 Sep 01	03 35	FQ
1976 Sep 08	12 52	FM
1976 Sep 16	17 20	LQ
1976 Sep 23	19 55	NM
1976 Sep 30	11 12	FQ
1976 Oct 08	04 55	FM
1976 Oct 16	08 59	LQ
1976 Oct 23	05 10	NM
1976 Oct 29	22 05	FQ
1976 Nov 06	23 15	FM
1976 Nov 14	22 39	LQ
1976 Nov 21	15 11	NM
1976 Nov 28	12 59	FQ
1976 Dec 06	18 15	FM
1976 Dec 14	10 14	LQ
1976 Dec 21	02 08	NM
1976 Dec 28	07 48	FQ
1977 Jan 05	12 10	FM
1977 Jan 12	19 55	LQ
1977 Jan 19	14 11	NM
1977 Jan 27	05 11	FQ
1977 Feb 04	03 56	FM
1977 Feb 11	04 07	LQ
1977 Feb 18	03 37	NM
1977 Feb 26	02 50	FQ
1977 Mar 05	17 13	FM
1977 Mar 12	11 35	LQ
1977 Mar 19	18 33	NM
1977 Mar 27	22 27	FQ
1977 Apr 04	04 09	FM
1977 Apr 10	19 15	LQ
1977 Apr 18	10 35	NM
1977 Apr 26	14 42	FQ
1977 May 03	13 03	FM
1977 May 10	04 08	LQ
1977 May 18	02 51	NM
1977 May 26	03 20	FQ
1977 Jun 01	20 31	FM
1977 Jun 08	15 07	LQ
1977 Jun 16	18 23	NM
1977 Jun 24	12 44	FQ
1977 Jul 01	03 24	FM
1977 Jul 08	04 39	LQ
1977 Jul 16	08 37	NM
1977 Jul 23	19 38	FQ
1977 Jul 30	10 52	FM
1977 Aug 06	20 40	LQ
1977 Aug 14	21 31	NM
1977 Aug 22	01 04	FQ
1977 Aug 28	20 10	FM
1977 Sep 05	14 33	LQ
1977 Sep 13	09 23	NM
1977 Sep 20	06 18	FQ
1977 Sep 27	08 17	FM
1977 Oct 05	09 21	LQ
1977 Oct 12	20 31	NM
1977 Oct 19	12 46	FQ
1977 Oct 26	23 35	FM
1977 Nov 04	03 58	LQ
1977 Nov 11	07 09	NM
1977 Nov 17	21 52	FQ
1977 Nov 25	17 31	FM
1977 Dec 03	21 16	LQ
1977 Dec 10	17 33	NM
1977 Dec 17	10 37	FQ
1977 Dec 25	12 49	FM
1978 Jan 02	12 07	LQ
1978 Jan 09	04 00	NM
1978 Jan 16	03 03	FQ
1978 Jan 24	07 56	FM
1978 Jan 31	23 51	LQ
1978 Feb 07	14 54	NM
1978 Feb 14	22 11	FQ
1978 Feb 23	01 26	FM
1978 Mar 02	08 34	LQ
1978 Mar 09	02 36	NM
1978 Mar 16	18 21	FQ
1978 Mar 24	16 20	FM
1978 Mar 31	15 11	LQ
1978 Apr 07	15 15	NM
1978 Apr 15	13 56	FQ
1978 Apr 23	04 11	FM
1978 Apr 29	21 02	LQ
1978 May 07	04 47	NM
1978 May 15	07 39	FQ
1978 May 22	13 17	FM
1978 May 29	03 30	LQ
1978 Jun 05	19 01	NM
1978 Jun 13	22 44	FQ
1978 Jun 20	20 30	FM
1978 Jun 27	11 44	LQ
1978 Jul 05	09 50	NM
1978 Jul 13	10 49	FQ
1978 Jul 20	03 05	FM
1978 Jul 26	22 31	LQ
1978 Aug 04	01 01	NM
1978 Aug 11	20 06	FQ
1978 Aug 18	10 14	FM
1978 Aug 25	12 18	LQ
1978 Sep 02	16 09	NM
1978 Sep 10	03 20	FQ
1978 Sep 16	19 01	FM
1978 Sep 24	05 08	LQ
1978 Oct 02	06 41	NM
1978 Oct 09	09 38	FQ
1978 Oct 16	06 10	FM
1978 Oct 24	00 34	LQ
1978 Oct 31	20 07	NM
1978 Nov 07	16 18	FQ
1978 Nov 14	20 00	FM
1978 Nov 22	21 24	LQ
1978 Nov 30	08 19	NM
1978 Dec 07	00 34	FQ
1978 Dec 14	12 31	FM
1978 Dec 22	17 42	LQ
1978 Dec 29	19 36	NM
1979 Jan 05	11 15	FQ
1979 Jan 13	07 09	FM
1979 Jan 21	11 23	LQ
1979 Jan 28	06 19	NM
1979 Feb 04	00 36	FQ
1979 Feb 12	02 39	FM
1979 Feb 20	01 17	LQ
1979 Feb 26	16 45	NM
1979 Mar 05	16 23	FQ
1979 Mar 13	21 14	FM
1979 Mar 21	11 22	LQ
1979 Mar 28	02 59	NM
1979 Apr 04	09 57	FQ
1979 Apr 12	13 15	FM
1979 Apr 19	18 30	LQ
1979 Apr 26	13 15	NM
1979 May 04	04 25	FQ
1979 May 12	02 01	FM
1979 May 18	23 57	LQ
1979 May 26	00 00	NM
1979 Jun 02	22 37	FQ
1979 Jun 10	11 55	FM
1979 Jun 17	05 01	LQ
1979 Jun 24	11 58	NM
1979 Jul 02	15 24	FQ
1979 Jul 09	19 59	FM
1979 Jul 16	10 59	LQ
1979 Jul 24	01 41	NM
1979 Aug 01	05 57	FQ
1979 Aug 08	03 21	FM
1979 Aug 14	19 02	LQ
1979 Aug 22	17 10	NM
1979 Aug 30	18 09	FQ
1979 Sep 06	10 58	FM
1979 Sep 13	06 15	LQ
1979 Sep 21	09 47	NM
1979 Sep 29	04 20	FQ
1979 Oct 05	19 35	FM
1979 Oct 12	21 24	LQ
1979 Oct 21	02 23	NM
1979 Oct 28	13 06	FQ
1979 Nov 04	05 47	FM
1979 Nov 11	16 24	LQ
1979 Nov 19	18 04	NM
1979 Nov 26	21 09	FQ
1979 Dec 03	18 08	FM
1979 Dec 11	13 59	LQ
1979 Dec 19	08 23	NM
1979 Dec 26	05 11	FQ
1980 Jan 02	09 02	FM
1980 Jan 10	11 50	LQ
1980 Jan 17	21 19	NM
1980 Jan 24	13 58	FQ
1980 Feb 01	02 21	FM
1980 Feb 09	07 35	LQ
1980 Feb 16	08 51	NM
1980 Feb 23	00 14	FQ
1980 Mar 01	21 00	FM
1980 Mar 09	23 49	LQ
1980 Mar 16	18 56	NM
1980 Mar 23	12 31	FQ
1980 Mar 31	15 14	FM
1980 Apr 08	12 06	LQ
1980 Apr 15	03 46	NM
1980 Apr 22	02 59	FQ
1980 Apr 30	07 35	FM
1980 May 07	20 51	LQ
1980 May 14	12 00	NM
1980 May 21	19 16	FQ
1980 May 29	21 28	FM
1980 Jun 06	02 53	LQ
1980 Jun 12	20 38	NM
1980 Jun 20	12 32	FQ
1980 Jun 28	09 02	FM
1980 Jul 05	07 27	LQ
1980 Jul 12	06 46	NM
1980 Jul 20	05 51	FQ
1980 Jul 27	18 54	FM
1980 Aug 03	12 00	LQ
1980 Aug 10	19 09	NM
1980 Aug 18	22 28	FQ
1980 Aug 26	03 42	FM
1980 Sep 01	18 08	LQ
1980 Sep 09	10 00	NM
1980 Sep 17	13 54	FQ
1980 Sep 24	12 08	FM

1980 Oct 01	03 18	LQ
1980 Oct 09	02 50	NM
1980 Oct 17	03 47	FQ
1980 Oct 23	20 52	FM
1980 Oct 30	16 33	LQ
1980 Nov 07	20 43	NM
1980 Nov 15	15 47	FQ
1980 Nov 22	06 39	FM
1980 Nov 29	09 59	LQ
1980 Dec 07	14 35	NM
1980 Dec 15	01 47	FQ
1980 Dec 21	18 08	FM
1980 Dec 29	06 32	LQ
1981 Jan 06	07 24	NM
1981 Jan 13	10 10	FQ
1981 Jan 20	07 39	FM
1981 Jan 28	04 19	LQ
1981 Feb 04	22 14	NM
1981 Feb 11	17 49	FQ
1981 Feb 18	22 58	FM
1981 Feb 27	01 14	LQ
1981 Mar 06	10 31	NM
1981 Mar 13	01 51	FQ
1981 Mar 20	15 22	FM
1981 Mar 28	19 34	LQ
1981 Apr 04	20 19	NM
1981 Apr 11	11 11	FQ
1981 Apr 19	07 59	FM
1981 Apr 27	10 14	LQ
1981 May 04	04 19	NM
1981 May 10	22 22	FQ
1981 May 19	00 04	FM
1981 May 26	21 00	LQ
1981 Jun 02	11 32	NM
1981 Jun 09	11 33	FQ
1981 Jun 17	15 04	FM
1981 Jun 25	04 25	LQ
1981 Jul 01	19 03	NM
1981 Jul 09	02 39	FQ
1981 Jul 17	04 39	FM
1981 Jul 24	09 40	LQ
1981 Jul 31	03 52	NM
1981 Aug 07	19 26	FQ
1981 Aug 15	16 37	FM
1981 Aug 22	14 16	LQ
1981 Aug 29	14 43	NM
1981 Sep 06	13 26	FQ
1981 Sep 14	03 09	FM
1981 Sep 20	19 47	LQ
1981 Sep 28	04 07	NM
1981 Oct 06	07 45	FQ
1981 Oct 13	12 49	FM
1981 Oct 20	03 41	LQ
1981 Oct 27	20 13	NM
1981 Nov 05	01 09	FQ
1981 Nov 11	22 26	FM
1981 Nov 18	14 54	LQ
1981 Nov 26	14 38	NM
1981 Dec 04	16 22	FQ
1981 Dec 11	08 41	FM
1981 Dec 18	05 47	LQ
1981 Dec 26	10 10	NM
1982 Jan 03	04 46	FQ
1982 Jan 09	19 53	FM
1982 Jan 16	23 58	LQ
1982 Jan 25	04 56	NM
1982 Feb 01	14 28	FQ
1982 Feb 08	07 57	FM
1982 Feb 15	20 21	LQ
1982 Feb 23	21 13	NM
1982 Mar 02	22 15	FQ
1982 Mar 09	20 45	FM
1982 Mar 17	17 15	LQ
1982 Mar 25	10 18	NM
1982 Apr 01	05 08	FQ
1982 Apr 08	10 18	FM
1982 Apr 16	12 42	LQ
1982 Apr 23	20 29	NM
1982 Apr 30	12 07	FQ
1982 May 08	00 45	FM
1982 May 16	05 11	LQ
1982 May 23	04 40	NM
1982 May 29	20 07	FQ
1982 Jun 06	15 59	FM
1982 Jun 14	18 06	LQ
1982 Jun 21	11 52	NM
1982 Jun 28	05 56	FQ
1982 Jul 06	07 32	FM
1982 Jul 14	03 47	LQ
1982 Jul 20	18 57	NM
1982 Jul 27	18 22	FQ
1982 Aug 04	22 34	FM
1982 Aug 12	11 09	LQ
1982 Aug 19	02 45	NM
1982 Aug 26	09 49	FQ
1982 Sep 03	12 28	FM
1982 Sep 10	17 19	LQ
1982 Sep 17	12 09	NM
1982 Sep 25	04 07	FQ
1982 Oct 03	01 09	FM
1982 Oct 09	23 26	LQ
1982 Oct 17	00 04	NM
1982 Oct 25	00 08	FQ
1982 Nov 01	12 57	FM
1982 Nov 08	06 38	LQ
1982 Nov 15	15 10	NM
1982 Nov 23	20 06	FQ
1982 Dec 01	00 21	FM
1982 Dec 07	15 53	LQ
1982 Dec 15	09 18	NM
1982 Dec 23	14 17	FQ
1982 Dec 30	11 33	FM
1983 Jan 06	04 00	LQ
1983 Jan 14	05 08	NM
1983 Jan 22	05 33	FQ
1983 Jan 28	22 26	FM
1983 Feb 04	19 17	LQ
1983 Feb 13	00 32	NM
1983 Feb 20	17 32	FQ
1983 Feb 27	08 58	FM
1983 Mar 06	13 16	LQ
1983 Mar 14	17 43	NM
1983 Mar 22	02 25	FQ
1983 Mar 28	19 27	FM
1983 Apr 05	08 38	LQ
1983 Apr 13	07 58	NM
1983 Apr 20	08 58	FQ
1983 Apr 27	06 31	FM
1983 May 05	03 43	LQ
1983 May 12	19 25	NM
1983 May 19	14 17	FQ
1983 May 26	18 48	FM
1983 Jun 03	21 07	LQ
1983 Jun 11	04 38	NM
1983 Jun 17	19 46	FQ
1983 Jun 25	08 32	FM
1983 Jul 03	12 12	LQ
1983 Jul 10	12 18	NM
1983 Jul 17	02 50	FQ
1983 Jul 24	23 27	FM
1983 Aug 02	00 52	LQ
1983 Aug 08	19 18	NM
1983 Aug 15	12 47	FQ
1983 Aug 23	14 59	FM
1983 Aug 31	11 22	LQ
1983 Sep 07	02 35	NM
1983 Sep 14	02 24	FQ
1983 Sep 22	06 36	FM
1983 Sep 29	20 05	LQ
1983 Oct 06	11 16	NM
1983 Oct 13	19 42	FQ
1983 Oct 21	21 53	FM
1983 Oct 29	03 37	LQ
1983 Nov 04	22 21	NM
1983 Nov 12	15 49	FQ
1983 Nov 20	12 29	FM
1983 Nov 27	10 50	LQ
1983 Dec 04	12 26	NM
1983 Dec 12	13 09	FQ
1983 Dec 20	02 00	FM
1983 Dec 26	18 52	LQ
1984 Jan 03	05 16	NM
1984 Jan 11	09 48	FQ
1984 Jan 18	14 05	FM
1984 Jan 25	04 48	LQ
1984 Feb 01	23 46	NM
1984 Feb 10	04 00	FQ
1984 Feb 17	00 41	FM
1984 Feb 23	17 12	LQ
1984 Mar 02	18 31	NM
1984 Mar 10	18 28	FQ
1984 Mar 17	10 10	FM
1984 Mar 24	07 58	LQ
1984 Apr 01	12 10	NM
1984 Apr 09	04 51	FQ
1984 Apr 15	19 11	FM
1984 Apr 23	00 26	LQ
1984 May 01	03 45	NM
1984 May 08	11 50	FQ
1984 May 15	04 29	FM
1984 May 22	17 45	LQ
1984 May 30	16 48	NM
1984 Jun 06	16 42	FQ
1984 Jun 13	14 42	FM
1984 Jun 21	11 10	LQ
1984 Jun 29	03 18	NM
1984 Jul 05	21 04	FQ
1984 Jul 13	02 20	FM
1984 Jul 21	04 01	LQ
1984 Jul 28	11 51	NM
1984 Aug 04	02 33	FQ
1984 Aug 11	15 43	FM
1984 Aug 19	19 41	LQ
1984 Aug 26	19 25	NM
1984 Sep 02	10 30	FQ
1984 Sep 10	07 01	FM
1984 Sep 18	09 31	LQ
1984 Sep 25	03 11	NM
1984 Oct 01	21 53	FQ
1984 Oct 09	23 58	FM
1984 Oct 17	21 14	LQ
1984 Oct 24	12 08	NM
1984 Oct 31	13 07	FQ
1984 Nov 08	17 43	FM
1984 Nov 16	06 59	LQ
1984 Nov 22	22 57	NM
1984 Nov 30	08 01	FQ
1984 Dec 08	10 53	FM
1984 Dec 15	15 25	LQ
1984 Dec 22	11 47	NM
1984 Dec 30	05 27	FQ
1985 Jan 07	02 16	FM
1985 Jan 13	23 27	LQ
1985 Jan 21	02 28	NM
1985 Jan 29	03 29	FQ
1985 Feb 05	15 19	FM
1985 Feb 12	07 57	LQ
1985 Feb 19	18 43	NM
1985 Feb 27	23 41	FQ
1985 Mar 07	02 13	FM
1985 Mar 13	17 34	LQ
1985 Mar 21	11 59	NM
1985 Mar 29	16 11	FQ
1985 Apr 05	11 32	FM
1985 Apr 12	04 42	LQ
1985 Apr 20	05 22	NM
1985 Apr 28	04 25	FQ
1985 May 04	19 53	FM
1985 May 11	17 34	LQ
1985 May 19	21 41	NM
1985 May 27	12 56	FQ
1985 Jun 03	03 50	FM
1985 Jun 10	08 19	LQ
1985 Jun 18	11 58	NM
1985 Jun 25	18 53	FQ
1985 Jul 02	12 08	FM
1985 Jul 10	00 49	LQ
1985 Jul 17	23 56	NM
1985 Jul 24	23 39	FQ
1985 Jul 31	21 41	FM
1985 Aug 08	18 29	LQ
1985 Aug 16	10 06	NM
1985 Aug 23	04 36	FQ
1985 Aug 30	09 27	FM
1985 Sep 07	12 16	LQ
1985 Sep 14	19 20	NM
1985 Sep 21	11 03	FQ
1985 Sep 29	00 08	FM
1985 Oct 07	05 04	LQ
1985 Oct 14	04 33	NM
1985 Oct 20	20 13	FQ
1985 Oct 28	17 38	FM
1985 Nov 05	20 07	LQ
1985 Nov 12	14 20	NM
1985 Nov 19	09 04	FQ
1985 Nov 27	12 42	FM
1985 Dec 05	09 01	LQ
1985 Dec 12	00 54	NM
1985 Dec 19	01 58	FQ
1985 Dec 27	07 30	FM
1986 Jan 03	19 47	LQ
1986 Jan 10	12 22	NM
1986 Jan 17	22 13	FQ
1986 Jan 26	00 31	FM
1986 Feb 02	04 41	LQ
1986 Feb 09	00 55	NM
1986 Feb 16	19 55	FQ
1986 Feb 24	15 02	FM
1986 Mar 03	12 17	LQ
1986 Mar 10	14 52	NM
1986 Mar 18	16 39	FQ
1986 Mar 26	03 02	FM
1986 Apr 01	19 30	LQ
1986 Apr 09	06 08	NM
1986 Apr 17	10 35	FQ
1986 Apr 24	12 46	FM
1986 May 01	03 22	LQ
1986 May 08	22 10	NM
1986 May 17	01 00	FQ
1986 May 23	20 45	FM
1986 May 30	12 55	LQ
1986 Jun 07	14 00	NM
1986 Jun 15	12 00	FQ
1986 Jun 22	03 42	FM
1986 Jun 29	00 53	LQ
1986 Jul 07	04 55	NM
1986 Jul 14	20 10	FQ
1986 Jul 21	10 40	FM
1986 Jul 28	15 34	LQ
1986 Aug 05	18 36	NM
1986 Aug 13	02 21	FQ
1986 Aug 19	18 54	FM
1986 Aug 27	08 39	LQ
1986 Sep 04	07 10	NM
1986 Sep 11	07 41	FQ
1986 Sep 18	05 34	FM
1986 Sep 26	03 17	LQ
1986 Oct 03	18 55	NM
1986 Oct 10	13 28	FQ
1986 Oct 17	19 22	FM
1986 Oct 25	22 26	LQ
1986 Nov 02	06 02	NM
1986 Nov 08	21 11	FQ
1986 Nov 16	12 12	FM
1986 Nov 24	16 50	LQ
1986 Dec 01	16 43	NM
1986 Dec 08	08 01	FQ
1986 Dec 16	07 04	FM
1986 Dec 24	09 17	LQ
1986 Dec 31	03 10	NM
1987 Jan 06	22 34	FQ
1987 Jan 15	02 30	FM
1987 Jan 22	22 45	LQ
1987 Jan 29	13 44	NM
1987 Feb 05	16 21	FQ
1987 Feb 13	20 58	FM
1987 Feb 21	08 56	LQ
1987 Feb 28	00 51	NM
1987 Mar 07	11 58	FQ
1987 Mar 15	13 13	FM
1987 Mar 22	16 22	LQ
1987 Mar 29	12 46	NM
1987 Apr 06	07 48	FQ
1987 Apr 14	02 31	FM
1987 Apr 20	22 15	LQ
1987 Apr 28	01 34	NM
1987 May 06	02 26	FQ
1987 May 13	12 50	FM
1987 May 20	04 02	LQ
1987 May 27	15 13	NM
1987 Jun 04	18 53	FQ
1987 Jun 11	20 49	FM
1987 Jun 18	11 03	LQ
1987 Jun 26	05 37	NM
1987 Jul 04	08 34	FQ
1987 Jul 11	03 32	FM
1987 Jul 17	20 17	LQ
1987 Jul 25	20 38	NM
1987 Aug 02	19 24	FQ
1987 Aug 09	10 17	FM
1987 Aug 16	08 25	LQ
1987 Aug 24	11 59	NM
1987 Sep 01	03 48	FQ
1987 Sep 07	18 13	FM
1987 Sep 14	23 44	LQ
1987 Sep 23	03 08	NM
1987 Sep 30	10 39	FQ
1987 Oct 07	04 12	FM
1987 Oct 14	18 06	LQ
1987 Oct 22	17 28	NM
1987 Oct 29	17 10	FQ
1987 Nov 05	16 46	FM
1987 Nov 13	14 38	LQ
1987 Nov 21	06 33	NM
1987 Nov 28	00 37	FQ
1987 Dec 05	08 01	FM
1987 Dec 13	11 41	LQ
1987 Dec 20	18 25	NM
1987 Dec 27	10 01	FQ
1988 Jan 04	01 40	FM
1988 Jan 12	07 04	LQ
1988 Jan 19	05 26	NM
1988 Jan 25	21 54	FQ
1988 Feb 02	20 51	FM
1988 Feb 10	23 01	LQ
1988 Feb 17	15 54	NM
1988 Feb 24	12 15	FQ
1988 Mar 03	16 01	FM
1988 Mar 11	10 56	LQ
1988 Mar 18	02 02	NM
1988 Mar 25	04 42	FQ
1988 Apr 02	09 21	FM
1988 Apr 09	19 21	LQ
1988 Apr 16	12 00	NM
1988 Apr 23	22 32	FQ
1988 May 01	23 41	FM
1988 May 09	01 23	LQ
1988 May 15	22 11	NM
1988 May 23	16 49	FQ
1988 May 31	10 54	FM
1988 Jun 07	06 22	LQ
1988 Jun 14	09 14	NM
1988 Jun 22	10 23	FQ
1988 Jun 29	19 46	FM
1988 Jul 06	11 36	LQ
1988 Jul 13	21 53	NM
1988 Jul 22	02 14	FQ
1988 Jul 29	03 25	FM
1988 Aug 04	18 22	LQ
1988 Aug 12	12 31	NM
1988 Aug 20	15 51	FQ
1988 Aug 27	10 56	FM
1988 Sep 03	03 50	LQ
1988 Sep 11	04 49	NM
1988 Sep 19	03 18	FQ
1988 Sep 25	19 07	FM
1988 Oct 02	16 58	LQ
1988 Oct 10	21 49	NM
1988 Oct 18	13 01	FQ
1988 Oct 25	04 36	FM
1988 Nov 01	10 11	LQ
1988 Nov 09	14 20	NM
1988 Nov 16	21 35	FQ
1988 Nov 23	15 53	FM
1988 Dec 01	06 49	LQ
1988 Dec 09	05 36	NM
1988 Dec 16	05 40	FQ
1988 Dec 23	05 29	FM
1988 Dec 31	04 57	LQ
1989 Jan 07	19 22	NM
1989 Jan 14	13 58	FQ
1989 Jan 21	21 34	FM
1989 Jan 30	02 02	LQ
1989 Feb 06	07 37	NM
1989 Feb 12	23 15	FQ
1989 Feb 20	15 32	FM
1989 Feb 28	20 08	LQ
1989 Mar 07	18 19	NM
1989 Mar 14	10 11	FQ
1989 Mar 22	09 58	FM
1989 Mar 30	10 21	LQ
1989 Apr 06	03 33	NM
1989 Apr 12	23 13	FQ
1989 Apr 21	03 13	FM
1989 Apr 28	20 46	LQ
1989 May 05	11 46	NM
1989 May 12	14 20	FQ
1989 May 20	18 16	FM
1989 May 28	04 01	LQ
1989 Jun 03	19 53	NM
1989 Jun 11	06 59	FQ
1989 Jun 19	06 57	FM
1989 Jun 26	09 09	LQ
1989 Jul 03	04 59	NM
1989 Jul 11	00 19	FQ
1989 Jul 18	17 42	FM
1989 Jul 25	13 31	LQ
1989 Aug 01	16 06	NM
1989 Aug 09	17 29	FQ
1989 Aug 17	03 07	FM
1989 Aug 23	18 40	LQ
1989 Aug 31	05 45	NM
1989 Sep 08	09 49	FQ
1989 Sep 15	11 51	FM
1989 Sep 22	02 10	LQ
1989 Sep 29	21 47	NM
1989 Oct 08	00 52	FQ
1989 Oct 14	20 32	FM
1989 Oct 21	13 19	LQ
1989 Oct 29	15 27	NM
1989 Nov 06	14 11	FQ
1989 Nov 13	05 51	FM
1989 Nov 20	04 44	LQ
1989 Nov 28	09 41	NM
1989 Dec 06	01 26	FQ
1989 Dec 12	16 30	FM
1989 Dec 19	23 55	LQ
1989 Dec 28	03 20	NM
1990 Jan 04	10 40	FQ
1990 Jan 11	04 57	FM
1990 Jan 18	21 17	LQ
1990 Jan 26	19 20	NM
1990 Feb 02	18 32	FQ
1990 Feb 09	19 16	FM
1990 Feb 17	18 48	LQ
1990 Feb 25	08 54	NM
1990 Mar 04	02 05	FQ
1990 Mar 11	10 59	FM
1990 Mar 19	14 30	LQ
1990 Mar 26	19 48	NM
1990 Apr 02	10 24	FQ
1990 Apr 10	03 18	FM
1990 Apr 18	07 03	LQ
1990 Apr 25	04 27	NM
1990 May 01	20 18	FQ
1990 May 09	19 31	FM
1990 May 17	19 45	LQ
1990 May 24	11 47	NM
1990 May 31	08 11	FQ
1990 Jun 08	11 01	FM
1990 Jun 16	04 48	LQ
1990 Jun 22	18 55	NM
1990 Jun 29	22 07	FQ
1990 Jul 08	01 23	FM
1990 Jul 15	11 04	LQ
1990 Jul 22	02 54	NM
1990 Jul 29	14 01	FQ
1990 Aug 06	14 19	FM
1990 Aug 13	15 54	LQ
1990 Aug 20	12 39	NM
1990 Aug 28	07 34	FQ
1990 Sep 05	01 46	FM
1990 Sep 11	20 53	LQ
1990 Sep 19	00 46	NM
1990 Sep 27	02 06	FQ
1990 Oct 04	12 02	FM
1990 Oct 11	03 31	LQ
1990 Oct 18	15 37	NM
1990 Oct 26	20 26	FQ
1990 Nov 02	21 48	FM
1990 Nov 09	13 02	LQ
1990 Nov 17	09 05	NM
1990 Nov 25	13 12	FQ
1990 Dec 02	07 50	FM
1990 Dec 09	02 04	LQ
1990 Dec 17	04 22	NM
1990 Dec 25	03 16	FQ
1990 Dec 31	18 35	FM
1991 Jan 07	18 35	LQ
1991 Jan 15	23 50	NM
1991 Jan 23	14 22	FQ

Moon Charts

122

1991 Jan 30	06 10	FM
1991 Feb 06	13 52	LQ
1991 Feb 14	17 32	NM
1991 Feb 21	22 58	FQ
1991 Feb 28	18 25	FM
1991 Mar 08	10 32	LQ
1991 Mar 16	08 10	NM
1991 Mar 23	06 03	FQ
1991 Mar 30	07 17	FM
1991 Apr 07	06 45	LQ
1991 Apr 14	19 38	NM
1991 Apr 21	12 39	FQ
1991 Apr 28	20 58	FM
1991 May 07	00 46	LQ
1991 May 14	04 36	NM
1991 May 20	19 46	FQ
1991 May 28	11 37	FM
1991 Jun 05	15 30	LQ
1991 Jun 12	12 06	NM
1991 Jun 19	04 19	FQ
1991 Jun 27	02 58	FM
1991 Jul 05	02 50	LQ
1991 Jul 11	19 06	NM
1991 Jul 18	15 11	FQ
1991 Jul 26	18 24	FM
1991 Aug 03	11 25	LQ
1991 Aug 10	02 28	NM
1991 Aug 17	05 01	FQ
1991 Aug 25	09 07	FM
1991 Sep 01	18 16	LQ
1991 Sep 08	11 01	NM
1991 Sep 15	22 01	FQ
1991 Sep 23	22 40	FM
1991 Oct 01	00 30	LQ
1991 Oct 07	21 39	NM
1991 Oct 15	17 33	FQ
1991 Oct 23	11 08	FM
1991 Oct 30	07 11	LQ
1991 Nov 06	11 11	NM
1991 Nov 14	14 02	FQ
1991 Nov 21	22 56	FM
1991 Nov 28	15 21	LQ
1991 Dec 06	03 56	NM
1991 Dec 14	09 32	FQ
1991 Dec 21	10 23	FM
1991 Dec 28	01 55	LQ
1992 Jan 04	23 10	NM
1992 Jan 13	02 32	FQ
1992 Jan 19	21 28	FM
1992 Jan 26	15 27	LQ
1992 Feb 03	19 00	NM
1992 Feb 11	16 15	FQ
1992 Feb 18	08 04	FM
1992 Feb 25	07 56	LQ
1992 Mar 04	13 22	NM
1992 Mar 12	02 36	FQ
1992 Mar 18	18 18	FM
1992 Mar 26	02 30	LQ
1992 Apr 03	05 01	NM
1992 Apr 10	10 06	FQ
1992 Apr 17	04 42	FM
1992 Apr 24	21 40	LQ
1992 May 02	17 44	NM
1992 May 09	15 44	FQ
1992 May 16	16 03	FM
1992 May 24	15 53	LQ
1992 Jun 01	03 57	NM
1992 Jun 07	20 47	FQ
1992 Jun 15	04 50	FM
1992 Jun 23	08 11	LQ
1992 Jun 30	12 18	NM
1992 Jul 07	02 43	FQ
1992 Jul 14	19 06	FM
1992 Jul 22	22 12	LQ
1992 Jul 29	19 35	NM
1992 Aug 05	10 59	FQ
1992 Aug 13	10 27	FM
1992 Aug 21	10 01	LQ
1992 Aug 28	02 42	NM
1992 Sep 03	22 39	FQ
1992 Sep 12	02 17	FM
1992 Sep 19	19 53	LQ
1992 Sep 26	10 40	NM
1992 Oct 03	14 12	FQ
1992 Oct 11	18 03	FM
1992 Oct 19	04 12	LQ
1992 Oct 25	20 34	NM
1992 Nov 02	09 11	FQ
1992 Nov 10	09 20	FM
1992 Nov 17	11 39	LQ
1992 Nov 24	09 11	NM
1992 Dec 02	06 17	FQ
1992 Dec 09	23 41	FM
1992 Dec 16	19 13	LQ
1992 Dec 24	00 43	NM
1993 Jan 01	03 38	FQ
1993 Jan 08	12 37	FM
1993 Jan 15	04 01	LQ
1993 Jan 22	18 27	NM
1993 Jan 30	23 20	FQ
1993 Feb 06	23 55	FM
1993 Feb 13	14 57	LQ
1993 Feb 21	13 05	NM
1993 Mar 01	15 47	FQ
1993 Mar 08	09 46	FM
1993 Mar 15	04 17	LQ
1993 Mar 23	07 14	NM
1993 Mar 31	04 10	FQ
1993 Apr 06	18 43	FM
1993 Apr 13	19 39	LQ
1993 Apr 21	23 49	NM
1993 Apr 29	12 41	FQ
1993 May 06	03 34	FM
1993 May 13	12 20	LQ
1993 May 21	14 07	NM
1993 May 28	18 21	FQ
1993 Jun 04	13 02	FM
1993 Jun 12	05 36	LQ
1993 Jun 20	01 52	NM
1993 Jun 26	22 43	FQ
1993 Jul 03	23 45	FM
1993 Jul 11	22 49	LQ
1993 Jul 19	11 24	NM
1993 Jul 26	03 25	FQ
1993 Aug 02	12 10	FM
1993 Aug 10	15 19	LQ
1993 Aug 17	19 28	NM
1993 Aug 24	09 57	FQ
1993 Sep 01	02 33	FM
1993 Sep 09	06 26	LQ
1993 Sep 16	03 10	NM
1993 Sep 22	19 32	FQ
1993 Sep 30	18 54	FM
1993 Oct 08	19 35	LQ
1993 Oct 15	11 36	NM
1993 Oct 22	08 52	FQ
1993 Oct 30	12 38	FM
1993 Nov 07	06 36	LQ
1993 Nov 13	21 34	NM
1993 Nov 21	02 03	FQ
1993 Nov 29	06 31	FM
1993 Dec 06	15 49	LQ
1993 Dec 13	09 27	NM
1993 Dec 20	22 26	FQ
1993 Dec 28	23 05	FM
1994 Jan 05	00 01	LQ
1994 Jan 11	23 10	NM
1994 Jan 19	20 27	FQ
1994 Jan 27	13 23	FM
1994 Feb 03	08 06	LQ
1994 Feb 10	14 30	NM
1994 Feb 18	17 47	FQ
1994 Feb 26	01 15	FM
1994 Mar 04	16 53	LQ
1994 Mar 12	07 05	NM
1994 Mar 20	12 14	FQ
1994 Mar 27	11 09	FM
1994 Apr 03	02 55	LQ
1994 Apr 11	00 17	NM
1994 Apr 19	02 34	FQ
1994 Apr 25	19 45	FM
1994 May 02	14 32	LQ
1994 May 10	17 07	NM
1994 May 18	12 50	FQ
1994 May 25	03 39	FM
1994 Jun 01	04 02	LQ
1994 Jun 09	08 26	NM
1994 Jun 16	19 56	FQ
1994 Jun 23	11 33	FM
1994 Jun 30	19 31	LQ
1994 Jul 08	21 37	NM
1994 Jul 16	01 12	FQ
1994 Jul 22	20 16	FM
1994 Jul 30	12 40	LQ
1994 Aug 07	08 45	NM
1994 Aug 14	05 57	FQ
1994 Aug 21	06 47	FM
1994 Aug 29	06 41	LQ
1994 Sep 05	18 33	NM
1994 Sep 12	11 34	FQ
1994 Sep 19	20 01	FM
1994 Sep 28	00 23	LQ
1994 Oct 05	03 55	NM
1994 Oct 11	19 17	FQ
1994 Oct 19	12 18	FM
1994 Oct 27	16 44	LQ
1994 Nov 03	13 35	NM
1994 Nov 10	06 14	FQ
1994 Nov 18	06 57	FM
1994 Nov 26	07 04	LQ
1994 Dec 02	23 54	NM
1994 Dec 09	21 06	FQ
1994 Dec 18	02 17	FM
1994 Dec 25	19 06	LQ
1995 Jan 01	10 56	NM
1995 Jan 08	15 46	FQ
1995 Jan 16	20 26	FM
1995 Jan 24	04 58	LQ
1995 Jan 30	22 48	NM
1995 Feb 07	12 54	FQ
1995 Feb 15	12 15	FM
1995 Feb 22	13 04	LQ
1995 Mar 01	11 48	NM
1995 Mar 09	10 14	FQ
1995 Mar 17	01 26	FM
1995 Mar 23	20 10	LQ
1995 Mar 31	02 09	NM
1995 Apr 08	05 35	FQ
1995 Apr 15	12 08	FM
1995 Apr 22	03 18	LQ
1995 Apr 29	17 36	NM
1995 May 07	21 44	FQ
1995 May 14	20 48	FM
1995 May 21	11 36	LQ
1995 May 29	09 27	NM
1995 Jun 06	10 26	FQ
1995 Jun 13	04 03	FM
1995 Jun 19	22 01	LQ
1995 Jul 05	20 02	FQ
1995 Jul 12	10 49	FM
1995 Jul 19	11 10	LQ
1995 Jul 27	15 13	NM
1995 Aug 04	03 16	FQ
1995 Aug 10	18 16	FM
1995 Aug 18	03 04	LQ
1995 Aug 26	04 31	NM
1995 Sep 02	09 03	FQ
1995 Sep 09	03 37	FM
1995 Sep 16	21 09	LQ
1995 Sep 24	16 55	NM
1995 Oct 01	14 36	FQ
1995 Oct 08	15 52	FM
1995 Oct 16	16 26	LQ
1995 Oct 24	04 36	NM
1995 Oct 30	21 17	FQ
1995 Nov 07	07 20	FM
1995 Nov 15	11 40	LQ
1995 Nov 22	15 43	NM
1995 Nov 29	06 28	FQ
1995 Dec 07	01 27	FM
1995 Dec 15	05 31	LQ
1995 Dec 22	02 22	NM
1995 Dec 28	19 06	FQ
1996 Jan 05	20 51	FM
1996 Jan 13	20 45	LQ
1996 Jan 20	12 50	NM
1996 Jan 27	11 14	FQ
1996 Feb 04	15 58	FM
1996 Feb 12	08 37	LQ
1996 Feb 18	23 30	NM
1996 Feb 26	05 52	FQ
1996 Mar 05	09 23	FM
1996 Mar 12	17 15	LQ
1996 Mar 19	10 45	NM
1996 Mar 27	01 31	FQ
1996 Apr 04	00 07	FM
1996 Apr 10	23 36	LQ
1996 Apr 17	22 49	NM
1996 Apr 25	20 40	FQ
1996 May 03	11 48	FM
1996 May 10	05 04	LQ
1996 May 17	11 46	NM
1996 May 25	14 13	FQ
1996 Jun 01	20 47	FM
1996 Jun 08	11 05	LQ
1996 Jun 16	01 36	NM
1996 Jun 24	05 23	FQ
1996 Jul 01	03 58	FM
1996 Jul 07	18 55	LQ
1996 Jul 15	16 15	NM
1996 Jul 23	17 49	FQ
1996 Jul 30	10 35	FM
1996 Aug 06	05 25	LQ
1996 Aug 14	07 34	NM
1996 Aug 22	03 36	FQ
1996 Aug 28	17 52	FM
1996 Sep 04	19 06	LQ
1996 Sep 12	23 07	NM
1996 Sep 20	11 23	FQ
1996 Sep 27	02 51	FM
1996 Oct 04	12 04	LQ
1996 Oct 12	14 14	NM
1996 Oct 19	18 09	FQ
1996 Oct 26	14 11	FM
1996 Nov 03	07 50	LQ
1996 Nov 11	04 16	NM
1996 Nov 18	01 09	FQ
1996 Nov 25	04 10	FM
1996 Dec 03	05 06	LQ
1996 Dec 10	16 56	NM
1996 Dec 17	09 31	FQ
1996 Dec 24	20 41	FM
1997 Jan 02	01 45	LQ
1997 Jan 09	04 26	NM
1997 Jan 15	20 02	FQ
1997 Jan 23	15 11	FM
1997 Jan 31	19 40	LQ
1997 Feb 07	15 06	NM
1997 Feb 14	08 58	FQ
1997 Feb 22	10 27	FM
1997 Mar 02	09 38	LQ
1997 Mar 09	01 14	NM
1997 Mar 16	00 06	FQ
1997 Mar 24	04 45	FM
1997 Mar 31	19 38	LQ
1997 Apr 07	11 02	NM
1997 Apr 14	17 00	FQ
1997 Apr 22	20 33	FM
1997 Apr 30	02 37	LQ
1997 May 06	20 46	NM
1997 May 14	10 55	FQ
1997 May 22	09 13	FM
1997 May 29	07 51	LQ
1997 Jun 05	07 04	NM
1997 Jun 13	04 51	FQ
1997 Jun 20	19 09	FM
1997 Jun 27	12 42	LQ
1997 Jul 04	18 40	NM
1997 Jul 12	21 44	FQ
1997 Jul 20	03 20	FM
1997 Jul 26	18 28	LQ
1997 Aug 03	08 14	NM
1997 Aug 11	12 42	FQ
1997 Aug 18	10 55	FM
1997 Aug 25	02 23	LQ
1997 Sep 01	23 52	NM
1997 Sep 10	01 31	FQ
1997 Sep 16	18 50	FM
1997 Sep 23	13 35	LQ
1997 Oct 01	16 51	NM
1997 Oct 09	12 22	FQ
1997 Oct 16	03 46	FM
1997 Oct 23	04 48	LQ
1997 Oct 31	10 01	NM
1997 Nov 07	21 43	FQ
1997 Nov 14	14 12	FM
1997 Nov 21	23 58	LQ
1997 Nov 30	02 14	NM
1997 Dec 07	06 09	FQ
1997 Dec 14	02 37	FM
1997 Dec 21	21 43	LQ
1997 Dec 29	16 57	NM
1998 Jan 05	14 18	FQ
1998 Jan 12	17 24	FM
1998 Jan 20	19 40	LQ
1998 Jan 28	06 01	NM
1998 Feb 03	22 53	FQ
1998 Feb 11	10 23	FM
1998 Feb 19	15 27	LQ
1998 Feb 26	17 26	NM
1998 Mar 05	08 41	FQ
1998 Mar 13	04 34	FM
1998 Mar 21	07 38	LQ
1998 Mar 28	03 13	NM
1998 Apr 03	20 18	FQ
1998 Apr 11	22 23	FM
1998 Apr 19	19 53	LQ
1998 Apr 26	11 41	NM
1998 May 03	10 04	FQ
1998 May 11	14 29	FM
1998 May 19	04 35	LQ
1998 May 25	19 32	NM
1998 Jun 02	01 45	FQ
1998 Jun 10	04 18	FM
1998 Jun 17	10 38	LQ
1998 Jun 24	03 50	NM
1998 Jul 01	18 43	FQ
1998 Jul 09	16 01	FM
1998 Jul 16	15 13	LQ
1998 Jul 23	13 44	NM
1998 Jul 31	12 05	FQ
1998 Aug 08	02 10	FM
1998 Aug 14	19 48	LQ
1998 Aug 22	02 03	NM
1998 Aug 30	05 06	FQ
1998 Sep 06	11 21	FM
1998 Sep 13	01 58	LQ
1998 Sep 20	17 01	NM
1998 Sep 28	21 11	FQ
1998 Oct 05	20 12	FM
1998 Oct 12	11 11	LQ
1998 Oct 20	10 09	NM
1998 Oct 28	11 46	FQ
1998 Nov 04	05 18	FM
1998 Nov 11	00 28	LQ
1998 Nov 19	04 27	NM
1998 Nov 27	00 23	FQ
1998 Dec 03	15 19	FM
1998 Dec 10	17 54	LQ
1998 Dec 18	22 42	NM
1998 Dec 26	10 46	FQ
1999 Jan 02	02 50	FM
1999 Jan 09	14 22	LQ
1999 Jan 17	15 46	NM
1999 Jan 24	19 15	FQ
1999 Jan 31	16 06	FM
1999 Feb 08	11 58	LQ
1999 Feb 16	06 39	NM
1999 Feb 23	02 43	FQ
1999 Mar 02	06 58	FM
1999 Mar 10	08 40	LQ
1999 Mar 17	18 48	NM
1999 Mar 24	10 18	FQ
1999 Mar 31	22 49	FM
1999 Apr 09	02 51	LQ
1999 Apr 16	04 22	NM
1999 Apr 22	19 02	FQ
1999 Apr 30	14 55	FM
1999 May 08	17 28	LQ
1999 May 15	12 05	NM
1999 May 22	05 34	FQ
1999 May 30	06 40	FM
1999 Jun 07	04 20	LQ
1999 Jun 13	19 03	NM
1999 Jun 20	18 13	FQ
1999 Jun 28	21 37	FM
1999 Jul 06	11 57	LQ
1999 Jul 13	02 24	NM
1999 Jul 20	09 00	FQ
1999 Jul 28	11 25	FM
1999 Aug 04	17 27	LQ
1999 Aug 11	11 08	NM
1999 Aug 19	01 47	FQ
1999 Aug 26	23 48	FM
1999 Sep 02	22 17	LQ
1999 Sep 09	22 02	NM
1999 Sep 17	20 06	FQ
1999 Sep 25	10 51	FM
1999 Oct 02	04 02	LQ
1999 Oct 09	11 34	NM
1999 Oct 17	15 00	FQ
1999 Oct 24	21 02	FM
1999 Oct 31	12 04	LQ
1999 Nov 08	03 53	NM
1999 Nov 16	09 03	FQ
1999 Nov 23	07 04	FM
1999 Nov 29	23 19	LQ
1999 Dec 07	22 32	NM
1999 Dec 16	00 50	FQ
1999 Dec 22	17 31	FM
1999 Dec 29	14 04	LQ
2000 Jan 06	18 14	NM
2000 Jan 14	13 34	FQ
2000 Jan 21	04 40	FM
2000 Jan 28	07 57	LQ
2000 Feb 05	13 03	NM
2000 Feb 12	23 21	FQ
2000 Feb 19	16 27	FM
2000 Feb 27	03 53	LQ
2000 Mar 06	05 17	NM
2000 Mar 13	06 59	FQ
2000 Mar 20	04 44	FM
2000 Mar 28	00 21	LQ
2000 Apr 04	18 12	NM
2000 Apr 11	13 30	FQ
2000 Apr 18	17 41	FM
2000 Apr 26	19 30	LQ
2000 May 04	04 12	NM
2000 May 10	20 00	FQ
2000 May 18	07 34	FM
2000 May 26	11 55	LQ
2000 Jun 02	12 14	NM
2000 Jun 09	03 29	FQ
2000 Jun 16	22 27	FM
2000 Jun 25	01 00	LQ
2000 Jul 01	19 20	NM
2000 Jul 08	12 53	FQ
2000 Jul 16	13 55	FM
2000 Jul 24	11 02	LQ
2000 Jul 31	02 25	NM
2000 Aug 07	01 02	FQ
2000 Aug 15	05 13	FM
2000 Aug 22	18 51	LQ
2000 Aug 29	10 19	NM
2000 Sep 05	16 27	FQ
2000 Sep 13	19 37	FM
2000 Sep 21	01 28	LQ
2000 Sep 27	19 53	NM
2000 Oct 05	10 59	FQ
2000 Oct 13	08 53	FM
2000 Oct 20	07 59	LQ
2000 Oct 27	07 58	NM
2000 Nov 04	07 27	FQ
2000 Nov 11	21 15	FM
2000 Nov 18	15 24	LQ
2000 Nov 25	23 11	NM
2000 Dec 04	03 55	FQ
2000 Dec 11	09 03	FM
2000 Dec 18	00 41	LQ
2000 Dec 25	17 22	NM
2001 Jan 02	22 31	FQ
2001 Jan 09	20 24	FM
2001 Jan 16	12 35	LQ
2001 Jan 24	13 07	NM
2001 Feb 01	14 02	FQ
2001 Feb 08	07 11	FM
2001 Feb 15	03 23	LQ
2001 Feb 23	08 21	NM
2001 Mar 03	02 03	FQ
2001 Mar 09	17 23	FM
2001 Mar 16	20 45	LQ
2001 Mar 25	01 21	NM
2001 Apr 01	10 49	FQ
2001 Apr 08	03 22	FM
2001 Apr 15	15 31	LQ
2001 Apr 23	15 26	NM
2001 Apr 30	17 08	FQ
2001 May 07	13 52	FM
2001 May 15	10 11	LQ
2001 May 23	02 46	NM
2001 May 29	22 09	FQ

2001 Jun 06	01 39	FM
2001 Jun 14	03 28	LQ
2001 Jun 21	11 58	NM
2001 Jun 28	03 19	FQ
2001 Jul 05	15 04	FM
2001 Jul 13	18 45	LQ
2001 Jul 20	19 44	NM
2001 Jul 27	10 08	FQ
2001 Aug 04	05 56	FM
2001 Aug 12	07 53	LQ
2001 Aug 19	02 55	NM
2001 Aug 25	19 55	FQ
2001 Sep 02	21 43	FM
2001 Sep 10	18 59	LQ
2001 Sep 17	10 27	NM
2001 Sep 24	09 31	FQ
2001 Oct 02	13 49	FM
2001 Oct 10	04 20	LQ
2001 Oct 16	19 23	NM
2001 Oct 24	02 58	FQ
2001 Nov 01	05 41	FM
2001 Nov 08	12 21	LQ
2001 Nov 15	06 40	NM
2001 Nov 22	23 21	FQ
2001 Nov 30	20 49	FM
2001 Dec 07	19 52	LQ
2001 Dec 14	20 47	NM
2001 Dec 22	20 56	FQ
2001 Dec 30	10 40	FM
2002 Jan 06	03 55	LQ
2002 Jan 13	13 29	NM
2002 Jan 21	17 46	FQ
2002 Jan 28	22 50	FM
2002 Feb 04	13 33	LQ
2002 Feb 12	07 41	NM
2002 Feb 20	12 02	FQ
2002 Feb 27	09 16	FM
2002 Mar 06	01 24	LQ
2002 Mar 14	02 02	NM
2002 Mar 22	02 28	FQ
2002 Mar 28	18 25	FM
2002 Apr 04	15 29	LQ
2002 Apr 12	19 21	NM
2002 Apr 20	12 48	FQ
2002 Apr 27	03 00	FM
2002 May 04	07 16	LQ
2002 May 12	10 45	NM
2002 May 19	19 42	FQ
2002 May 26	11 51	FM
2002 Jun 03	00 05	LQ
2002 Jun 10	23 46	NM
2002 Jun 18	00 29	FQ
2002 Jun 24	21 42	FM
2002 Jul 02	17 19	LQ
2002 Jul 10	10 26	NM
2002 Jul 17	04 47	FQ
2002 Jul 24	09 07	FM
2002 Aug 01	10 22	LQ
2002 Aug 08	19 15	NM
2002 Aug 15	10 12	FQ
2002 Aug 22	22 29	FM
2002 Aug 31	02 31	LQ
2002 Sep 07	03 10	NM
2002 Sep 13	18 08	FQ
2002 Sep 21	13 59	FM
2002 Sep 29	17 03	LQ
2002 Oct 06	11 17	NM
2002 Oct 13	05 33	FQ
2002 Oct 21	07 20	FM
2002 Oct 29	05 28	LQ
2002 Nov 04	20 34	NM
2002 Nov 11	20 52	FQ
2002 Nov 20	01 34	FM
2002 Nov 27	15 46	LQ
2002 Dec 04	07 34	NM
2002 Dec 11	15 48	FQ
2002 Dec 19	19 10	FM
2002 Dec 27	00 31	LQ
2003 Jan 02	20 23	NM
2003 Jan 10	13 15	FQ
2003 Jan 18	10 48	FM
2003 Jan 25	08 33	LQ
2003 Feb 01	10 48	NM
2003 Feb 09	11 11	FQ
2003 Feb 16	23 51	FM
2003 Feb 23	16 46	LQ
2003 Mar 03	02 35	NM
2003 Mar 11	07 15	FQ
2003 Mar 18	10 34	FM
2003 Mar 25	01 51	LQ
2003 Apr 01	19 19	NM
2003 Apr 09	23 40	FQ
2003 Apr 16	19 36	FM
2003 Apr 23	12 18	LQ
2003 May 01	12 15	NM
2003 May 09	11 53	FQ
2003 May 16	03 36	FM
2003 May 23	00 31	LQ
2003 May 31	04 20	NM
2003 Jun 07	20 28	FQ
2003 Jun 14	11 16	FM
2003 Jun 21	14 45	LQ
2003 Jun 29	18 39	NM
2003 Jul 07	02 32	FQ
2003 Jul 13	19 21	FM
2003 Jul 21	07 01	LQ
2003 Jul 29	06 53	NM
2003 Aug 05	07 28	FQ
2003 Aug 12	04 48	FM
2003 Aug 20	00 48	LQ
2003 Aug 27	17 26	NM
2003 Sep 03	12 34	FQ
2003 Sep 10	16 36	FM
2003 Sep 18	19 03	LQ
2003 Sep 26	03 09	NM
2003 Oct 02	19 09	FQ
2003 Oct 10	07 27	FM
2003 Oct 18	12 31	LQ
2003 Oct 25	12 50	NM
2003 Nov 01	04 24	FQ
2003 Nov 09	01 13	FM
2003 Nov 17	04 15	LQ
2003 Nov 23	22 59	NM
2003 Nov 30	17 16	FQ
2003 Dec 08	20 37	FM
2003 Dec 16	17 42	LQ
2003 Dec 23	09 43	NM
2003 Dec 30	10 03	FQ
2004 Jan 07	15 40	FM
2004 Jan 15	04 46	LQ
2004 Jan 21	21 05	NM
2004 Jan 29	06 03	FQ
2004 Feb 06	08 47	FM
2004 Feb 13	13 39	LQ
2004 Feb 20	09 18	NM
2004 Feb 28	03 24	FQ
2004 Mar 06	23 14	FM
2004 Mar 13	21 01	LQ
2004 Mar 20	22 41	NM
2004 Mar 28	23 48	FQ
2004 Apr 05	11 03	FM
2004 Apr 12	03 46	LQ
2004 Apr 19	13 21	NM
2004 Apr 27	17 32	FQ
2004 May 04	20 33	FM
2004 May 11	11 04	LQ
2004 May 19	04 52	NM
2004 May 27	07 57	FQ
2004 Jun 03	04 19	FM
2004 Jun 09	20 02	LQ
2004 Jun 17	20 27	NM
2004 Jun 25	19 08	FQ
2004 Jul 02	11 09	FM
2004 Jul 09	07 33	LQ
2004 Jul 17	11 24	NM
2004 Jul 25	03 37	FQ
2004 Jul 31	18 05	FM
2004 Aug 07	22 01	LQ
2004 Aug 16	01 24	NM
2004 Aug 23	10 12	FQ
2004 Aug 30	02 22	FM
2004 Sep 06	15 10	LQ
2004 Sep 14	14 29	NM
2004 Sep 21	15 53	FQ
2004 Sep 28	13 09	FM
2004 Oct 06	10 12	LQ
2004 Oct 14	02 48	NM
2004 Oct 20	21 59	FQ
2004 Oct 28	03 07	FM
2004 Nov 05	05 53	LQ
2004 Nov 12	14 27	NM
2004 Nov 19	05 50	FQ
2004 Nov 26	20 07	FM
2004 Dec 05	00 53	LQ
2004 Dec 12	01 29	NM
2004 Dec 18	16 40	FQ
2004 Dec 26	15 06	FM
2005 Jan 03	17 46	LQ
2005 Jan 10	12 03	NM
2005 Jan 17	06 57	FQ
2005 Jan 25	10 32	FM
2005 Feb 02	07 27	LQ
2005 Feb 08	22 28	NM
2005 Feb 16	00 16	FQ
2005 Feb 24	04 54	FM
2005 Mar 03	17 36	LQ
2005 Mar 10	09 10	NM
2005 Mar 17	19 19	FQ
2005 Mar 25	20 58	FM
2005 Apr 02	00 50	LQ
2005 Apr 08	20 32	NM
2005 Apr 16	14 37	FQ
2005 Apr 24	10 06	FM
2005 May 01	06 24	LQ
2005 May 08	08 45	NM
2005 May 16	08 56	FQ
2005 May 23	20 18	FM
2005 May 30	11 47	LQ
2005 Jun 06	21 55	NM
2005 Jun 15	01 22	FQ
2005 Jun 22	04 14	FM
2005 Jun 28	18 23	LQ
2005 Jul 06	12 02	NM
2005 Jul 14	15 20	FQ
2005 Jul 21	11 00	FM
2005 Jul 28	03 19	LQ
2005 Aug 05	03 05	NM
2005 Aug 13	02 38	FQ
2005 Aug 19	17 53	FM
2005 Aug 26	15 18	LQ
2005 Sep 03	18 45	NM
2005 Sep 11	11 37	FQ
2005 Sep 18	02 01	FM
2005 Sep 25	06 41	LQ
2005 Oct 03	10 28	NM
2005 Oct 10	19 01	FQ
2005 Oct 17	12 14	FM
2005 Oct 25	01 17	LQ
2005 Nov 02	01 24	NM
2005 Nov 09	01 57	FQ
2005 Nov 16	00 57	FM
2005 Nov 23	22 11	LQ
2005 Dec 01	15 01	NM
2005 Dec 08	09 36	FQ
2005 Dec 15	16 15	FM
2005 Dec 23	19 36	LQ
2005 Dec 31	03 12	NM
2006 Jan 06	18 56	FQ
2006 Jan 14	09 48	FM
2006 Jan 22	15 14	LQ
2006 Jan 29	14 14	NM
2006 Feb 05	06 29	FQ
2006 Feb 13	04 44	FM
2006 Feb 21	07 17	LQ
2006 Feb 28	00 31	NM
2006 Mar 06	20 16	FQ
2006 Mar 14	23 35	FM
2006 Mar 22	19 10	LQ
2006 Mar 29	10 15	NM
2006 Apr 05	12 01	FQ
2006 Apr 13	16 40	FM
2006 Apr 21	03 28	LQ
2006 Apr 27	19 44	NM
2006 May 05	05 13	FQ
2006 May 13	06 51	FM
2006 May 20	09 20	LQ
2006 May 27	05 25	NM
2006 Jun 03	23 06	FQ
2006 Jun 11	18 03	FM
2006 Jun 18	14 08	LQ
2006 Jun 25	16 05	NM
2006 Jul 03	16 37	FQ
2006 Jul 11	03 02	FM
2006 Jul 17	19 12	LQ
2006 Jul 25	04 31	NM
2006 Aug 02	08 46	FQ
2006 Aug 09	10 54	FM
2006 Aug 16	01 51	LQ
2006 Aug 23	19 10	NM
2006 Aug 31	22 56	FQ
2006 Sep 07	18 42	FM
2006 Sep 14	11 15	LQ
2006 Sep 22	11 45	NM
2006 Sep 30	11 04	FQ
2006 Oct 07	03 13	FM
2006 Oct 14	00 25	LQ
2006 Oct 22	05 14	NM
2006 Oct 29	21 25	FQ
2006 Nov 05	12 58	FM
2006 Nov 12	17 45	LQ
2006 Nov 20	22 18	NM
2006 Nov 28	06 29	FQ
2006 Dec 05	00 25	FM
2006 Dec 12	14 32	LQ
2006 Dec 20	14 01	NM
2006 Dec 27	14 48	FQ
2007 Jan 03	13 57	FM
2007 Jan 11	12 44	LQ
2007 Jan 19	04 01	NM
2007 Jan 25	23 01	FQ
2007 Feb 02	05 45	FM
2007 Feb 10	09 51	LQ
2007 Feb 17	16 14	NM
2007 Feb 24	07 56	FQ
2007 Mar 03	23 17	FM
2007 Mar 12	03 54	LQ
2007 Mar 19	02 42	NM
2007 Mar 25	18 16	FQ
2007 Apr 02	17 15	FM
2007 Apr 10	18 04	LQ
2007 Apr 17	11 36	NM
2007 Apr 24	06 35	FQ
2007 May 02	10 09	FM
2007 May 10	04 27	LQ
2007 May 16	19 27	NM
2007 May 23	21 02	FQ
2007 Jun 01	01 04	FM
2007 Jun 08	11 43	LQ
2007 Jun 15	03 13	NM
2007 Jun 22	13 15	FQ
2007 Jun 30	13 49	FM
2007 Jul 07	16 53	LQ
2007 Jul 14	12 04	NM
2007 Jul 22	06 29	FQ
2007 Jul 30	00 48	FM
2007 Aug 05	21 19	LQ
2007 Aug 12	23 02	NM
2007 Aug 20	23 54	FQ
2007 Aug 28	10 35	FM
2007 Sep 04	02 32	LQ
2007 Sep 11	12 44	NM
2007 Sep 19	16 48	FQ
2007 Sep 26	19 45	FM
2007 Oct 03	10 06	LQ
2007 Oct 11	05 01	NM
2007 Oct 19	08 33	FQ
2007 Oct 26	04 51	FM
2007 Nov 01	21 18	LQ
2007 Nov 09	23 03	NM
2007 Nov 17	22 32	FQ
2007 Nov 24	14 30	FM
2007 Dec 01	12 44	LQ
2007 Dec 09	17 40	NM
2007 Dec 17	10 17	FQ
2007 Dec 24	01 15	FM
2007 Dec 31	07 51	LQ
2008 Jan 08	11 37	NM
2008 Jan 15	19 46	FQ
2008 Jan 22	13 35	FM
2008 Jan 30	05 03	LQ
2008 Feb 07	03 44	NM
2008 Feb 14	03 33	FQ
2008 Feb 21	03 30	FM
2008 Feb 29	02 18	LQ
2008 Mar 07	17 14	NM
2008 Mar 14	10 45	FQ
2008 Mar 21	18 40	FM
2008 Mar 29	21 47	LQ
2008 Apr 06	03 55	NM
2008 Apr 12	18 32	FQ
2008 Apr 20	10 25	FM
2008 Apr 28	14 12	LQ
2008 May 05	12 18	NM
2008 May 12	03 47	FQ
2008 May 20	02 11	FM
2008 May 28	02 56	LQ
2008 Jun 03	19 22	NM
2008 Jun 10	15 03	FQ
2008 Jun 18	17 30	FM
2008 Jun 26	12 10	LQ
2008 Jul 03	02 18	NM
2008 Jul 10	04 35	FQ
2008 Jul 18	07 59	FM
2008 Jul 25	18 41	LQ
2008 Aug 01	10 12	NM
2008 Aug 08	20 20	FQ
2008 Aug 16	21 16	FM
2008 Aug 23	23 49	LQ
2008 Aug 30	19 58	NM
2008 Sep 07	14 04	FQ
2008 Sep 15	09 13	FM
2008 Sep 22	05 04	LQ
2008 Sep 29	08 12	NM
2008 Oct 07	09 04	FQ
2008 Oct 14	20 02	FM
2008 Oct 21	11 54	LQ
2008 Oct 28	23 14	NM
2008 Nov 06	04 03	FQ
2008 Nov 13	06 17	FM
2008 Nov 19	21 31	LQ
2008 Nov 27	16 54	NM
2008 Dec 05	21 25	FQ
2008 Dec 12	16 37	FM
2008 Dec 19	10 29	LQ
2008 Dec 27	12 22	NM
2009 Jan 04	11 56	FQ
2009 Jan 11	03 27	FM
2009 Jan 18	02 46	LQ
2009 Jan 26	07 55	NM
2009 Feb 02	23 13	FQ
2009 Feb 09	14 49	FM
2009 Feb 16	21 37	LQ
2009 Feb 25	01 35	NM
2009 Mar 04	07 46	FQ
2009 Mar 11	02 38	FM
2009 Mar 18	17 47	LQ
2009 Mar 26	16 06	NM
2009 Apr 02	14 34	FQ
2009 Apr 09	14 56	FM
2009 Apr 17	13 36	LQ
2009 Apr 25	03 22	NM
2009 May 01	20 44	FQ
2009 May 09	04 01	FM
2009 May 17	07 26	LQ
2009 May 24	12 11	NM
2009 May 31	03 22	FQ
2009 Jun 07	18 12	FM
2009 Jun 15	22 14	LQ
2009 Jun 22	19 35	NM
2009 Jun 29	11 28	FQ
2009 Jul 07	09 21	FM
2009 Jul 15	09 53	LQ
2009 Jul 22	02 34	NM
2009 Jul 28	22 00	FQ
2009 Aug 06	00 55	FM
2009 Aug 13	18 55	LQ
2009 Aug 20	10 01	NM
2009 Aug 27	11 42	FQ
2009 Sep 04	16 02	FM
2009 Sep 12	02 16	LQ
2009 Sep 18	18 44	NM
2009 Sep 26	04 50	FQ
2009 Oct 04	06 10	FM
2009 Oct 11	08 56	LQ
2009 Oct 18	05 33	NM
2009 Oct 26	00 42	FQ
2009 Nov 02	19 14	FM
2009 Nov 09	15 56	LQ
2009 Nov 16	19 14	NM
2009 Nov 24	21 39	FQ
2009 Dec 02	07 30	FM
2009 Dec 09	00 13	LQ
2009 Dec 16	12 02	NM
2009 Dec 24	17 36	FQ
2009 Dec 31	19 13	FM
2010 Jan 07	10 39	LQ
2010 Jan 15	07 11	NM
2010 Jan 23	10 53	FQ
2010 Jan 30	06 17	FM
2010 Feb 05	23 48	LQ
2010 Feb 14	02 51	NM
2010 Feb 22	00 42	FQ
2010 Feb 28	16 38	FM
2010 Mar 07	15 42	LQ
2010 Mar 15	21 01	NM
2010 Mar 23	11 00	FQ
2010 Mar 30	02 25	FM
2010 Apr 06	09 37	LQ
2010 Apr 14	12 29	NM
2010 Apr 21	18 20	FQ
2010 Apr 28	12 18	FM
2010 May 06	04 15	LQ
2010 May 14	01 04	NM
2010 May 20	23 42	FQ
2010 May 27	23 07	FM
2010 Jun 04	22 13	LQ
2010 Jun 12	11 14	NM
2010 Jun 19	04 29	FQ
2010 Jun 26	11 30	FM
2010 Jul 04	14 35	LQ
2010 Jul 11	19 40	NM
2010 Jul 18	10 10	FQ
2010 Jul 26	01 36	FM
2010 Aug 03	04 58	LQ
2010 Aug 10	03 08	NM
2010 Aug 16	18 14	FQ
2010 Aug 24	17 04	FM
2010 Sep 01	17 22	LQ
2010 Sep 08	10 29	NM
2010 Sep 15	05 50	FQ
2010 Sep 23	09 17	FM
2010 Oct 01	03 52	LQ
2010 Oct 07	18 44	NM
2010 Oct 14	21 27	FQ
2010 Oct 23	01 36	FM
2010 Oct 30	12 46	LQ
2010 Nov 06	04 52	NM
2010 Nov 13	16 38	FQ
2010 Nov 21	17 27	FM
2010 Nov 28	20 36	LQ
2010 Dec 05	17 36	NM
2010 Dec 13	13 59	FQ
2010 Dec 21	08 13	FM
2010 Dec 28	04 18	LQ
2011 Jan 04	09 02	NM
2011 Jan 12	11 31	FQ
2011 Jan 19	21 21	FM
2011 Jan 26	12 57	LQ
2011 Feb 03	02 30	NM
2011 Feb 11	07 18	FQ
2011 Feb 18	08 35	FM
2011 Feb 24	23 26	LQ
2011 Mar 04	20 46	NM
2011 Mar 12	23 45	FQ
2011 Mar 19	18 10	FM
2011 Mar 26	12 07	LQ
2011 Apr 03	14 32	NM
2011 Apr 11	12 05	FQ
2011 Apr 18	02 44	FM
2011 Apr 25	02 47	LQ
2011 May 03	06 51	NM
2011 May 10	20 33	FQ
2011 May 17	11 08	FM
2011 May 24	18 52	LQ
2011 Jun 01	21 02	NM
2011 Jun 09	02 10	FQ
2011 Jun 15	20 13	FM
2011 Jun 23	11 48	LQ
2011 Jul 01	08 54	NM
2011 Jul 08	06 29	FQ
2011 Jul 15	06 39	FM
2011 Jul 23	05 02	LQ
2011 Jul 30	18 40	NM
2011 Aug 06	11 08	FQ
2011 Aug 13	18 57	FM
2011 Aug 21	21 54	LQ
2011 Aug 29	03 04	NM
2011 Sep 04	17 39	FQ
2011 Sep 12	09 26	FM
2011 Sep 20	13 38	LQ
2011 Sep 27	11 08	NM

Moon Charts
124
Moon Charts

2011 Oct 04	03 15	FQ
2011 Oct 12	02 06	FM
2011 Oct 20	03 30	LQ
2011 Oct 26	19 55	NM
2011 Nov 02	16 38	FQ
2011 Nov 10	20 16	FM
2011 Nov 18	15 09	LQ
2011 Nov 25	06 09	NM
2011 Dec 02	09 52	FQ
2011 Dec 10	14 36	FM
2011 Dec 18	00 47	LQ
2011 Dec 24	18 06	NM
2012 Jan 01	06 14	FQ
2012 Jan 09	07 30	FM
2012 Jan 16	09 08	LQ
2012 Jan 23	07 39	NM
2012 Jan 31	04 09	FQ
2012 Feb 07	21 54	FM
2012 Feb 14	17 04	LQ
2012 Feb 21	22 34	NM
2012 Mar 01	01 21	FQ
2012 Mar 08	09 39	FM
2012 Mar 15	01 25	LQ
2012 Mar 22	14 37	NM
2012 Mar 30	19 40	FQ
2012 Apr 06	19 18	FM
2012 Apr 13	10 49	LQ
2012 Apr 21	07 18	NM
2012 Apr 29	09 57	FQ
2012 May 06	03 35	FM
2012 May 12	21 47	LQ
2012 May 20	23 47	NM
2012 May 28	20 16	FQ
2012 Jun 04	11 11	FM
2012 Jun 11	10 41	LQ
2012 Jun 19	15 02	NM
2012 Jun 27	03 30	FQ
2012 Jul 03	18 52	FM
2012 Jul 11	01 48	LQ
2012 Jul 19	04 24	NM
2012 Jul 26	08 56	FQ
2012 Aug 02	03 27	FM
2012 Aug 09	18 55	LQ
2012 Aug 17	15 54	NM
2012 Aug 24	13 53	FQ
2012 Aug 31	13 58	FM
2012 Sep 08	13 15	LQ
2012 Sep 16	02 10	NM
2012 Sep 22	19 41	FQ
2012 Sep 30	03 18	FM
2012 Oct 08	07 33	LQ
2012 Oct 15	12 02	NM
2012 Oct 22	03 32	FQ
2012 Oct 29	19 49	FM
2012 Nov 07	00 35	LQ
2012 Nov 13	22 08	NM
2012 Nov 20	14 31	FQ
2012 Nov 28	14 46	FM
2012 Dec 06	15 31	LQ
2012 Dec 13	08 41	NM
2012 Dec 20	05 19	FQ
2012 Dec 28	10 21	FM
2013 Jan 05	03 58	LQ
2013 Jan 11	19 43	NM
2013 Jan 18	23 45	FQ
2013 Jan 27	04 38	FM
2013 Feb 03	13 56	LQ
2013 Feb 10	07 20	NM
2013 Feb 17	20 30	FQ
2013 Feb 25	20 26	FM
2013 Mar 04	21 53	LQ
2013 Mar 11	19 51	NM
2013 Mar 19	17 26	FQ
2013 Mar 27	09 27	FM
2013 Apr 03	04 36	LQ
2013 Apr 10	09 35	NM
2013 Apr 18	12 31	FQ
2013 Apr 25	19 57	FM
2013 May 02	11 14	LQ
2013 May 10	00 28	NM
2013 May 18	04 34	FQ
2013 May 25	04 25	FM
2013 May 31	18 58	LQ
2013 Jun 08	15 56	NM
2013 Jun 16	17 23	FQ
2013 Jun 23	11 32	FM
2013 Jun 30	04 53	LQ
2013 Jul 08	07 14	NM
2013 Jul 16	03 18	FQ
2013 Jul 22	18 15	FM
2013 Jul 29	17 43	LQ
2013 Aug 06	21 50	NM
2013 Aug 14	10 56	FQ
2013 Aug 21	01 44	FM
2013 Aug 28	09 35	LQ
2013 Sep 05	11 36	NM
2013 Sep 12	17 08	FQ
2013 Sep 19	11 13	FM
2013 Sep 27	03 55	LQ
2013 Oct 05	00 34	NM
2013 Oct 11	23 02	FQ
2013 Oct 18	23 37	FM
2013 Oct 26	23 40	LQ
2013 Nov 03	12 50	NM
2013 Nov 10	05 57	FQ
2013 Nov 17	15 16	FM
2013 Nov 25	19 27	LQ
2013 Dec 03	00 22	NM
2013 Dec 09	15 12	FQ
2013 Dec 17	09 28	FM
2013 Dec 25	13 47	LQ
2014 Jan 01	11 14	NM
2014 Jan 08	03 39	FQ
2014 Jan 16	04 52	FM
2014 Jan 24	05 19	LQ
2014 Jan 30	21 38	NM
2014 Feb 06	19 22	FQ
2014 Feb 14	23 53	FM
2014 Feb 22	17 15	LQ
2014 Mar 01	07 59	NM
2014 Mar 08	13 27	FQ
2014 Mar 16	17 08	FM
2014 Mar 24	01 46	LQ
2014 Mar 30	18 44	NM
2014 Apr 07	08 30	FQ
2014 Apr 15	07 42	FM
2014 Apr 22	07 51	LQ
2014 Apr 29	06 14	NM
2014 May 07	03 15	FQ
2014 May 14	19 16	FM
2014 May 21	12 59	LQ
2014 May 28	18 40	NM
2014 Jun 05	20 39	FQ
2014 Jun 13	04 11	FM
2014 Jun 19	18 39	LQ
2014 Jun 27	08 08	NM
2014 Jul 05	11 59	FQ
2014 Jul 12	11 25	FM
2014 Jul 19	02 08	LQ
2014 Jul 26	22 42	NM
2014 Aug 04	00 49	FQ
2014 Aug 10	18 09	FM
2014 Aug 17	12 26	LQ
2014 Aug 25	14 13	NM
2014 Sep 02	11 11	FQ
2014 Sep 09	01 38	FM
2014 Sep 16	02 05	LQ
2014 Sep 24	06 14	NM
2014 Oct 01	19 32	FQ
2014 Oct 08	10 50	FM
2014 Oct 15	19 12	LQ
2014 Oct 23	21 56	NM
2014 Oct 31	02 48	FQ
2014 Nov 06	22 23	FM
2014 Nov 14	15 15	LQ
2014 Nov 22	12 32	NM
2014 Nov 29	10 06	FQ
2014 Dec 06	12 27	FM
2014 Dec 14	12 51	LQ
2014 Dec 22	01 36	NM
2014 Dec 28	18 31	FQ
2015 Jan 05	04 53	FM
2015 Jan 13	09 46	LQ
2015 Jan 20	13 13	NM
2015 Jan 27	04 48	FQ
2015 Feb 03	23 09	FM
2015 Feb 12	03 50	LQ
2015 Feb 18	23 47	NM
2015 Feb 25	17 14	FQ
2015 Mar 05	18 05	FM
2015 Mar 13	17 48	LQ
2015 Mar 20	09 36	NM
2015 Mar 27	07 42	FQ
2015 Apr 04	12 05	FM
2015 Apr 12	03 44	LQ
2015 Apr 18	18 57	NM
2015 Apr 25	23 55	FQ
2015 May 04	03 42	FM
2015 May 11	10 36	LQ
2015 May 18	04 13	NM
2015 May 25	17 19	FQ
2015 Jun 02	16 19	FM
2015 Jun 09	15 42	LQ
2015 Jun 16	14 05	NM
2015 Jun 24	11 02	FQ
2015 Jul 02	02 19	FM
2015 Jul 08	20 24	LQ
2015 Jul 16	01 24	NM
2015 Jul 24	04 04	FQ
2015 Jul 31	10 43	FM
2015 Aug 07	02 02	LQ
2015 Aug 14	14 53	NM
2015 Aug 22	19 31	FQ
2015 Aug 29	18 35	FM
2015 Sep 05	09 54	LQ
2015 Sep 13	06 41	NM
2015 Sep 21	08 59	FQ
2015 Sep 28	02 50	FM
2015 Oct 04	21 06	LQ
2015 Oct 13	00 05	NM
2015 Oct 20	20 31	FQ
2015 Oct 27	12 05	FM
2015 Nov 03	12 24	LQ
2015 Nov 11	17 47	NM
2015 Nov 19	06 27	FQ
2015 Nov 25	22 44	FM
2015 Dec 03	07 40	LQ
2015 Dec 11	10 29	NM
2015 Dec 18	15 14	FQ
2015 Dec 25	11 11	FM
2016 Jan 02	05 30	LQ
2016 Jan 10	01 30	NM
2016 Jan 16	23 26	FQ
2016 Jan 24	01 46	FM
2016 Feb 01	03 28	LQ
2016 Feb 08	14 39	NM
2016 Feb 15	07 46	FQ
2016 Feb 22	18 20	FM
2016 Mar 01	23 10	LQ
2016 Mar 09	01 54	NM
2016 Mar 15	17 03	FQ
2016 Mar 23	12 01	FM
2016 Mar 31	15 17	LQ
2016 Apr 07	11 23	NM
2016 Apr 14	03 59	FQ
2016 Apr 22	05 23	FM
2016 Apr 30	03 28	LQ
2016 May 06	19 29	NM
2016 May 13	17 02	FQ
2016 May 21	21 14	FM
2016 May 29	12 12	LQ
2016 Jun 05	02 59	NM
2016 Jun 12	08 10	FQ
2016 Jun 20	11 02	FM
2016 Jun 27	18 18	LQ
2016 Jul 04	11 01	NM
2016 Jul 12	00 52	FQ
2016 Jul 19	22 56	FM
2016 Jul 26	22 59	LQ
2016 Aug 02	20 44	NM
2016 Aug 10	18 21	FQ
2016 Aug 18	09 26	FM
2016 Aug 25	03 41	LQ
2016 Sep 01	09 03	NM
2016 Sep 09	11 49	FQ
2016 Sep 16	19 05	FM
2016 Sep 23	09 56	LQ
2016 Oct 01	00 11	NM
2016 Oct 09	04 33	FQ
2016 Oct 16	04 23	FM
2016 Oct 22	19 14	LQ
2016 Oct 30	17 38	NM
2016 Nov 07	19 51	FQ
2016 Nov 14	13 52	FM
2016 Nov 21	08 33	LQ
2016 Nov 29	12 18	NM
2016 Dec 07	09 03	FQ
2016 Dec 14	00 05	FM
2016 Dec 21	01 55	LQ
2016 Dec 29	06 53	NM
2017 Jan 05	19 47	FQ
2017 Jan 12	11 34	FM
2017 Jan 19	22 13	LQ
2017 Jan 28	00 07	NM
2017 Feb 04	04 19	FQ
2017 Feb 11	00 33	FM
2017 Feb 18	19 33	LQ
2017 Feb 26	14 58	NM
2017 Mar 05	11 32	FQ
2017 Mar 12	14 54	FM
2017 Mar 20	15 58	LQ
2017 Mar 28	02 57	NM
2017 Apr 03	18 39	FQ
2017 Apr 11	06 08	FM
2017 Apr 19	09 56	LQ
2017 Apr 26	12 16	NM
2017 May 03	02 47	FQ
2017 May 10	21 42	FM
2017 May 19	00 33	LQ
2017 May 25	19 44	NM
2017 Jun 01	12 42	FQ
2017 Jun 09	13 09	FM
2017 Jun 17	11 32	LQ
2017 Jun 24	02 30	NM
2017 Jul 01	00 51	FQ
2017 Jul 09	04 06	FM
2017 Jul 16	19 25	LQ
2017 Jul 23	09 45	NM
2017 Jul 30	15 23	FQ
2017 Aug 07	18 10	FM
2017 Aug 15	01 15	LQ
2017 Aug 21	18 30	NM
2017 Aug 29	08 13	FQ
2017 Sep 06	07 03	FM
2017 Sep 13	06 25	LQ
2017 Sep 20	05 30	NM
2017 Sep 28	02 53	FQ
2017 Oct 05	18 40	FM
2017 Oct 12	12 25	LQ
2017 Oct 19	19 12	NM
2017 Oct 27	22 22	FQ
2017 Nov 04	05 23	FM
2017 Nov 10	20 36	LQ
2017 Nov 18	11 42	NM
2017 Nov 26	17 03	FQ
2017 Dec 03	15 47	FM
2017 Dec 10	07 51	LQ
2017 Dec 18	06 30	NM
2017 Dec 26	09 20	FQ
2018 Jan 02	02 24	FM
2018 Jan 08	22 25	LQ
2018 Jan 17	02 17	NM
2018 Jan 24	22 20	FQ
2018 Jan 31	13 26	FM
2018 Feb 07	15 54	LQ
2018 Feb 15	21 05	NM
2018 Feb 23	08 09	FQ
2018 Mar 02	00 51	FM
2018 Mar 09	11 20	LQ
2018 Mar 17	13 11	NM
2018 Mar 24	15 35	FQ
2018 Mar 31	12 37	FM
2018 Apr 08	07 17	LQ
2018 Apr 16	01 57	NM
2018 Apr 22	21 45	FQ
2018 Apr 30	00 58	FM
2018 May 08	02 08	LQ
2018 May 15	11 48	NM
2018 May 22	03 49	FQ
2018 May 29	14 19	FM
2018 Jun 06	18 31	LQ
2018 Jun 13	19 43	NM
2018 Jun 20	10 51	FQ
2018 Jun 28	04 53	FM
2018 Jul 06	07 50	LQ
2018 Jul 13	02 47	NM
2018 Jul 19	19 52	FQ
2018 Jul 27	20 20	FM
2018 Aug 04	18 18	LQ
2018 Aug 11	09 57	NM
2018 Aug 18	07 48	FQ
2018 Aug 26	11 56	FM
2018 Sep 03	02 37	LQ
2018 Sep 09	18 01	NM
2018 Sep 16	23 15	FQ
2018 Sep 25	02 52	FM
f2018 Oct 02	09 45	LQ
2018 Oct 09	03 47	NM
2018 Oct 16	18 01	FQ
2018 Oct 24	16 45	FM
2018 Oct 31	16 40	LQ
2018 Nov 07	16 02	NM
2018 Nov 15	14 54	FQ
2018 Nov 23	05 39	FM
2018 Nov 30	00 19	LQ
2018 Dec 07	07 20	NM
2018 Dec 15	11 49	FQ
2018 Dec 22	17 48	FM
2018 Dec 29	09 34	LQ
2019 Jan 06	01 28	NM
2019 Jan 14	06 45	FQ
2019 Jan 21	05 16	FM
2019 Jan 27	21 10	LQ
2019 Feb 04	21 03	NM
2019 Feb 12	22 26	FQ
2019 Feb 19	15 53	FM
2019 Feb 26	11 27	LQ
2019 Mar 06	16 04	NM
2019 Mar 14	10 27	FQ
2019 Mar 21	01 43	FM
2019 Mar 28	04 09	LQ
2019 Apr 05	08 50	NM
2019 Apr 12	19 06	FQ
2019 Apr 19	11 12	FM
2019 Apr 26	22 18	LQ
2019 May 04	22 45	NM
2019 May 12	01 12	FQ
2019 May 18	21 11	FM
2019 May 26	16 33	LQ
2019 Jun 03	10 02	NM
2019 Jun 10	05 59	FQ
2019 Jun 17	08 30	FM
2019 Jun 25	09 46	LQ
2019 Jul 02	19 16	NM
2019 Jul 09	10 55	FQ
2019 Jul 16	21 38	FM
2019 Jul 25	01 18	LQ
2019 Aug 01	03 12	NM
2019 Aug 07	17 31	FQ
2019 Aug 15	12 29	FM
2019 Aug 23	14 56	LQ
2019 Aug 30	10 37	NM
2019 Sep 06	03 10	FQ
2019 Sep 14	04 32	FM
2019 Sep 22	02 41	LQ
2019 Sep 28	18 26	NM
2019 Oct 05	16 47	FQ
2019 Oct 13	21 08	FM
2019 Oct 21	12 39	LQ
2019 Oct 28	03 38	NM
2019 Nov 04	10 23	FQ
2019 Nov 12	13 34	FM
2019 Nov 19	21 11	LQ
2019 Nov 26	15 05	NM
2019 Dec 04	06 58	FQ
2019 Dec 12	05 12	FM
2019 Dec 19	04 57	LQ
2019 Dec 26	05 13	NM
2020 Jan 03	04 45	FQ
2020 Jan 10	19 21	FM
2020 Jan 17	12 58	LQ
2020 Jan 24	21 42	NM
2020 Feb 02	01 41	FQ
2020 Feb 09	07 33	FM
2020 Feb 15	22 17	LQ
2020 Feb 23	15 32	NM
2020 Mar 02	19 57	FQ
2020 Mar 09	17 47	FM
2020 Mar 16	09 34	LQ
2020 Mar 24	09 28	NM
2020 Apr 01	10 21	FQ
2020 Apr 08	02 35	FM
2020 Apr 14	22 56	LQ
2020 Apr 23	02 26	NM
2020 Apr 30	20 38	FQ
2020 May 07	10 45	FM
2020 May 14	14 02	LQ
2020 May 22	17 39	NM
2020 May 30	03 30	FQ
2020 Jun 05	19 12	FM
2020 Jun 13	06 23	LQ
2020 Jun 21	06 41	NM
2020 Jun 28	08 15	FQ
2020 Jul 05	04 44	FM
2020 Jul 12	23 29	LQ
2020 Jul 20	17 33	NM
2020 Jul 27	12 32	FQ
2020 Aug 03	15 58	FM
2020 Aug 11	16 44	LQ
2020 Aug 19	02 41	NM
2020 Aug 25	17 57	FQ
2020 Sep 02	05 22	FM
2020 Sep 10	09 25	LQ
2020 Sep 17	11 00	NM
2020 Sep 24	01 55	FQ
2020 Oct 01	21 05	FM
2020 Oct 10	00 39	LQ
2020 Oct 16	19 31	NM
2020 Oct 23	13 23	FQ
2020 Oct 31	14 49	FM
2020 Nov 08	13 46	LQ
2020 Nov 15	05 07	NM
2020 Nov 22	04 45	FQ
2020 Nov 30	09 29	FM
2020 Dec 08	00 36	LQ
2020 Dec 14	16 16	NM
2020 Dec 21	23 41	FQ
2020 Dec 30	03 28	FM

ECLIPSE TABLES

SOLAR ECLIPSES

FOR THE YEARS 1920–2020

Year	Date	Time:GMT	Sign
1920	May 18	06:25	TAU
	Nov 10	18:05	SCO
1921	Apr 08	09:05	ARI
	Oct 01	12:26	LIB
1922	Mar 28	13:03	ARI
	Sep 21	04:38	VIR
1923	Mar 17	12:51	PIS
	Sep 10	20:52	VIR
1924	Mar 05	15:58	PIS
	Jul 31	19:42	LEO
	Aug 30	08:37	VIR
1925	Jan 24	14:45	AQU
	Jul 20	21:40	CAN
1926	Jan 14	06:34	CAP
	Jul 09	23:06	CAN
1927	Jan 03	20:28	CAP
	Jun 29	06:32	CAN
	Dec 24	04:13	CAP
1928	May 19	13:14	TAU
	Jun 17	20:42	GEM
	Nov 12	09:35	SCO
1929	May 09	06:07	TAU
	Nov 01	12:01	SCO
1930	Apr 28	19:08	TAU
	Oct 21	21:47	LIB
1931	Apr 18	01:00	ARI
	Sep 12	04:26	VIR
	Oct 11	13:06	LIB
1932	Mar 07	07:44	PIS
	Aug 31	19:54	VIR
1933	Feb 24	12:44	PIS
	Aug 21	05:48	LEO
1934	Feb 14	00:43	AQU
	Aug 10	08:45	LEO
1935	Jan 05	05:20	CAP
	Feb 03	16:27	AQU
	Jun 30	19:44	CAN
	Jul 30	09:32	LEO
	Dec 25	17:49	CAP
1936	Jun 19	05:14	GEM
	Dec 13	23:25	SAG
1937	Jun 08	20:43	GEM
	Dec 02	23:11	SAG
1938	May 29	13:59	GEM
	Nov 22	00:05	SCO
1939	Apr 19	16:35	ARI
	Oct 12	20:30	LIB
1940	Apr 07	20:18	ARI
	Oct 01	12:41	LIB
1941	Mar 27	20:14	ARI
	Sep 21	04:38	VIR
1942	Mar 16	23:50	PIS
	Aug 12	02:28	LEO
	Sep 10	15:33	VIR
1943	Feb 04	23:29	AQU
	Aug 01	04:08	LEO
1944	Jan 25	15:24	AQU
	Jul 20	05:42	CAN
1945	Jan 14	05:06	CAP
	Jul 09	13:35	CAN
1946	Jan 03	12:30	CAP
	May 30	20:49	GEM
	Jun 29	04:06	CAN
	Nov 23	17:24	SAG
1947	May 20	13:44	TAU
	Nov 12	20:01	SCO
1948	May 09	02:30	TAU
	Nov 01	06:03	SCO
1949	Apr 28	08:02	TAU
	Oct 21	21:23	LIB
1950	Mar 18	15:20	PIS
	Sep 12	03:29	VIR
1951	Mar 07	20:51	PIS
	Sep 01	12:50	VIR
1952	Feb 25	09:16	PIS
	Aug 20	15:20	LEO
1953	Feb 14	01:10	AQU
	Jul 11	02:28	CAN
	Aug 09	16:10	LEO
1954	Jan 05	02:21	CAP
	Jun 30	12:26	CAN
	Dec 25	07:33	CAP
1955	Jun 20	04:12	GEM
	Dec 14	07:07	SAG
1956	Jun 08	21:29	GEM
	Dec 02	08:13	SAG
1957	Apr 29	23:54	TAU
	Oct 23	04:43	LIB
1958	Apr 19	03:23	ARI
	Oct 12	20:52	LIB
1959	Apr 08	03:29	ARI
	Oct 02	12:31	LIB
1960	Mar 27	07:37	ARI
	Sep 20	23:12	VIR
1961	Feb 15	08:10	AQU
	Aug 11	10:36	LEO
1962	Feb 05	00:10	AQU
	Jul 31	12:24	LEO
1963	Jan 25	13:42	AQU
	Jul 20	20:43	CAN
1964	Jan 14	20:43	CAP
	Jun 10	04:22	GEM
	Jul 09	11:31	CAN
	Dec 04	01:18	SAG
1965	May 30	21:13	GEM
	Nov 23	04:10	SAG
1966	May 20	09:42	TAU
	Nov 12	14:26	SCO
1967	May 09	14:55	TAU
	Nov 02	05:48	SCO
1968	Mar 28	22:48	ARI
	Sep 22	11:08	VIR
1969	Mar 18	04:51	PIS
	Sep 11	19:56	VIR
1970	Mar 07	17:42	PIS
	Aug 31	22:01	VIR
1971	Feb 25	09:48	PIS
	Jul 22	09:15	CAN
	Aug 20	22:53	LEO
1972	Jan 18	10:52	CAP
	Jul 10	19:39	CAN
1973	Jan 04	15:42	CAP
	Jun 30	11:39	CAN
	Dec 24	15:07	CAP
1974	Jun 20	04:56	GEM
	Dec 13	16:25	SAG
1975	May 11	07:05	TAU
	Nov 03	13:05	SCO
1976	Apr 29	10:19	TAU
	Oct 23	05:10	LIB
1977	Apr 18	10:35	ARI
	Oct 12	20:31	LIB
1978	Apr 07	15:15	ARI
	Oct 02	06:41	LIB
1979	Feb 26	16:45	PIS
	Aug 22	17:10	LEO
1980	Feb 16	08:51	AQU
	Aug 10	19:09	LEO
1981	Feb 04	22:14	AQU
	Jul 31	03:52	LEO
1982	Jan 25	04:56	AQU
	Jun 21	11:52	GEM
	Jul 20	18:57	CAN
	Dec 15	09:18	SAG
1983	Jun 11	04:37	GEM
	Dec 04	12:26	SAG
1984	May 30	16:48	GEM
	Nov 22	22:57	SAG
1985	May 19	21:41	TAU
	Nov 12	14:20	SCO
1986	Apr 09	06:08	ARI
	Oct 03	18:55	LIB
1987	Mar 29	12:46	ARI
	Sep 23	03:08	VIR
1988	Mar 18	02:02	PIS
	Sep 11	04:49	VIR
1989	Mar 07	18:19	PIS
	Aug 31	05:45	VIR
1990	Jan 26	19:20	AQU
	Jul 22	02:54	CAN
1991	Jan 15	23:50	CAP
	Jul 11	19:06	CAN
1992	Jan 04	23:10	CAP
	Jun 30	12:18	CAN
	Dec 24	00:43	CAP
1993	May 21	14:07	GEM
	Nov 13	21:34	SCO
1994	May 10	17:07	TAU
	Nov 03	13:35	SCO
1995	Apr 29	17:36	SCO
	Oct 24	04:36	SCO
1996	Apr 17	22:49	ARI
	Oct 12	14:14	LIB
1997	Mar 09	01:15	PIS
	Sep 01	23:52	VIR
1998	Feb 26	17:26	PIS
	Aug 22	02:03	LEO
1999	Feb 16	06:39	AQU
	Aug 11	11:09	LEO
2000	Feb 05	13:03	AQU
	Jul 01	19:20	CAN
	Jul 31	02:25	LEO
	Dec 25	17:22	CAP
2001	Jun 21	12:04	CAN
	Dec 14	20:53	SAG
2002	Jun 10	23:48	GEM
	Dec 04	07:35	SAG
2003	May 31	04:21	GEM
	Nov 23	23:00	SAG
2004	Apr 19	13:22	ARI
	Oct 14	02:49	LIB
2005	Apr 08	20:33	ARI
	Oct 03	10:29	LIB
2006	Apr 29	10:18	ARI
	Sep 22	11:46	VIR
2007	Mar 19	02:44	PIS
	Sep 11	12:45	VIR
2008	Feb 07	03:46	AQU
	Aug 01	10:14	LEO
2009	Jan 26	07:56	AQU
	Jul 22	02:36	CAN
2010	Jan 15	07:12	CAP
	Jul 11	19:42	CAN
2011	Jan 04	09:04	CAP
	Jun 01	21:04	GEM
	Jul 01	08:55	CAN
	Nov 25	06:11	SAG
2012	May 20	23:48	GEM
	Nov 13	22:09	SCO
2013	May 10	00:30	TAU
	Nov 03	12:51	SCO
2014	Apr 29	06:15	TAU
	Oct 23	21:58	SCO
2015	Mar 20	09:37	PIS
	Sep 13	06:42	VIR
2016	Mar 09	01:56	PIS
	Sep 01	09:04	VIR
2017	Feb 26	14:59	PIS
	Aug 21	18:31	LEO
2018	Feb 15	21:06	AQU
	Jul 13	02:49	CAN
	Aug 11	09:59	LEO
2019	Jan 06	01:29	CAP
	Jul 02	18:17	CAN
	Dec 26	05:14	CAP
2020	Jun 21	06:43	CAN
	Dec 14	16:18	SAG

Moon Charts

ECLIPSE TABLES

LUNAR ECLIPSES

FOR THE YEARS 1920–2020

Year	Date	Time:GMT	Sign
1920	May 03	01.47	SCO
	Oct 27	14.11	TAU
1921	Apr 22	07.49	SCO
	Oct 16	22.59	ARI
1922	Mar 13	11.14	VIR
	Apr 11	20.43	LIB
	Oct 08	00.58	ARI
1923	Mar 03	03.23	VIR
	Aug 26	10.29	PIS
1924	Feb 20	18.07	VIR
	Aug 14	20.19	AQU
1925	Feb 08	21.49	LEO
	Aug 04	11.59	AQU
1926	Jan 28	21.35	LEO
	Jun 25	21:13	CAP
	Jul 25	05.13	AQU
	Dec 19	08.09	GEM
1927	Jun 15	08.19	SAG
	Dec 08	17.32	GEM
1928	Jun 03	12.13	SAG
	Nov 27	09.05	GEM
1929	May 23	12.50	SAG
	Nov 17	00.14	TAU
1930	Apr 13	05.48	LIB
	Oct 07	18.55	ARI
1931	Apr 02	20.05	LIB
	Sep 28	19.45	ARI
1932	Mar 22	12.37	LIB
	Sep 14	21.08	PIS
1933	Feb 10	13.00	LEO
	Mar 12	02.48	VIR
	Aug 05	19.32	AQU
	Sep 04	05.04	PIS
1934	Jan 30	18.31	LEO
	Jul 28	12.09	AQU
1935	Jan 19	15.44	CAN
	Jul 16	05.00	CAP
1936	Jan 08	18.15	CAN
	Jul 04	17.34	CAP
	Dec 28	04.00	CAN
1937	May 25	07.38	SAG
	Nov 18	08.09	TAU
1938	May 14	08.39	SCO
	Nov 07	22.23	TAU
1939	May 03	15.15	SCO
	Oct 28	06.42	TAU
1940	Mar 23	19.33	LIB
	Apr 22	04.37	SCO
	Oct 16	08.15	ARI
1941	Mar 13	11.47	VIR
	Sep 05	17.36	PIS
1942	Mar 03	00.20	VIR
	Aug 26	03.46	PIS
1943	Feb 20	05.45	VIR
	Aug 15	19.34	AQU
1944	Feb 09	05.29	LEO
	Jul 06	04.27	CAP
	Aug 04	12.39	AQU
	Dec 29	14.38	CAN
1945	Jun 25	15.08	CAP
	Dec 19	02.17	GEM
1946	Jun 14	18.42	SAG
	Dec 08	17.52	GEM
1947	Jun 03	19.27	SAG
	Nov 28	08.45	GEM
1948	Apr 23	13.28	SCO
	Oct 18	02.23	ARI
1949	Apr 13	04.08	LIB
	Oct 07	02.53	ARI
1950	Apr 02	20.49	LIB
	Sep 26	04.21	ARI
1951	Mar 23	10.50	LIB

Year	Date	Time:GMT	Sign
	Aug 17	02.59	AQU
	Sep 15	12.38	PIS
1952	Feb 11	00.28	LEO
	Aug 05	19.40	AQU
1953	Jan 29	23.44	LEO
	Jul 26	12.21	AQU
1954	Jan 19	02.37	CAN
	Jul 16	00.29	CAP
1955	Feb 08	12.44	CAN
	Jun 05	14.08	SAG
	Nov 29	16.50	GEM
1956	May 24	15.26	SAG
	Nov 18	06.45	TAU
1957	May 13	22.34	SCO
	Nov 07	14.32	TAU
1958	Apr 04	03.45	LIB
	Oct 27	15.41	TAU
1959	Mar 24	20.02	LIB
	Sep 17	00.52	PIS
1960	Mar 13	08.26	VIR
	Sep 05	11.19	PIS
1961	Mar 02	13.35	VIR
	Aug 26	03.13	PIS
1962	Feb 19	13.18	VIR
	Jul 17	11.40	CAP
	Aug 15	20.09	AQU
1963	Jan 09	23.08	CAN
	Jul 06	21.55	CAP
	Dec 30	11.04	CAN
1964	Jun 25	01.08	CAP
	Dec 19	02.41	GEM
1965	Jun 14	01.59	SAG
	Dec 08	17.21	GEM
1966	May 04	21.00	SCO
	Oct 29	10.00	TAU
1967	Apr 24	12:03	SCO
	Oct 18	10.11	ARI
1968	Apr 13	04.52	LIB
	Oct 08	11.46	ARI
1969	Apr 02	18.45	LIB
	Aug 27	10.32	PIS
	Oct 25	20.21	ARI
1970	Feb 21	08.19	VIR
	Aug 17	03.15	AQU
1971	Feb 10	07.41	LEO
	Aug 08	19.42	AQU
1972	Jan 30	10.58	LEO
	Jul 26	07:23	AQU
1973	Jan 18	21.28	CAN
	Jun 15	20.50	SAG
	Dec 10	01.35	GEM
1974	Jun 04	22.10	SAG
	Nov 29	15.10	GEM
1975	May 25	05.51	SAG
	Nov 18	22.28	TAU
1976	May 13	20.04	SCO
	Nov 08	23.15	TAU
1977	Apr 04	04.09	LIB
	Sep 27	08.17	ARI
1978	Mar 24	16.20	LIB
	Sep 16	19.01	PIS
1979	Mar 13	21.14	VIR
	Sep 06	10.59	PIS
1980	Mar 01	21.00	VIR
	Jul 27	18.54	AQU
	Aug 26	03.42	PIS
1981	Jan 20	07.39	LEO
	Jul 17	04.39	CAP
1982	Jan 09	19:53	CAN
	Jul 06	07.32	CAP
	Dec 30	11.33	CAN
1983	Jun 25	08.32	CAP
	Dec 20	02.00	GEM
1984	May 15	04.29	SCO
	Jun 13	14.42	SAG
	Nov 08	17.43	TAU
1985	May 04	19.53	SCO
	Oct 28	17.38	TAU
1986	Apr 24	12.46	SCO

Year	Date	Time:GMT	Sign
	Oct 17	19.22	ARI
1987	Apr 14	02.31	LIB
	Oct 07	04:12	ARI
1988	Mar 03	16.01	VIR
	Aug 27	10:58	PIS
1989	Feb 20	15.32	VIR
	Aug 17	03.07	AQU
1990	Feb 09	19.16	LEO
	Aug 06	14.19	AQU
1991	Jan 30	06.10	LEO
	Jun 27	02.58	CAP
	Jul 26	18.24	AQU
	Dec 21	10.23	GEM
1992	Jun 15	04.50	SAG
	Dec 09	23.41	GEM
1993	Jun 04	13.02	SAG
	Nov 29	06.31	GEM
1994	May 25	03.39	SAG
	Nov 18	06.57	TAU
1995	Apr 15	12.08	LIB
	Oct 08	15.52	ARI
1996	Apr 04	00.07	LIB
	Sep 27	02.51	ARI
1997	Mar 24	04.45	LIB
	Sep 18	18:51	PIS
1998	Mar 13	04.34	VIR
	Aug 08	02.10	AQU
	Sep 06	11.21	PIS
1999	Jan 31	16.07	LEO
	Jul 28	11.25	AQU
2000	Jan 21	04.41	LEO
	Jul 16	13.55	CAP
2001	Jan 09	20.25	CAN
	Jul 05	15.05	CAP
	Dec 30	10.42	CAN
2002	May 26	11.52	SAG
	Jun 24	21.43	CAP
	Nov 20	01.35	TAU
2003	May 16	03.37	SCO
	Nov 09	01.14	TAU
2004	May 04	20.34	SCO
	Oct 28	03.08	TAU
2005	Apr 24	10.07	SCO
	Oct 17	12.15	ARI
2006	Mar 14	22.37	VIR
	Sep 07	18.43	PIS
2007	Mar 03	23.18	VIR
	Aug 28	10.36	PIS
2008	Feb 21	03.32	VIR
	Aug 01	21.18	AQU
2009	Feb 09	14.50	LEO
	Jul 07	09.23	CAP
	Aug 06	00.56	AQU
	Dec 31	19.14	CAN
2010	Jun 26	11:31	CAP
	Dec 21	08.15	GEM
2011	Jun 15	20.15	SAG
	Dec 10	14.37	GEM
2012	Jun 04	11.13	SAG
	Nov 28	14.47	GEM
2013	Apr 25	19.58	SCO
	May 25	04.26	SAG
	Oct 18	23.39	ARI
2014	Apr 15	07.43	LIB
	Oct 08	10.52	ARI
2015	Apr 04	12.07	LIB
	Sep 28	02.52	ARI
2016	Mar 23	12.02	LIB
	Sep 16	19.06	PIS
2017	Feb 11	00.34	LEO
	Aug 07	18.12	AQU
2018	Jan 31	13.28	LEO
	Jul 27	20.21	AQU
2019	Jan 21	05.17	LEO
	Jul 16	21.39	CAP
2020	Jan 10	19.22	CAN
	Jun 05	19.14	SAG
	Jul 05	04.46	CAP
	Nov 30	09.31	GEM

MOON SIGN TABLES

FOR THE YEARS 1920–2020

TABLE 1

YEAR OF BIRTH						JAN	FEB	MAR	APR	MAY	JUN	JUL	AUG	SEP	OCT	NOV	DEC
1920	1939	1958	1977	1996	2015	TAU	CAN	CAN	VIR	LIB	SAG	CAP	AQU	ARI	TAU	CAN	LEO
1921	1940	1959	1978	1997	2016	LIB	SCO	SAG	CAP	AQU	ARI	TAU	CAN	LEO	VIR	SCO	SAG
1922	1941	1960	1979	1998	2017	AQU	ARI	ARI	GEM	CAN	LEO	VIR	SCO	CAP	AQU	ARI	TAU
1923	1942	1961	1980	1999	2018	GEM	LEO	LEO	LIB	SCO	CAP	AQU	ARI	TAU	GEM	LEO	VIR
1924	1943	1962	1981	2000	2019	SCO	SAG	CAP	AQU	ARI	TAU	GEM	LEO	LIB	SCO	SAG	CAP
1925	1944	1963	1982	2001	2020	PIS	TAU	TAU	CAN	LEO	LIB	SCO	SAG	AQU	PIIS	TAU	GEM
1926	1945	1964	1983	2002		LEO	VIR	LIB	SCO	SAG	AQU	PIS	TAU	CAN	LEO	VIR	LIB
1927	1946	1965	1984	2003		SAG	CAP	AQU	PIS	TAU	GEM	LEO	VIR	SCO	SAG	AQU	PIS
1928	1947	1966	1985	2004		ARI	GEM	GEM	LEO	VIR	SCO	SAG	AQU	PIS	ARI	GEM	CAN
1929	1948	1967	1986	2005		VIR	SCO	SCO	CAP	AQU	PIS	TAU	GEM	LEO	VIR	LIB	SAG
1930	1949	1968	1987	2006		CAP	PIS	PIS	TAU	GEM	LEO	VIR	SCO	SAG	CAP	PIS	ARI
1931	1950	1969	1988	2007		TAU	CAN	CAN	VIR	LIB	SAG	CAP	PIS	ARI	GEM	CAN	LEO
1932	1951	1970	1989	2008		LIB	SAG	SAG	AQU	PIS	TAU	GEM	CAN	VIR	LIB	SAG	CAP
1933	1952	1971	1990	2009		PIS	ARI	TAU	GEM	CAN	VIR	LIB	SAG	CAP	AQU	ARI	TAU
1934	1953	1972	1991	2010		CAN	VIR	VIR	LIB	SAG	CAP	PIS	ARI	GEM	CAN	VIR	LIB
1935	1954	1973	1992	2011		SCO	CAP	CAP	PIS	ARI	GEM	CAN	VIR	SCO	SAG	CAP	AQU
1936	1955	1974	1993	2012		ARI	TAU	GEM	LEO	VIR	LIB	SCO	CAP	PIS	ARI	TAU	CAN
1937	1956	1975	1994	2013		LEO	UB	LIB	SAG	CAP	PIS	ARI	TAU	CAN	LEO	LIB	SCO
1938	1957	1976	1995	2014		CAP	AQU	PIS	ARI	TAU	CAN	LEO	LIB	SCO	CAP	AQU	ARI

TABLE 2: NUMBER OF SIGNS TO BE ADDED FOR EACH DAY OF THE MONTH

Day	Add (signs)	Day	Add (signs)
1	0	16	7
2	1	17	7
3	1	18	8
4	1	19	8
5	2	20	9
6	2	21	9
7	3	22	10
8	3	23	10
9	4	24	10
10	4	25	11
11	5	26	11
12	5	27	12
13	5	28	12
14	6	29	1
15	6	30	1
		31	2

TABLE 3: SIGNS OF THE ZODIAC

1 ARIES (ARI)	7 LIBRA (LIB)
2 TAURUS (TAU)	8 SCORPIO (SCO)
3 GEMINI (GEM)	9 SAGITTARIUS (SAG)
4 CANCER (CAN)	10 CAPRICORN (CAP)
5 LEO (LEO)	11 AQUARIUS (AQU)
6 VIRGO (VIR)	12 PISCES (PIS)

Note: count through the signs in a continuous loop, so number 1 follows on from number 12.

sign the Moon is in at any given time, simply apply this principle. This method is fairly accurate in most cases, but if you disagree with the characteristics of the sign you come up with, it may be because your birthday falls on a day when the Moon changes sign. Turn to the preceding or following sign to see if either of these seem more fitting.

Example 1:
To find the Moon sign for a person born on October 12, 1975:
From Table 1: On October 1, 1975, Moon was in Leo
From Table 2: 12 days means counting on five signs
from Table 3: counting on five signs brings us to Capricorn – the person's Moon sign.

Example 2:
Here's someone you might recognize. The most famous male Russian ballet dancer of the 20th century was born on March 17, 1938. To find his Moon sign, follow the above procedure to find that he is a Libra – the sign of perfect balance and beauty (the person in question is Rudolph Nureyev).

HOW TO FIND YOUR MOON SIGN USING THE TABLES ABOVE

The Moon takes about 2¼ days to pass through each sign of the Zodiac and completes one Zodiac circuit in about 27 days. It returns to the same position in the Zodiac on the same date every 19 years. This cycle means that tables can be drawn up, from which you can find your sign. To find your Moon sign, first use Table 1 to reveal the sign occupied by the Moon on the first day of the month of your birth. Now turn to Table 2 and find the number of the day on which you were born and the number of signs you need to count on through the Zodiac (Table 3) to discover which sign the Moon occupied on your birthday. To find out which

INDEX